Jessamyn West, Revised Edition

Twayne's United States Authors Series

Frank Day, Editor
Clemson University

TUSAS 192

Jessamyn West
Courtesy of the Bancroft Library, University of California, Berkely

Jessamyn West, Revised Edition

Alfred S. Shivers

Stephen F. Austin State University

Twayne Publishers ■ New York

Maxwell Macmillan Canada ■ Toronto

Maxwell Macmillan International ■ New York Oxford Singapore Sydney

Jessamyn West, Revised Edition
Alfred S. Shivers

Copyright 1992 by Twayne Publishers

Twayne Publishers   Maxwell Macmillan Canada, Inc.
Macmillan Publishing Company 1200 Eglinton Avenue East
866 Third Avenue   Suite 200
New York, New York 10022   Don Mills, Ontario M3C 3N1

Macmillan Publishing Company is part of the Maxwell Communications Group of Companies.

Library of Congress Cataloging-in-Publication Data

Shivers, Alfred S.
    Jessamyn West revised edition / Shivers, Alfred S.
    p. cm. – (Twayne's United States authors series; TUSAS 192)
    Rev. ed. of: Jessamyn West. 1972.
    Includes bibliographical references and index.
    ISBN 0-8057-3979-3
    1. West, Jessamyn – Criticism and interpretation. I. Shivers, Alfred S. Jessamyn West II. Title. III. Series.
PS3545.E8315Z88 1992
813'.54 – dc20   92-29077
                                                               CIP

The paper used in this publication meets the minimum requirements of American National Standard for Information Sciences – Permanence of Paper for Printed Library Materials, ANSI Z39.48-1984.

10 9 8 7 6 5 4 3 2 1

Printed in the United States of America.

for my wife, Clare Ann, with love

Contents

Preface

The intended readers for this revised edition of my 1972 book *Jessamyn West* are those who want an accurate synoptic and analytical study of such works as *The Friendly Persuasion*, *Except for Me and Thee*, *South of the Angels*, *Cress Delahanty*, *Leafy Rivers*, *The Massacre at Fall Creek*, *The Life I Really Lived*, and *The State of Stony Lonesome*. Because Mary Jessamyn West had brought out a total of seven books – three of them novels – after my research on her was completed, and because some valuable new material on her life and art had reached the press, I thought it high time to assimilate this new material into a revised edition. But not only did I want to make this second work up-to-date, I wanted to make it better organized and more readable as well. Too, there was consolation in the knowledge that the passage of time, which does wonders in winnowing chaff from the grain, would allow me to give a sounder valuation and to place Jessamyn West more accurately in the context of American literary history.

Jessamyn West, Revised Edition begins with a biographical chapter taking the career of the author up to the year of her death, 1984. Here I discuss Jessamyn West as an "unconventional Quaker" author only incidentally, for the major concern of this chapter is how her art is related to her artistic theory, practice, and vita (including ancestry). Nevertheless, any Friend who devotes most of his or her talent to composing secular stories that are not overtly spiritually improving would *have* to be unconventional. That West deals with sexual matters is another point, one that alienated some of her sectarian readers after the publication of *Witch Diggers* and *South of the Angels*.

The remaining three chapters consist of practical criticism, all mine unless otherwise indicated, including summaries of the best of what criticism has been written about West's literature, whether by reviewers, explicators, or West herself. All the new fiction is dealt with. In chapters 2 and 3 I ignore the chronology of publication some of the time and treat her work as related to two distinct geographic regions, the Midwest and southern California, respectively, and discuss the books accordingly. I take the liberty of using *The Life I Really Lived* as a transitional work to introduce the California phase even though the novel comes late in her career; I do this because the novel opens in Kentucky and shifts to California about halfway through. The last work covered is *The State of Stony Lonesome*, which happens to be the last West novel to see print.

In my revision I left some sections almost intact; others I changed considerably in organization, style, and content; and the net result is a longer and much more comprehensive book. Here are some of the substantive changes: The first chapter contains more biography, including more information on the author's modus operandi as well as her adoption of her Irish daughter, the full story of which West forbade me to disclose in *Jessamyn West*. The following chapters update the older criticism, discuss her late fiction, and bring in whatever criticism pertains to this fiction.

As this study deals almost exclusively with the short stories and novels readily available in West books, surely her best work, most of the stories that were not collected or reworked into book form are omitted. Among these omitted ones are some, like "There'll Come a Day," which do not do justice to her art. The study devotes little attention to West's single venture into operetta (*A Mirror for the Sky*), and it concerns itself not at all with her poetry, despite the existence of her collection called *The Secret Look*, the main reason being that she was a far better fiction writer than a poet. I discuss her autobiographical and philosophical writings (*To See the Dream, Love Is Not What You Think, Hide and Seek, The Woman Said Yes, Double Discovery*) only as they contribute to the biographical sketch and the literary criticism.

For at least a decade, 1965-75, during which the first edition of this book was put together, I had the inestimable advantage of knowing Jessamyn West through not only several telephone calls and private interviews but dozens of letters in which she patiently answered my numerous questions. But she went far beyond being a correspondent, supplying me with addresses of childhood friends and teachers, photographs, copies of unpublished sketches and stories, even a writer's notebook. I was wary of being overinfluenced in this way, but much of her material I gratefully used because neither a full-length biography of the woman nor her letters or journals had yet reached print, which omissions are still the case today. By means of her help I received correspondence from a few people who had known her personally during her formative years. After the final draft of the first edition was ready, West took the opportunity to study it in my presence; her only response was that she found nothing in it that "bothered" her. Not long afterward her husband, Dr. Harry Maxwell McPherson, told me privately that she was pleased. West died long before the second edition got started.

The scholar takes obvious risks in relying on the literary figure herself for biographical data (some famous authors have been known to lie or suffer quirks of memory, especially as they grow old), but I am confident that my product – both in its biography and its literary criticism – is much more reliable for this help than many other books are which were done on the lives and works of literati no longer around to assist. West's friends and acquaintances and even her husband supplied ample corroboration with respect to vita. In doubtful cases I tried wherever possible to check one source against another, even at the risk of displeasing Jessamyn West herself, who once showed me the peppery side of her nature when she wanted her letters back because I appeared to be relying too much on the anecdotes of a certain midwestern matron who supposedly knew her. (West and I were soon reconciled.)

In April 1966 I made a special visit to the area around North Vernon, Indiana, to research the background of *Witch Diggers*, and later checked my findings with the author herself. And in December 1990 I had the pleasure of a lengthy interview with her husband, Dr. McPherson, at his home in Napa, California; there I also interviewed his adopted daughter, Ann McCarthy Cash, along with her husband, Alan, and the young novelist Karen Ray, who had long been a friend of West's.

Putting together the whole account was a slow and painstaking endeavor. Sometimes childhood friends of West's furnished colorful anecdotes that would have spiced up my narrative considerably, but after I checked these out they proved to be apocryphal. Therefore, I scrupulously excluded these gems from my work. Such is the price the scholar pays for the truth.

But getting to know West was one of the most engrossing experiences of my life. Her career is an inspiring example of what talent can achieve even in the face of imminent death, of how one can break free of the bonds of tradition and religious restraint if the will is strong enough, and go on to fulfill a childhood dream.

West was exuberant, vivacious, and witty; she relished every hour as if it were a reprieve from death (which it was, she being for decades a victim of TB). Somewhere in our correspondence she remarked that, despite her years, she had no plans to retire from her craft, that she intended to write on and on into old age as Thomas Hardy did. Living nearly 82 years, she got her wish – though she did not live quite as long as Hardy.

I hope this book will help readers better understand the life and art of this remarkable woman who, despite her considerable merit, goes too often neglected these days.

Acknowledgments

I must acknowledge my debt to the late Jessamyn West for providing vita, books, galleys, family papers, a writing notebook, photographs, help in locating obscure stories, and written explanations of her artistic aims and methods, almost always in response to specific questions I raised.

Many are the correspondents to whom I am indebted for aid. Of prime service for biographical details are the memoirs of West's former teachers, relatives, friends, and acquaintances: Dr. William T. Boyce (Claremont, California), President Paul S. Smith (Whittier College), Mr. Merritt T. Burdg and Mrs. Olive Marshburn (both of Whittier, California), Mrs. Gladys Gauldin (La Habra, California), Mrs. Esther T. Mendenhall (Santa Ana, California), Mrs. Allie Clark and Mrs. John Woolf (both of North Vernon, Indiana), Mrs. Hellen Oches (Columbus, Ohio), Mr. Richard Scowcroft (Stanford University), former president Richard M. Nixon, Mrs. Sue Lucas and Mr. Donald Kelly Lucas (both of Earp, California), and one relative who has requested not to be listed here.

I am particularly grateful to Dr. Harry Maxwell McPherson (Napa, California), the author's husband, for a lengthy interview; to Mr. and Mrs. Alan Cash (Rodeo, California) for interviews; to Karen Ray (Arlington, Texas) for an interview; to the author's brother, Merle West (Whittier, California), for information about his sister; to Mrs. Lois C. McClure (formerly librarian at the William T. Boyce Library, Fullerton Junior College, Fullerton, California) for much information about West's student life at Fullerton; to Wilhelmina Bevers and Horace W. Robinson and Alyce R. Sheetz (Eugene, Oregon) for information on the production of *Mirror for the Sky*; to Mr. Donald C. Johnson (University Library, Northern Illinois University) for reproductions of early stories and for help in tracking down out-of-the-way periodicals; to Mrs. Lorraine Hartwick (Milwaukee Public Library) for statistical data; to Mr. E. M. Adams and Miss Jan C. Todd (Steen Library, Stephen F. Austin State University) for interlibrary loan materials; and to the officials of the Library of Congress for photocopied stories and bibliographical aid.

For financial assistance I am indebted to Stephen F. Austin State University for several faculty research grants, without which much of my research on Jessamyn West could not have been done. For reasons too various to single out here I also owe a note of thanks to Dr. Edwin W. Gaston, Jr., and Mr. Edwin D. Shake (both of them friends of mine as well as former colleagues at Stephen F. Austin State University); to Dr. Hensley C. Woodbridge (Southern Illinois University, Carbondale); to Mr. Ralph D. Olive (my lifelong friend on the *Milwaukee Journal*); to Mr. Horace W. Robinson, the director of the University Theater, and Mrs. Wilhelmina Bevers, the business manager of the University Theater (University of Washington); to Mrs. Ozella Dew (Tyler, Texas); to Professor D. Elton Trueblood (Earlham College); to Professor Joyce Ann Diemer (Napa Valley College); to Mr. Julian P. Muller (former editor for Jessamyn West at Harcourt Brace Jovanovich); and to Mr. Henry Volkening (Russell & Volkening, Inc., New York City).

I wish to thank Harcourt Brace Jovanovich for permission to quote from books by Jessamyn West and, of course, the Jessamyn West estate for permission to quote from the letters and other unpublished documents.

Chronology

1902   Mary Jessamyn West born 18 July near North Vernon, Indiana, daughter of Eldo Roy and Grace Anna Milhous West.

1909   In April West family moves to Los Angeles County and settles briefly on an orange ranch; within two years moves to nearby Yorba Linda.

1914   Opening of a public library in Yorba Linda marks the beginning of her "adult intellectual life," West says.

1919   After graduation from Fullerton High School, attends Whittier College for one year.

1920-1921   Attends Fullerton Junior College.

1921-1923   Returns to Whittier College; graduates with bachelor of arts in English. On 16 August 1923 marries Harry Maxwell McPherson.

1924-1929   McPhersons move to Hemet. West is school secretary for one year, followed by four years as teacher in a one-room public school. In 1929 attends Oxford University for summer session; visits Paris.

1929-1931   Becomes graduate student at the University of California. In August 1931, following tuberculosis hemorrhage, enters La Vina Sanitorium; long period of "horizontal life" ensues.

1933   In November joins husband in Yuba City, where he is vice-principal of high school; "99.6" written here.

1934-1935   Moves to Mt. Shasta, where McPherson is principal of high school.

1936-1940   Moves to St. Helena, where McPherson is again principal. Publishes first short story, "99.6," in *Broun's Nutmeg* on 10 June 1939.

1940	Moves to Napa, last home, where McPherson is superintendent of public schools and later college president.
1944	West's adopted daughter, Ann McCarthy, is born 29 October in Limerick, Ireland.
1945	First collection of stories, *The Friendly Persuasion*.
1948	Operetta, *A Mirror for the Sky*, based on an idea by Raoul Péne Dubois. *The Pismire Plan* (science fiction novelette) published in *Cross Section 1948*.
1951	First novel, *The Witch Diggers*.
1952	Delivers speech, *The Reading Public* (privately printed).
1953	*Cress Delahanty* (stories).
1955	*Love Death and the Ladies' Drill Team* (stories). Does nine months of scriptwriting in Hollywood.
1957	Receives Indiana Authors' Day Award for *Love Death and the Ladies' Drill Team*. *To See the Dream*, autobiography covering the Hollywood experience of filming *The Friendly Persuasion*.
1958	Receives Thormod Monsen Award for *To See the Dream*. Sees staging, 22-24 May, of *A Mirror for the Sky* in Eugene, Oregon.
1959	*Love Is Not What You Think* (essay). Mother, Grace West, dies.
1960	Travels to England and Europe with sister, Carmen. Second novel, *South of the Angels*.
1962	*The Quaker Reader*.
1963	Sister, Carmen, commits suicide on 26 October.
1966	Third novel, *A Matter of Time*, based on Carmen's death.
1967	Fourth novel, *Leafy Rivers*. *The Chilekings* (science fiction novelette originally published in collection as *Little Men*).
1969	*Except for Me and Thee* – more "Friendly Persuasion" stories.

1970   *Crimson Ramblers of the World, Farewell* (stories). Father, Eldo Roy West, dies.

1973   *Hide and Seek* (autobiography).

1974   *The Secret Look* (poems).

1975   Fifth novel, *The Massacre at Fall Creek*.

1976   *The Woman Said Yes* (memoirs of her mother and sister).

1979   Sixth novel, *The Life I Really Lived*.

1980   *Double Discovery* (memoirs).

1984   Following a stroke, Jessamyn West dies 23 February. Eighth novel, *The State of Stony Lonesome* (posthumous).

1986   *Collected Stories of Jessamyn West.*

Chapter One

Not a Sweet Little Old Quaker Lady

At first thought it seems amazing that Mary Jessamyn West (1902-84), whom the doctors at a tuberculosis asylum considered "incurable," whose Quaker heritage forbade using one's talents for belletristic purposes, and whose family background contained no known writers, theatrical folk, or artists of any kind, should survive to pen books that have sold more than 6 million copies and been translated into at least 19 foreign languages. Robert Kirsch, writing for the *Los Angeles Times Book Review* (18 November 1979), surely speaks for many West admirers in declaring, "It is time, I think, to recognize Jessamyn West as one of the treasures of this state's literature, and, in fact, of the nation's." Indeed, it is high time.

Most critics exaggerate the importance of the Quaker element in West's writings and continue citing *The Friendly Persuasion* as if she had never written anything else of value comparable to that remarkable work. All this is unfair. On the other hand, since *Jessamyn West, Revised Edition* is about an author in whose life and art Quakerism has a special role, it is proper to open this study with a short record of the sect in American letters, including how Jessamyn West relates to it. The relatively tiny Religious Society of Friends, formed in England during the seventeenth century, has generated in America a correspondingly small number of literary artists who have achieved national or world fame. But when we consider that the Friends have always been a minority in this country, that *The World Almanac and Book of Facts 1991* lists their number at 111,286 as compared with the general population of close to 250 million, it is easy to account for their scarcity among the famous; yet they have certainly done well in relation to other minorities of similar size in America. Doubtless their numbers in belles lettres would be larger did not the Quakers believe that any member gifted with language ought to employ that talent more or less exclusively to benefit the faith. John Woolman's *Journal* (1774), a spiritual autobiography in plain, unadorned style, is a beautiful model that a Friend might be expected to emulate.

One finds in the eighteenth century at least three Quakers, born in America, whose writings demonstrate distinct literary flavor: The humanitarian Woolman, already mentioned; the darling of the English romantics, William Bartram; and the novelist of Gothic romance, Charles Brockden Brown. In the keeping of journals and the choice of so-called useful or practical subject matter, Woolman and Bartram followed in a long tradition of Quaker practice.

John Greenleaf Whittier, of a later period, long held the reputation of being one of America's foremost poets, although his absorption with abolition and his stylistic virtues of directness, simplicity, and emotion have regrettably run afoul of the metaphysical revival that favors obscurity and tortured syntax. Walt Whitman, although not formally a Quaker, had Quaker parentage, grew up in a section of Long Island where Quaker influence was pronounced, took an admiring and prolonged interest in the evangelist Elias Hicks, and introduced into *Leaves of Grass* ideas, terminology, and techniques that are often strikingly consonant with traditional Quakerism. Like the Friends, he pursued a course of pacifism (even becoming a male nurse during the Civil War).

It should be emphasized at this point that since the Quakers have no ecclesiastical organization, there is no central church; nor do they have formal creeds or liturgical worship. Instead, the Quakers constitute a rather loosely confederated Society of Friends whose members worship in meetinghouses that may or may not be buildings devoted exclusively to that purpose. Unlike the traditional Quakers of *Friendly Persuasion* back on the eastern seaboard – the ones we read about in Hawthorne and other early writers – those in California now, represented in West's *The Life I Really Lived*, do not practice silent worship; they even have a vested choir and a hired pastor. Sometimes these "modern" Quakers hold revivals and send missionaries abroad (West's 7 September 1965 letter to me). Outwardly they resemble nowadays the fundamentalist Protestant sects in going in for faith healing and noisy emotionalism. Nor have the American Friends always been unified in their traditional opposition to war, as witness the fact that the future playwright Maxwell Anderson, a pacifist, was fired from the faculty of Whittier College largely because of his public opposition to the draft in World War I.[1]

As for the minor Quaker literati of the present century, such as Daisy Newman, Janet Whitney, Elizabeth Gray Vining, Logan Pearsall Smith, Nora Waln, James Baldwin (1841 – 1925), and Maude Robinson (1859 – 1950), this book will mention only the last two. When the Englishwoman Maude Robinson issued her collection of pious and sentimental chronicles called *Wedded in Prison* (London, 1925), the preface bore a revealing statement of the aims and limitations that a Quaker story writer might be expected to follow in using her talents to advance the church: "Nothing sensational will be found in these stories – no 'plots,' no 'villains of the piece,' but sketches from real life of men and women who lived and labored for the spreading of the Truth . . . and for the help and healing of their fellowmen." However improving such sketches may be, they are sadly deficient in dramatic content, and the dialogue rings wooden and monotonous.

That Jessamyn West actually escaped from the backwoods of the genteel tradition represented by Robinson and her kind in the Quaker faith is nothing less than astonishing if we pause to consider that the strength of the genteel tradition in older members of the sect today is still a very real thing, as West herself warned me. By remaining within the Society of Friends, West must have felt a divided loyalty when she had to decide between religious tradition and literary fashion. But, fortunately for American literature, she ended up resisting the moralizing impulse in favor of the ostensibly amoral demands of objective art.

Jessamyn West is probably the first Quaker author in the media of the novel *and* the short story to gain an international reputation as well as the approval of serious readers. Even so, apprehensive of the goody-goody image that the *Friendly Persuasion* stories created even after several of her erotic novels had appeared, she repeatedly begged interviewers not to think of her as a sweet little old Quaker lady. To this end she sometimes went out of her way to raise eyebrows, such as by announcing in public that she had once slept with Richard Milhous Nixon, and followed by explaining that as a little girl out babysitting she had slept on the same bed with baby Nixon.[2]

Partly because her books draw so much on her family's past, of which she was proud, it is best to turn next to her forebears.

Forebears

Of the ancestry of Jessamyn West's father, Eldo Roy West, relatively little is known, but his family seems to have been predominately English.[3] Eldo West's mother was a Clark, a woman tall, dark, and gaunt, who relished fishing. Family history has it that the grandmother of this particular Clark was the Indian "blanket wife" of George Rogers Clark, the hero of the Battle of Vincennes. Eldo West, born in Indiana in 1879, grew up on a farm under meager circumstances (a humble beginning that his future wife, however devoted, never let him forget). His famous daughter describes him as "six feet one, black-haired, olive-skinned . . . a quiet man, easily discouraged, and given to melancholy" (*Woman*, 14-15). Evidently far more intelligent than his nine years of formal education indicated, he studied law and taught school in Indiana, and later achieved relative prosperity in California through various kinds of work. He wrote poems in praise of California, poems that he sent back East for printing in the Vernon, Indiana, *Banner Plain-Dealer*, and verses to put on place cards at luncheons.

Grace Anna Milhous West, the mother of Jessamyn, came from a background of Welsh, Scottish, and, particularly, Irish people. It is this side of the family that the daughter drew on almost exclusively for anecdotes and characters. The Quaker family of Grace's father sailed from Timahoe, Ireland, in the early eighteenth century to settle in America. A member of the Milhous line then married a Welsh woman of the Griffith patronym, who had voyaged to America on the same ship that had carried William Penn. The genealogy from this stage onward includes the Prices, the Sharps (Irish), and the McManamans (Scotch-Irish) – all thrifty landowners, nurserymen, teachers, or preachers. In various avatars Grace turns up in many of her daughter's stories as the practical, amusing, sex-fearing mother.

West's great-grandmother, Elizabeth Price Griffith Milhous, was a Quaker minister who suggests by religious calling and name (but little else) the Eliza Milhous of the early magazine stories in the *Friendly Persuasion* group. Her nurseryman husband, Joshua Vickers Milhous, is chronologically the Jess of *Friendly Persuasion*. This Joshua, along with his twin sister, were the youngest in a family that resided near Mt. Pleasant, Ohio. When 27, Joshua journeyed into

Pennsylvania and returned with his bride, Elizabeth, who in due time bore him eight children. In 1854, after the birth of his sons Jesse and Frank and of a daughter, Edith, he moved with his family to Jennings County, Indiana.[4] One of Frank's descendants was Richard Milhous Nixon, who became president of the United States.

Jesse G. Milhous chose as his bride Mary Frances McManaman, an educated woman blessed with spirit and energy who, according to her famous granddaughter, was more or less the model for the Eliza of *Friendly Persuasion*.[5]

To this couple, Grace Anna was born in 1884 near Butlerville in southern Indiana. Her father ran the Maple Grove Nursery and raised for sale and for the family table a veritable cornucopia of fruits.[6] After Grace moved to southern California, she took sensuous delight in recounting this abundance to her daughter, along with divers anecdotes that ultimately helped Jessamyn re-create for herself and millions of her readers the vanished forests and hamlets of the Indiana-Kentucky region. Jessamyn heard in the mother's lonely yearnings for life back East suggestive hints – mere wisps of story situations – and turned them into literature.

One of Grace's memorable experiences at age 16 or 17 was to spend a winter on the County Farm about five miles south of Vernon, Indiana, where her stern grandfather, blue-eyed and snowy whiskered James McManaman, was then superintendent. This "poor farm," as the neighbors called it, whose inmates – the derelicts, the paupers, the feeble-minded, an insane old woman, a former schoolteacher turned kleptomaniac, and sexual offenders – so horrified and fascinated the impressionable Grace that she continued to relate stories about the bizarre place and people to her children.[7] This "poor farm" became the setting for *The Witch Diggers*. It also figures in *The Life I Really Lived*.

At 21 Eldo Roy West married Grace against the objections of her parents, who eyed him as a non-Quaker of little means, or promise, who was presumptively trying to butt into a well-established Quaker family.[8] Eldo, who had tried his hand at various jobs, at last settled down near North Vernon as a renter on some land now covered by the Jefferson Proving Ground, and he worked for his father-in-law as a day laborer. At the time it seemed that he would remain as poor as his family. To worsen matters, Grace ailed in health.

On 18 July 1902 their first child was born, Mary Jessamyn. (Grace's love of word games had resulted in the name Jessamyn; the "Jess" she took from her maternal uncle, and added the remainder to keep the name from sounding too common or plain.[9]) Between Jessamyn and her poetry-reciting, bookish grandmother a mutual affection soon blossomed. No doubt Grandmother Milhous proved to be an important intellectual as well as emotional stimulant for the young Jessamyn. Within a very few years were born Myron and Carmen, model for Blix in *A Matter of Time*.

Year after year the treadmill of farm work turned but, meanwhile, Uncle Frank Milhous invested in California real estate and moved his own family to the Quaker community of Whittier. Fortunately for Eldo, an excellent opportunity arose. Grace's father had been one of those interested enough in Whittier land investment to buy an orange grove that was to yield a considerable profit years later when subdivided into building lots. Such speculations were a sign of the new materialism rapidly entering into the lives of the erstwhile simple Friends almost everywhere, a materialism to be lamented in *A Matter of Time*. This orange grove Eldo was to manage temporarily until he had time to make his own investment. The change from the snows of Indiana to the sunshine of California would benefit Grace's health. And so, on a rainy April day in 1909, the Wests boarded the train for California.

In the Sun That Is Young Once Only

The grandmother, until her death three years later, saw that her hazel-eyed, befreckled, towheaded favorite received packages of books, magazines, and hand-decorated dresses. After reaching the "Golden State," the family lived for two years in a green bungalow that West's grandfather had bought along with an orange grove at East Whittier. To support his family Eldo West performed ranch work for his more prosperous neighbors and friends. Although surrounded by relatives on neighboring ranches, Grace became lonely for Indiana and began to tell her children stories of the "good old days" back East.

Eldo eventually bought some wilderness land in the Yorba Linda tract in Orange County and planted a lemon grove.[10] They roughed it in a tent at Yorba Linda for a while, then moved into a two-story house that Eldo had constructed on a windy hilltop at the edge of "town" north of Club Terrace and Yorba Linda Boulevard.[11] Around them lay rolling hills of cactus and sagebrush, some now planted in barley; the nearest neighbor lived a quarter-mile distant; clustered around them on neighboring ranches dwelt their relatives who had moved over from Indiana. The frail mother, troubled with caring for three small children and later a fourth, was doubtless grateful to get away from the crawling rattlers outdoors, but the centipedes had a way of sneaking in through cracks.

In his planting of lemons Eldo correctly anticipated the drift of agriculture toward citrus fruits, for by 1916 three-fourths of the original tract was in oranges and lemons.[12] Yorba Linda lay bare in the sun on the rim of what used to be the great arid, sandy waste jutting up through south-central California until, just after the turn of the century, the railroad and irrigation fostered an agricultural revolution for the state. Jessamyn grew up on a frontier in transition, increasingly domesticated with fruit orchards, truck gardens, and grain ranches.

Because the Yorba Linda of her childhood figures in four of West's books – *Cress Delahanty*, *South of the Angels*, *A Matter of Time*, and *The State of Stony Lonesome* – a little more should be said about this once-pioneer community that today is next door to Disneyland in one of the most densely populated regions of America. In the year of West's arrival in California, the undulating sagebrush and brown hills of Yorba Linda contained only one house ("Bare Hills," 1). The tract was largely the home of the ground squirrel, the trapdoor spider, and weird rolling balls of sagebrush that tumbled along with the dry Santa Ana wind. Aloft, coasting buzzards peered down on Saddle Back Mountain toward the east, cinnamon foothills toward the north, a black forest of oil rigs at Olinda in the Chino Hills to the northwest, and just three miles south the silver curve of the Santa Ana River as it rolled to the Pacific.

To West's eyes, when she first saw the area, all the "wild and spare and tawny" landscape was beautiful. In the spring, "Grass swept across the hillsides like green fire," she wrote feelingly in a hometown newspaper article in 1947. "Reservoir Hill was carpeted with yellow violets. . . . There were other flowers, of course, and on other hills . . . Indian paint brushes, baby blue eyes, Mariposa lilies, lupine. In Yorba Linda in the early days no one had to wait for

heaven to claim his bed of flowery ease," for every hillside had a
floral blanket.[13] With the joyous insouciance of youth, she did not
mind that the schoolhouse would not be ready on Olinda Street until
the coming September, that the Santa Ana blew loose shingles clattering from rooftops, that water had to be hauled in from Atwood
until the pipes and pumps of the recently incorporated Yorba Linda
Water Company[14] were ready, or that not until 1912 was there a
general merchandise store in town – let alone electricity. Contemporary photographs show a horse-and-buggy town with very few
automobiles on the streets.

Eldo quickly became influential through election to the board of
trustees for the school and, soon afterward, to the office of secretary
or president. Over the years he worked as postmaster, garage owner,
water company superintendent, owner of a dry cleaning plant, and
realtor.[15] He earned enough income to give his family ample
comforts (Jessamyn had no lack of silk dresses, she reports) and to
send three of the children to college.

To be sure, the girl Jessamyn was no angel, despite the relative
strictness of her upbringing. Though swimming was a forbidden but
enticing luxury in such a warm climate, she joined other urchins in
plunging into the irrigation canal when adults were not around. Her
children in *South of the Angels* take delight in this very peccadillo.

Gladys Gauldin, a playmate of this period, remembers in detail
one incident indicating how cruel West at age 13 could be to the
submissive. Accompanying the slightly older Gladys home one day
with her bucket full of strawberries intended for a strawberry short-
cake, West picked up a switch and switched the girl at intervals to
force her to give her berries to eat. When the victim reached home,
few berries were left. The memory of this little tyranny gave the adult
West insight into the "sickening pleasures of cruelty and of the
temptation the submissive offer to the aggressor to see just how far
his submissiveness will go."[16] So disgusted was she by this blemish in
herself that she gives a similar flaw to her villainess, Mrs. Prosper, in
"A Little Collar for the Monkey."

West had known even at age three or four that she was born to
read and write: She would sit in the corner crying because she was
unable to figure out the words in the book she was holding
(*Woman*, 73). She said that from age 12 onward she kept notebooks
of ideas for stories. In fact, she dated her adult intellectual life from

this very year, when one summer evening she checked out John Fox, Jr.'s novel *The Trail of the Lonesome Pine* from among 50 works in the newly opened "library" in the janitor's closet at school.[17] Thereafter, reading became a passion; even in her later years she could not remember any finer pleasure than that of walking back from the library, "book and magazine laden, in early autumn twilight, or under summer stars . . . with an evening's reading" before her. Her practice was to finish nightly one book and then begin another; she felt stronger through her ability to finish the first, and she was assured of an abundant tomorrow by having a book already started.[18] Neither her two brothers nor her sister shared this fascination with books. Even after he grew up and finished college as an engineer, her brother Myron regarded writing as a "show-off business" and boasted that he had never read one line of her stories.[19]

Thanks to the collection provided by Grandmother Milhous, West made inroads into the works of a fellow Hoosier, Gene Stratton-Porter, with whose literary technique and career she was to have a few striking resemblances. More meaty reading came with William Wordsworth, Edgar Allan Poe, Palgrave's *Golden Treasury*, *The Oxford Book of Victorian Poetry*, Thomas Carlyle's *Heroes and Hero Worship*, Hippolyte Taine's *History of English Literature*, Charles Dickens's *David Copperfield*, and the literature of Anton Chekhov, Hilaire Belloc, and G. B. Shaw. Her childhood reading diet consisted mainly, however, of poetry and novels, but there was also a generous helping of socialism à la Jane Addams and Jack London, a subject much favored then by avant-garde intelligentsia, that helped make her sympathetic toward downtrodden minority groups, such as the "greasers" (Mexican-Americans) in *South of the Angels*. West admits that much of what she read was trash, and that her father burned a copy of a paperbound novel called *Tempest and Sunshine* that she had been reading.[20]

As expected of a Quaker girl, West relished journal reading, but she was not restricted to those of George Fox, John Woolman, and their ilk; for instance, she especially favored Samuel Pepys. What seemed "uncanny" to her (using her own word) is that, long before she discovered she had TB, she was forcibly drawn to tubercular authors and those who wrote about the disease: John Keats, Henry D. Thoreau, the Brontës, Katherine Mansfield, the already mentioned Chekhov, Marie Bashkirtsev, Thomas Mann (*Magic Mountain*), and no doubt others. Perhaps it is best to accept West's word for it that she was drawn to tubercular writers and journal keepers because of "their ability to endure, their Stoicism." Her weakening health during her twenties may well have disposed her to seek out authors similarly handicapped who could, through the notable examples of their lives, offer implicit consolation. Mansfield, alluring her most strongly, early became her heroine both as a fiction writer about adolescent girls and as a personality. Henry D. Thoreau had an even greater impact on her; she put him into at least two of her literary works, and mentions him several times in *Dream* (42-43).

To certain modern authors she responded affectionately. Her fellow Californian William Saroyan is one who once had a slight (though unfortunate) influence on her as a beginning writer, in that the opening story of *Friendly Persuasion* was originally entitled "No Uncle of Saroyan" and had in it several Saroyan references that were later deleted.[21] But Saroyan also proved helpful too, as we shall see later. Along with Mansfield, Virginia Woolf became a favorite with West. About the time her writing career began, West had already decided to become the Virginia Woolf of the 1940s,[22] an ambition she soon fulfilled and even surpassed. From the beginning she was a deep admirer of Eudora Welty's writings.[23] It appears that she never consciously tried to imitate any of these authors, but she might have derived some of her skill at narration from Mansfield, Woolf, and maybe Welty.

West's brother Merle says that his sister made daily hoards of new words to improve her vocabulary (Mast, A2), a practice that Cress Delahanty used for her notebook of beautiful words and phrases. Nonetheless, this girlhood interest in vocabulary was not accompanied by any conscious effort at authorship, in contrast to the aims of her heroines the Brontës, for it took many years to overcome her awe of literary people so that she could dare compose a story (great writers seemed like magicians). But she unwittingly prepared for authorship by keeping a journal, at least 50 volumes of which were to accumulate by 1975.[24] (Her husband, following her instructions, destroyed some of these journals after her death.) From the age of 12 she kept notebooks of story ideas for use someday, but, as she later admitted, they were colored by the inhibitions of her Quaker upbringing:

I think I was affected by the Quaker attitude, don't stick your neck out, don't take a chance. My grandfather, I can remember, thought ill of people who boasted about what they were going to do. . . . A Quaker principle was that if you did have any aptitude for words, then your writing should be something that preaches a lesson. Stories should have a moral. The plots I wrote when I was fourteen had pretty good morals. In a story about a girl who disobeyed her mother, the mother said, "Don't go to a dance . . . don't wear a low-necked dress." The girl did. She went to the dance. She wore a low-necked dress. She caught a cold, the cold went to pneumonia, and she died. I have had people [Quaker relatives and acquaintances] feel that it was frivolous to write any other kind of stories.[25]

High School and College

In due time West began to commute to Fullerton Union High School, which shared a campus with the affiliated Fullerton Junior College. In high school she took the usual subjects, including Latin.[26] Her grades were far above average; one report card shows a predominance of B+'s and A's. Her English compositions were so outstanding that the faculty sent her to read them to other classes (*Dream*, 254-55). Among various extracurricular activities she edited *New Pleiades*, a weekly published jointly by the two schools.

Here, and later in the junior college, the students in organized forensics found they had an able new voice among them. Indeed, a notice in the school paper records that "Jessyman" West and Flora Walker roundly defeated the Santa Ana Junior College Team.[27] The debating coach and college director, Dr. William T. Boyce, taught her a course in the then-new subject of economics. From all the evidence, Dr. Boyce seems to have been one of those rare teachers who so inspire their students as to live on in their hearts and minds – and thereby extend indefinitely their subtle influence. He certainly was impressed by West: "Her face, then as now, lights up showing interest, enthusiasm. . . . There was no monotony in the flow of words. She played on many keys. She had a fine sense of humor and in a debate used it sparingly but with expressive results. The use of her hands was as natural as was her voice."[28]

A crude stanza about her in *The Pleiades* (high school yearbook) indicates that she spoke rapidly.[29] Her mature speech, although still

rapid, was precise, clear, intense, and animated, with a faint delicious warble to it, as I can well affirm from having talked with her
several times and hearing her on television and in the lecture hall.
Boyce, in the foregoing letter, remembers that she made friends
easily but seemed to have no "bosom pals." She revealed, he also
remembers, a strain of unconventionality by bobbing her hair when
this style was not yet fashionable. He recalls a delightful, unforget-
table girl who was generally "at loose-ends with books, sweaters,
rain togs. . . . Her mind was too occupied with her many facets of
interest and responsibility to keep track of her belongings."

A schoolmate from the Whittier period recollected that West
wore "a very stern look," yet smiled readily, enjoyed being around
other students, and was lively in a group.[30] Various reports from
contemporaries paint the overall image of a happy if somewhat
reserved and serious schoolgirl who was eager for knowledge and
experience; if anything, she was the superabundantly normal intellectual trying on her first blue stockings. A photograph of her in *The
Pleiades* shows a smiling, impish face, full of joyous self-possession
and animal spirits even though she was no beauty.

In the fall after high school graduation, West, age 17, matricu-
lated at Whittier College, which had been founded by the Society of
Friends in 1901. Her statement that she went to college mainly to
find boys should be taken with a pound of salt; she was too much
the scholar for that. She arrived a year too late to be a student under
the future playwright Maxwell Anderson. A little after West's time the
novelist Dorothy Baker attended the school, and still later West's
cousin Richard M. Nixon. As a freshman who was still aglow from her
triumphs at Fullerton, West had difficulties with a beautiful composition teacher named Miss Fisher, a "tall Rossetti-like woman" who
wore gloves during her walks in the hills, and who later, it is said,
suffered a mental breakdown. This redheaded Miss Fisher disliked
one of West's themes entitled "Braided Eye Beams," which was
based on her own discovery of the twisted eye beams motif used so
memorably by John Donne in a poem. After class the teacher told the
young woman to curb her imagination. But the theme that caused
West the most trouble was entitled "Live Life Deeply." The outraged
Miss Fisher copied the theme onto the blackboards for the class to
see and spent the rest of the period demonstrating the author's
moral and intellectual shortcomings. West was so profoundly

shocked and humiliated by this woman that she set out the next morning, dressed in white as befitted a sacrificial maiden, to drown herself. Providentially, the reservoir chosen was boarded over; therefore, she decided to have a bit of breakfast and then try again. But breakfast raised the would-be suicide's spirits so much that she postponed her attempt – and followed with other postponements.[31] The short story "Live Life Deeply" (not to be confused with the theme, which was never published) treats the attempted suicide.

The negative influence of this English teacher was surely one of the factors that caused West to delay until her late thirties the writing of stories. Notwithstanding the fact that her writing style early in college seems to have been studded with precious diction, any normal composition teacher ought to have been pleased with the prospect of having such brilliant talent to guide and improve. The opening of one of West's college themes written during that same year has been published; it is a dazzling exercise in the use of recherché words beginning with the letter *a*.[32]

For various reasons, including dating for the first time and her plan to be married by the end of her freshman year – living life *too* deeply? – her grade average plummeted.[33] Thereupon she transferred to Fullerton Junior College where she came under the stimulus of Director Boyce, raised her grades, and played basketball. Back at Whittier in the fall of 1921, she worked under the tutelage of Herbert Harris (Farmer, 8) and earned a series of A's in literature and in other subjects on her way to her bachelor's degree in English. Somewhere in all this collegiate experience there must have been an old spinster who taught a nominally informative course in sex education, "Hygiene," as it is dubbed in the slightly fictionalized story "Love." In that story the spinster warns the all-girl class with the shocking news that boys are "different" from them, that "if a boy attempts to embrace you, draw away from him gently but firmly and say 'Think of your future children.'"[34] This prissy Victorianism was then prevalent almost everywhere in small American schools. The remarkable thing about Jessamyn West is that, with such a tradition to build on – or, rather, revolt from – she even bothered to write at all, much less write truthfully about such controversial subjects as sex.

In her senior year West took sociology from a superb young teacher, Paul S. Smith, who later became president of the college, and she made a lasting impression on him as a vivacious and apt scholar.[35] Surviving is a paper that she did for his class; it covers a sociology trip to the courts of Los Angeles. Though rife with errors of punctuation and spelling, the style is crisp in its use of antithesis, irony, wide vocabulary, and occasional exclamatory phrases. The evaluations she made are seemingly based on objective evidence and proposed with an awareness of the difficulties of studying social phenomena. The paper has no literary merit, but it is interesting as an early example of the firsthand observation West had to practice, consciously or otherwise, to become a creative writer.[36]

Although Whittier College tolerated no dancing or card playing, West seems to have had an agreeable time. Evidently she continued to indulge her love of reading. As at Fullerton, she plunged into a variety of extracurricular activities, including holding offices in the Palmer Literary Society. Her dramatic interest, manifest in the high school years, extended to acting in skits and in the senior class play.[37]

The youth to whom West had become engaged in her freshman year was Harry Maxwell (Max) McPherson, the curly-haired son of a Quaker family in Whittier. He, like members of West's immediate family, cared little for literature as a fine art, but he made up for this in other ways. On 16 August 1923, two months after her graduation, Jessamyn and Max were married in the Yorba Linda Friends Church.[38] During the next few years the McPhersons moved about a good deal. McPherson himself was to return to finish college, earn a doctorate, and rise through various high school principalships to become a professor of education at the University of California, the longtime superintendent of the Napa Valley Unified School District, and the founder and first president of what is now Napa Valley College. So distinguished and well liked is he that the McPherson Elementary School is named after him, as is a building at the college. When an admiring local judge recently asked him whether he had any enemies, Dr. McPherson retorted in the negative, "I outlived the bastards!" (*Napa* [California] *Register*, 23 October 1990). He seems to have been that rarity among the spouses of famous writers, namely a very congenial mate who protected his wife's privacy and renovated their Napa house expressly to suit her needs, and, moreover, an eminently practical man who was so skillful at investing his wife's earnings that he doubled or quadrupled their value. At one time the McPhersons owned not only land in Oregon but a share in 1,500 acres around Napa.

In 1924 West and her husband went to live in his parents' apricot orchard at Hemet. At first she worked as a school secretary. But in 1925 she began four years of teaching in a clockless, plumbingless, one-room school a few miles from the ranch. She gives us a view of a school very much like it in the rhythmical opening sentences of "The Singing Lesson" in *Love Death and the Ladies' Drill Team*: "Liberty School is built on a piece of low, unusable alkaline land. There are no other buildings in sight. In spring it rises like a lighthouse above great fields of ripening barley; in fall its shadow is long morning and evening across far-reaching stretches of stubble. In winter it stands solitary in the center of a pool of shallow, wind-scalloped water."[39]

In this little isolated building she taught all six grades and, surprisingly, loved the work. Despite the demanding routine, she must have had her daydreams too, wondering when she would find time and sufficient excuse to write her books. The wind blowing about the schoolhouse in the aforementioned story is made to speak to the teacher, significantly named Miss Mary McManaman: "It said far. It said distant, strange, remote. It said someday" (*Love Death*, 234). Even if West had never read or were never to read any of the Katherine Mansfield stories about children, this experience in the school would have furnished her with numerous observations for stories and novels about young people. Hardly any student of human nature can read "The Singing Lesson" without feeling that West is someone who would establish excellent rapport with children. One of her friends, Richard Scowcroft of Stanford University, says that West's work speaks to children with directness and interest, never condescendingly.[40] Because the career of a college professor with a doctorate in English began to appeal to her, West resigned from her teaching post to attend graduate school. In the summer of 1929 she attended lectures at Oxford University; however, the lure of the Old World sights proved stronger than the boring lecture hall. After the summer session ended, she traveled to Paris. The whole account of this first trip abroad is laid out in her memoir *Double Discovery*. In midwinter she joined her husband at the University of California at Berkeley for a year and a half of study.

Although making rapid progress in the doctoral program, West soon realized that studying was another postponement of her dream, which was to write stories. One of her letters underscores the sense of failure: "I can remember (here in Berkeley, from where I write) getting up from my study table, going to a rain drenched window, to look out, I thought, and to review in my mind the French I had just memorized; and instead to weep and say, 'When am I ever going to write my stories?' "[41]

A far more serious problem arose that made her doubly damned. West had barely reached her twenty-ninth birthday when the date was set for her doctoral orals. Meanwhile she and her husband visited her parents' home. For a long time she had suspected that she had a medical problem; physicians, nevertheless, had failed to diagnose anything serious. Jumping from bed one morning, as Katherine Mansfield had done before her, she tasted some warm-salty arterial blood in her mouth – a tubercular hemorrhage. Within three days she entered La Vina Sanitorium near Pasadena, for X rays had revealed a "far advanced" infection in both lungs. The doctors thoughtlessly issued her a booklet indicating that 95 percent of patients with far advanced cases like hers perish within five years. Despondent, she began to plan suicide.[42] Indeed, as events proved, of the 18 women patients being treated in the cottages there at the time of her admission, she was to be the only one alive at the end of 10 years.[43] West mirrors the patient-physician relationship in her story "The Condemned Librarian."[44]

Nine anxious months followed before she at last went home to Yuba City, where her husband lived. But only a few weeks later the TB flared again, and she was brought back to La Vina on a stretcher. Not long afterward the doctor told her parents that nothing more could be done; they might as well take her home to die in the company of loved ones.[45]

Horizontal Life

And so West went to live in her parents' home, where Grace West would tolerate no nonsense about dying. A long period of couch or bed life began that did not end until 1945, when her youth was long past. Under her mother's care she began to improve. Had Grace not been the emotionally vital person she was – "a life-enhancer if there ever was one"[46] – her daughter might not have survived to write a single story. Grace West, who deeply influenced her daughter and her books far more than the more educated Eldo, was a woman of delightful contradictions. The repressive, backwoods Quaker in her, attributable partly to a tradition of numerous preachers in the family, gave her a fear about sex when it came to raising her children, and this overprotectiveness may be seen in Lib of *The Witch Diggers*. Both she and her husband avoided drinking anything stronger than frosted root beer and brought up the children to believe that dancing was sinful. Yet the lively McManamans and Sharps in her blood, the family strain of which her writing daughter took pride in, were constantly rubbing against the staid, conventional Milhouses. Shy and retiring by habit, she also wielded a switchblade tongue; moreover, she was given to pranks. Bored with the juvenile goings-on at a Girls' League party in West's high school gymnasium, Grace seized a dangling rope and swung from the balcony over the heads of the startled females (West's 28 January 1966 letter to me). Extant is a copy of a hilarious burlesque letter that she reportedly sent to one of West's former professors at Whittier who had praised the daughter in sentimental and profuse terms (unhappily, space does not permit its inclusion).[47]

Within half a year West recovered sufficiently to rejoin her husband, then employed in Yuba City; a photograph of her from this time shows a woman sadly altered from the college days. She looks pathetically ill, seemingly middle-aged already, and overweight from tubercular fat. With much leisure on her hands, she once more turned to reading books. She chanced on a story by William Saroyan, likewise a member of a minority group, whose expressed belief is that all one needs to do to compose a story is to ignore the rules of other people, forget how such-and-such a famous author wrote, never try to arrive at style, learn to typewrite, and pour out a torrent of words without regard to care. But what she found in the Saroyan story as representing maximum requirements, "a lot of feeling and a free-flowing pen," emboldened her to break down a psychological impediment – perhaps caused by Miss Fisher – and to construct her first story, "99.6," about sanitorium life ("Three R's," 159). Some of the published biographical articles might delude us into thinking that West's first stories originated in the sanitorium. In those days, however, she was too ill to manage serious writing or reading, for TB, though it is not a painful disease, makes one pitifully weak. Not until two years had passed, and she was out of the sanitorium, flat on her back in St. Helena in 1936, and unable to do anything else did she feel that it would not be presumptuous for her to begin to write, to expand her notebook writing into more or less finished "pieces." Thus, by depriving her of so much else, TB forced her into recognizing and making use of her talent.[48] It was about this time that a woman visited her and suggested that West piece a quilt so that, when she died, she would have something to leave her mother. "Hell," West responded, "if I've reached the end of the road, I'm not going to leave a quilt. I'll put Grace's stories down on paper. And I began writing" (Berges, 38).

Her husband told me that in St. Helena she yearned so intensely to enter a bookstore, as she had done in her glorious student days when she was strong and healthy, when the world of knowledge had flung open its doors, that she sometimes begged him to drive her to one of the bookstores at Berkeley – just to *smell* the pages and bindings of books again. And so he agreed to take her there on Saturday mornings once a month. To conserve her strength for the trip she would rest up for hours ahead of time and then lie down in the backseat of the car until they reached the store. By the time the McPhersons moved into their Napa house in 1940, West had recovered enough to be on her feet a good deal of the day. But during all her subsequent years she led the life of a valetudinarian, always careful not to overexert herself physically, or fail to get enough rest, for fear that the TB – impossible of final cure – might flare up again.

In the story "Home-Coming," which deals with the TB experience, West remarks that an organism under germ attack strives harder than ever at reproduction – meaning increased sexual desire, in the case of the asylum patient. Extrapolating this idea to the field of Freudian psychology, one might go on to say that, on the brink of imminent death, the libido of this childless and bookless Jessamyn West insisted on expressing its own special form of fertility, belles-lettres. And doubtless the realization that she could fulfill her dream made it even more important to live.

Although West's tubercular experience was to influence her writings – as is shown later – and to restrict them in significant ways, it did not make them pallid, squeamish, or preoccupied very long with disease or death. Probably the most striking and memorable result of the TB calamity, aside from shoving a wistful, five-foot-seven-inch scribbler of journals into writing literature, is something on the order of an aesthetic revelation enacted in several of her best works: It is where a character undergoes a preternatural awakening to the wonder of being alive and alert to all the senses, to a glory enwrapping even common things. Edna St. Vincent Millay expressed the feeling beautifully in her poem "Renascence." In a letter to me West told me about "that continuous elation which is the chief fact of my life."[49]

It appears the merest stroke of luck that her stories were ever published. Her husband, Dr. McPherson, had accidentally looked at some pages that fell open before him one day and he discovered "a number of very beautiful stories." "I praised her," he said, "but she simply glared at me" (Berges, 38). Her secret was discovered. But West refused to mail any stories off to publishers until his naggings became unbearable. To satisfy him, she finally consented to send a dozen to as many magazines on the condition that he cease talking about publication if they were all rejected. Fortunately, acceptance came quickly.[50]

Success

The upshot was that Jessamyn West, unlike many other authors, broke into print without difficulty, being quite satisfied to send most of her early work to "little magazines" that paid nothing. Thus she spared herself the heartbreak of those numerous rejections that plague aspiring authors who beat on the doors of the major presses. Anyway, having a husband with a good job, she had no need to support herself (Doty, 150). In the course of years she grew wealthy from her writings, but whether the magazines paid or not she was grateful for the encouragement and critical advice of such editors as Dudley Wynn (*New Mexico Quarterly*), Lowry C. Wimberley (*Prairie Schooner*), Mary Louise Aswell (*Harper's Bazaar*), Edward Weeks

(*Atlantic*), Katherine White (*New Yorker*), Kay Gauss Jackson (*Harper's Magazine*), and Hugh Kahler (*Ladies' Home Journal*).[51] An artist cannot live by bread alone; she needs orchids for her soul. Although the hesitant author kept "99.6" from the market for years, it won a prize when published in *Broun Nutmeg* in June 1939. That summer the story "Homecoming," also about sanitorium life, won no prize in *American Prefaces*, but it is clearly a much better work.[52] Having cured herself of the tuberculosis motif, West quickly turned to other subjects. She retained California as a favorite fictional locale and added to it southern Indiana, where the family roots lay. In the fall of 1939 *Foothills* carried "The Day of the Hawk," a psychological study of a neurotic woman whose sense of guilt over her infant's death eventually becomes an Albert Schweitzer-like "reverence for life." Not too surprisingly, the narrator is a convalescing female who lives in Yorba Linda and has a whole row of personal journals to her credit. The story is cleverly done, although the dialogue (as reported from a journal) sounds strained in places.

West's first publishing year is interesting for at least four reasons:

1. For stories she began quite early to draw on her own experience as a girl and young woman in southern California. Her life was to be for her the stuff of which books are made, but not in the intensely autobiographical fashion of Thomas Wolfe and Marcel Proust. Just as George Washington Cable had said that the best stories rest somewhere on a factual basis, Jessamyn West founded some but by no means all of her best work on a little isle of fact amid a great big sea of fancy, making use of identifiable personal experience and family tradition. On the other hand, she never wrote about places foreign to her experience, or about foreign lands either except in the short story "Hunting for Hoot Owls" and the nonfictional *Double Discovery*.

2. Her interest in juvenile figures, finally leading to some of her most popular books, found expression in "The Mush Pot," later cast into a *Cress Delahanty* story.

3. Her interest in backcountry Indiana life, which was to be for her a new frontier in source material, gave rise to the first of the *Friendly Persuasion* stories, "Music on the Muscatatuck."

4. An exquisitely wrought poetic prose marks some of her stories, for example "Music on the Muscatatuck." In 1945 Harcourt, Brace brought out *The Friendly Persuasion*, a unified collection of narratives about the Quaker couple Jess and Eliza Birdwell. With this book West finally reached an international audience. From now on there would be no more "horizontal life" for her, except in the sense of writing in bed or in a lounge chair by the swimming pool; instead, an active career of authorship, traveling, and teaching creative writing began.

During Grace West's final illness, following a series of strokes, she was unable to recall the identities of her children. On one occasion, reminding her mother who she was, West said that she was that woman who had written the Quaker stories. And what a startling response this got! "Oh Jessamyn," the mother misunderstood, "*did* I get them written? I was always going to write from the time I was a girl." This well-kept secret startled the daughter. But the latter had enough aplomb and kindness to answer, "Yes you did, Mama. You got them all written. There is a whole book of them . . . everything you ever thought about the Quakers and the old days in Indiana is down in print."[53]

Still, the student of West's life must be careful not to accept unqualified the daughter's adoring valuation of the mother. That Grace saved West's life goes without saying, and that she supplied some ideas for stories is also true; however, West furnished the labor and imagination that made all the difference between exhilarating and even provocative reportage and the sometimes striking literary artifact.

Jessamyn West and her husband wanted but were never to have children of their own. During the 1950s their affection for teenagers found outlet in taking a 16-year-old lad named Fred Oswald as a ward into the Napa household for three years.[54]

And then came Ann. The following true-life anecdote about her sounds fictitious – but it actually happened. While sightseeing in Limerick, Ireland, in 1955, West was trying to weigh herself in front of a Woolworth store. "Would you like me to hold your purse, ma'am?" asked a pert, red-headed girl named Ann McCarthy, who was "blue with cold" and more thinly clothed than the mendicant street fiddlers. West consented. After weighing, she invited the 11-year-old, as well as her girlfriend, out to tea at a restaurant – a tea that turned out to be a full dinner with chops and chips. The rich, creamy sauces proved too much for Ann, however. She threw up. The author became so intrigued by this "enchanting, witty little street gamine" that she stayed on in Limerick to get to know the family, which consisted of a hardworking, widowed scrubwoman struggling heroically to make ends meet with jobs that paid 75 cents a day (when jobs were available), a grandmother, and six children, all hungry, all crammed together in a converted barrack that contained few of the amenities that middle-class American families take for granted. West wrote to me, "We do not know the poverty, can not imagine the poverty of the slums of . . . Limerick."[55]

The upshot was that West determined – not out of pity, she said, but out of love – to take Ann back to Napa, California, to live with her for a few years. Her husband, Max, 57 at the time, and wary from his long experience in disciplining thousands of rambunctious children in the public schools, thought her plan was "crazy." But he finally yielded, provided that the sister Jean, age 13, come too to keep Ann company. The mother, who loved her children, resisted letting the girls go until a friend put it to her this way: Do you want your girls to end up living eight-to-a-room like you do? Canon Lee, of the Limerick diocese, consented to the arrangement but not so the Catholic archbishop of San Francisco, who objected that the Quaker McPhersons might tamper with the girls' religion. Better for the girls to starve in Limerick than to backslide in a Quaker household – even if the McPhersons had promised, which they did, to send Ann and Jean off to mass regularly. Worse still, the Irish civil authorities hung fire because of a law intended to keep Irish girls from entering into white slavery at the hands of vicious adoptive parents. Hearing of this impasse, two carloads of Catholics sympathetic with the McPhersons drove down to the archbishop's assistant and tried to intercede. But to no avail.

It required the intercession of Jessamyn West's second cousin, then vice-president Richard M. Nixon of the United States, to convince the Irish civil authorities that the McPhersons would be suitable parents. In March 1956 the girls flew in to New York, spent the night in the luxurious home of the Harcourt Brace Jovanovich president – an introduction to America that risked spoiling them – and thence to California. Of the two girls, Ann alone stayed with the McPhersons, finished high school, and even went to California State University, graduating magna cum laude. She married a man named Alan Cash, now a realtor, and has two daughters. In the spring of 1990 Dr. McPherson legally adopted Ann and willed the estate to her and her husband.[56]

It is not known whether West, consciously or otherwise, used Fred Oswald (the ward mentioned earlier) or Ann McCarthy as models for youths in her stories. But considering that children interested her exceedingly, and that Ann was the very type of loveable, amusing, and intelligent girl of Irish background that West liked to portray in fictional form, the possibility of influence cannot be discounted. Life often influences art, but the reverse can be true: a psychologist might say that the author in Limerick was consciously or unconsciously *looking* for that dream child, that counterpart to the Cress Delahantys of her imagination.

A Mirror for the Sky (1948) represented West's first and last attempt at operetta. She seems to have perceived fairly early where her forte lay: short stories and novels. The first of the novels, *The Witch Diggers* (1951), had a Hoosier setting around the turn of the century. In succeeding novels and story collections she usually moved forward chronologically, passing from the parental into personal recollections. The time and setting of *Cress Delahanty* (1953) are approximately those of West's own childhood in Yorba Linda. In *Love Death and the Ladies' Drill Team* (1955) West collected many of her better short stories that had been printed in magazines.

To See the Dream (1957), based on her hitherto unpublished journals covering the filming of the *Friendly Persuasion* stories, was West's first extended piece of autobiography. In 1959 appeared the philosophical essay *Love is Not What You Think*.

West's second novel, *South of the Angels*, was somehow delayed until 1960. Traveling about on speaking engagements, receiving honorary doctorates (nine before her life was over),[57] attending writer's conferences, and teaching creative writing at universities, all these seriously interfered with whatever she might be writing. *A Matter of Time* (1966), the third novel, brought her finally to the present-day setting, thereby marking for her a radical departure. The following year the fourth novel, *Leafy Rivers*, signaled the first of several returns to the Indiana past. Early 1969 saw the publication of the best-seller *Except for Me and Thee*, which consisted of additional Jess Birdwell stories that round out the scheme of *Friendly Persuasion*. In September 1970 came her second collection of miscellaneous stories, under the colorful title *Crimson Ramblers of the World, Farewell*. Old age did nothing to slow the stream of books.

More autobiography appeared with *Hide and Seek* (1973), actually a discursive account of her life in a trailer alongside the Colorado River (her substitute for Walden Pond) while she tells about such things as her childhood, her readings, her mother's refusal to educate her about sex, her mature reflections on sex and love (always candid and illuminating), her encounters with Jesus-lovers and even a violent drunk who bites dogs, and her continual fascination with the writings and life-style of Henry David Thoreau. Next we have the West book that generated the greatest volume of mail to her, whether praising or condemning: *The Woman Said Yes* (1976), which is about the lives of her mother and sister, the latter of whom ended up killing herself. *Double Discovery* followed four years later, an account of West's 1929 trip alone to Oxford and Paris when she was a naive young woman, seen both from the perspective of her letters at that time and from her own reflections a half-century later. Because she left no single autobiography that covers her entire life or even most of it, her future Boswell will have much to do with these last three books.

West's poems, which practically everyone ignored when they appeared in magazines, got ignored all over again when they finally appeared in the thin volume *The Secret Look* (1974), but the poetry for which she will be remembered is of another kind: Her many instances of jewel-like prose in such works as *Friendly Persuasion* and *The Life I Really Lived*.

Like the late novels of Willa Cather, those by Jessamyn West consisted of a retreat to the past, a past that she had already used for some of her best work. It was not that the present displeased her; it was that the past provided materials she felt familiar and comfortable with, even if she had to do some research (hated word!), as when she wrote what was the most profitable book of all, *The Massacre at Fall Creek* (1975). Other late novels included *The Life I Really Lived* (1979) and *The State of Stony Lonesome* (1984).

West had always been something of a ham at the lectern, always loving to give speeches (but never reading from her stories), putting everything she had into the performance, glowing with pleasure when all went well. Her husband recalls scenes in which hundreds in the auditorium would jump to their feet afterward and clap and clap and clap. Having personally witnessed her oratory on two occasions, I can testify to the charisma she emanated. But during her last years West suffered a series of minor strokes that caused thickening of speech, loss of memory, and inability to orient herself to her surroundings. At a 1982 meeting of the Friends of San Marino Library, she shuffled her three-by-five-inch cards as if she had not seen them before, forgot parts of her speech, foundered, and had to extemporize. It was sad to see a veteran fail. But a year later, feeling her powers return, she consented to give a speech at the annual meeting of the Bancroft Library in the Wheeler Auditorium, University of California. This time, however, her husband begged her to decline – he feared she would fail and open herself to still more embarrassment. But West said no, she welcomed the opportunity; no cause to worry. As it turned out, the speech succeeded so well that it "electrified everybody." It was a "beautiful end to her speaking career," her husband recalls. But otherwise her powers continued to decline. On Wednesday, 22 February 1984, she suffered her last stroke. She had entered the house carrying an armful of daffodils and went into the little TV room, where she sat down on the settee. "I'm kind of hungry," she said to her husband, and he left for the kitchen to get her something, and while he was gone she cried out, "Max!" and collapsed. She was taken to the local Queen of the Valley Hospital, where she died the following morning about 5:00 without ever regaining consciousness. She was 81, having defeated TB to the very end. True to her request, no funeral service attended the cremation. Her ashes were buried in back of the house on the little hill where she loved to sit.[58]

Jessamyn West at Work

Like many other authors, West occasionally did screenwriting. She received sole credit for the script *Stolen Hours*, partial credit for *The Big Country*, but none at all for *The Friendly Persuasion*, despite her undoubted collaboration with the director William Wyler, because the studio, aware that a blacklisted Michael Wilson had written an earlier screenplay, wanted to avoid legal troubles with the Screen Writers Guild.[59] Although she resented the corporate method of originating scripts, she still welcomed the challenges of the film medium. The motion picture rights to *Friendly Persuasion* earned West $17,500,[60] and *South of the Angels*, picked up by Metro-Goldwyn-Mayer, was even more lucrative.

But what was it like to find her at work in Napa?[61] Let us pretend for a moment that we can recover that lost period and make a visit to Napa, the hilly wine district north of San Francisco, just a few miles away from the Beauty Ranch of her near-contemporary Jack London. We would find her living on three acres just outside of town in a russet, two-story, redwood-and-shingle house. Rising from a flag-stone patio in back of the house is a terraced slope of flower beds, on the crest of which lies her solar-heated swimming pool, which she likes to bathe in nude. Despite the azaleas, camellias, rhododendrons, and lilies – and more lilies – that her amateur horticulturist husband has set out, she herself never does a tap of work at gardening. She tires easily. Any partying or other recreation is done up here on the slope, where the noise will not disturb her if she happens to be working in the house. A white rooster strutting about the yard gives the setting a distinctly rural air. In the pasture we might see West's favorite gelding, named Dandy; elsewhere, a hunting dog (belonging to her husband – she herself prefers cats). We notice alongside the curving driveway a Dodge motor home that she uses on trips, in lieu of hotels; sometimes she takes it over to Parker, Arizona, during the summer to write in in the solitude of her beloved desert. After entering a glassed-in sun porch used for dining, we reach the comfortable living room lined with books, and a narrow staircase that leads up to an attic containing still more books. Roaming about the house are her latest cats, two Pekinese, and also a cross-eyed gray cat that lives in a cupboard. This is not a mansion but a simple farmhouse that cost the McPhersons only $7,500 and was then enlarged to provide not only comfort but the isolation that West required for her work. The only servants are a housekeeper and a part-time gardener.

West has few friends in the community, where her husband is a popular and well-known educator, for she absolutely refuses to take on the numerous social obligations expected of a school superinten-dent's wife. Fortunately, people realize that she needs to conserve her energies for the task of writing. Even speech making, which she loves to do, is fatiguing.

She has a bedroom all to herself, the bed itself built into a windowed alcove that overlooks the wooded front grounds. After a light breakfast of orange juice and coffee, she customarily goes in pajamas back to bed (like Mark Twain and Marcel Proust), for here she can put words on paper without delay and interruption; other-wise, if she were to leave bed and start looking around, her house-keeping instincts would take over and a hundred unnecessary chores would beg for attention. Like Thoreau, she has learned to simplify her life. Now, about nine o'clock, she places a portable desk over her legs and sets to work – unless interrupted by one of the migraine headaches that strike at least twice a week, or by some of the many visitors who drop by to see her gregarious husband. Always she writes her stories with a fountain pen, producing a small, neat script on pads of legal paper. The huge adjoining bathroom shows her love of nature that turns up so often in the writings: Instead of a wall behind the sunken Jacuzzi, a big window there looks out over the garden under the trees. So much for what a visit might have shown us.

West first preferred to write short stories but then switched to novels, which is "an easier form, because the short story requires a far tighter construction. With the novel you simply live with the people for a considerable length of time and you write as things happen, whereas the short story, like the poem, must be convoluted for a purpose . . . a shaft of light into that particular happening." Her husband, who is not a literary person and who knows well his limits, sometimes offered criticism but with mixed results: He told her not to send off some of the *Friendly Persuasion* stories (they were "too trivial"). On the other hand, he was good at advising on geography in *Massacre at Fall Creek*, a novel that excited him (Doty, 152). He, no doubt supposing that her fictional creation reflected on him, was, she said, "hurt to the quick" if "*any* young man [were] ineffective" in her stories. For the same reason her mother was "hurt to the quick because *a* mother wore a dirty night gown. Even a novel about crusaders might not escape this family criticism," West wrote me apprehensively.[62] Although these reactions pained her, there is no evidence that they actually shaped her work, for rascals and other flawed people did appear in her books up until her last years. She ranked the describing of scenery as the most difficult aspect of her art; the rendering of conversation, the "easiest and most exhilarating" (Doty, 153). Unlike her former neighbor, Jack London, over at Glen Ellen, she did not hustle to achieve a minimum number of words per day. Nor did she send just anything off to the publishers, good work and bad, even though her name attached to something might have ensured its publication, for she absolutely did not write for the money (uncashed checks from publishers piled up in her desk drawer). Success in her eyes was not to be equated with income or material possessions; consequently, she spent surprisingly little on clothes and, according to her husband, did not give "one hot damn about jewelry . . . no interest in it, period."[63]

Nevertheless, this woman so easy to please with clothes and jewelry was exceedingly particular when it came to her art. Writing was too private even to share with the family: She never took such ego trips as reading her stories aloud to them, nor did she read to local writers' groups. After doing a draft, she revised so much that the acquaintance who typed her work would have to turn out three or four successive copies before reaching the final version.

West edited herself tightly. Not typically a writer of picturesque, long-winded, flamboyant passages, she wrote in a spare style in which even the characters economize on their words. Perhaps this is one of her Hemingway legacies.

Apparently she never outlined. "Perhaps I could be a better writer if I outlined. But, basically, thinking, plotting, planning is not the way I write" (Tooker and Hofheins, 186).[64] The act of writing was to her in the nature of a fresh adventure, not the keeping of a tightly scheduled appointment. West put it this way: "Some writers have their stories so carefully planned that they never change a word once it is on paper. Some writers keep elaborate notebooks and files of ideas. I have no files or real story notebooks [she excepted the notebooks from childhood], but I do rewrite many times. I rewrite not only to get a sentence to suit me, but because I do not know all of my story until I have written it." Further, "I expect my characters to reveal more of themselves as the story progresses. I think the writer, as well as the reader, deserves a few surprises in the story" ("Where," 6-7).

These statements imply that a certain character might undergo a good deal of unforeseen development; then the author must go back and make changes to prepare for the twists of plot necessitated by the new characterization. In an interview reported in the May, 1967 issue of *Writer's Digest* West admitted that what came first to her mind was "the person in a situation" – not anything to prove and not any complete plot – after which she learned about the story as she wrote.[65] Her fiction apparently did take form in this way. The following description of her method is applicable to at least one of her stories, and it reveals that the chief characters were formed early, before the story became clear.

In a letter West wrote that "things as they actually happen rarely make good stories. . . . There's no satisfaction in 'repeating' – only in creating."[66] What matters is the tiny bud of suggestion that alights like yeast in the imagination and works away until wine develops. In "The Story of a Story" West described in detail how her account of the schizoid physician, Dr. Chooney, emerged. On a driving trip with her husband up the Silverado Trail, about 15 miles from Napa, she saw a large, isolated house with a physiotherapist sign posted by the highway, a rundown, mysterious place. In this instance the locale or setting preceded both character and plot in the story that would ultimately coalesce. The remote and rundown situation of the house caused her to speculate on its occupant. Immediately Gothic over-tones arose; these are discernible in the significant questions she asked herself about the house. And in explaining the questions, she stated that "There is a self beneath the surface who knows all the answers – to the right questions." The general method suggests the "organic theory" of art, wherein the story assumes its own form independent of any preconceived design on the part of the artist. And West sounded almost like a Transcendentalist when, affirming the values of intuition, she added: "One must be careful only to ask the right question, to ask it in a low voice, and to wait."[67] In this case West waited six months – but meanwhile she was working on other stories – until she had a name for the doctor (later changed), gave him a daughter (later changed to a patient-victim), and knew that he was somehow evil.

Other significant questions were posed, followed by another six months of waiting. In the meantime, she heard from her house-keeper a certain anecdote that somehow appealed to the uncon-

scious part of herself as a storyteller. She luckily set down this anecdote in her journal. In due time she discovered that what she had
recorded was the answer she had been seeking. Three years after
first sighting the house she began "Horace Chooney, M.D."

This history of creation is the only detailed one that Jessamyn
West ever gave us, it seems. But for two reasons the foregoing explanation is not typical of her procedure: (a) Her stories are in practically every instance constructed much, much faster than was this
one. (b) "Horace Chooney, M.D." is one of the few in the West
corpus having, as she said, a "considerable basis in the external
world." As a rule she shied away from the ready-made story handed
her by someone else; she preferred the glittering fragment on which
the imagination can play and envision the shining whole.

Even though she could not tell (she said) how a given story of
hers would end, she did commence with definite ideas about where
her characters were going. But her unwillingness to outline, or at
least to see clearly in the beginning how a story would end, led to a
certain looseness in plot construction.

In critical theory West agreed with V. S. Pritchett that what writers strive to do is to learn their own identity, and do so by removing
as many of the veils as possible that hide them from themselves
(unpublished autobiography typescript, 1). She posited in "The
Story of a Story" that the artist searching for his private identity
"assumes in turn the identities of as many of his fellow men as the
breadth of his genius permits. In his search for himself he discovers
us." This romantic idea also has its parallel in "The American
Scholar" of Emerson, whom she read early: Said Emerson, "He then
learns that in going down into the secrets of his own mind he has
descended into the secrets of all minds. He learns that he who has
mastered any law in his private thoughts, is master to that extent of
all men whose language he speaks, and of all into whose language
his own can be translated."

Accordingly, the novelist at work peels off layers of her personality as if she were an onion, somewhere down disclosing all possibilities, even the sadistic and selfish Mrs. Prosper of "A Little Collar
for the Monkey" – for West must have known what it was like to be
Mrs. Prosper and other nasty types. And so it must have been too for
proud Lib Conboy of *Witch Diggers*, and lonely Asa Brice and lustful
Tom Mount of *South of the Angels*.

With such a theory, West naturally leaned toward realism, her own life being the principal quarry out of which she carved her literary valuables. Even the two science fiction stories, *The Pismire Plan* (1948) and *Little Men* (1954), bound her to her native earth in southern California. The realism of Jessamyn West included fidelity not only to physical detail and historical accuracy but to human psychology in the tradition of Henry James, whose critical observations she had read approvingly by 1949. She seems to have shared James's high regard for writing as a consummate art form, his interest in fine consciences, and his use of interior monologue, but insisted on making her own dialogue much more lifelike with colloquialisms, dialect, and period vocabulary. Her writing is far more sensuous too. Nor did she, unlike the later James, rely heavily on merely cerebral happenings as opposed to direct physical action. Moreover, as indicated earlier, Jessamyn West was quite un-Victorian despite her Quaker faith, and tolerably "modern" in treating human sexuality.

Chapter Two

Olden Days Back "East"

Among the Hoosiers

Almost all of Jessamyn West's writing ignores the street crime, drugs, poverty, and artificiality of today's urban life and ensconces itself amid the small town or rural America of generations past, roughly in the period from the early nineteenth century through the first half of the twentieth. Her personal love for solitude as a homemaker among her chores; her predilection for the writings of Thoreau; her childhood spent on ranches without (it seems) any important regrets; her dislike of, or at least uneasiness with, highway commercialism; her fascination with her mother's tales of life back in the "good old days" – all of these found expression in such books as *The Friendly Persuasion*, *Except for Me and Thee*, *A Mirror for the Sky*, *The Witch Diggers*, *Leafy Rivers*, *The Massacre at Fall Creek*, and the first half of *The Life I Really Lived* (covered in chapter 3). Early West discovered that, by choosing her literary materials from an era already securely established in the past, she could avoid the pain of dealing with her own valetudinarian condition, a subject soon exhausted, in any event, as well as the disadvantage of having led a sheltered life. To a woman who had spent many years confined to bed and couch, whose youth had burned up in tubercular fever, the family past meant release, romance, and freedom for the imagination. If it had worked for the bedridden Marcel Proust and Robert Louis Stevenson, it might work for her. Of course, the accessibility of bits of story material related to her by her mother made it irresistible to use the old days in the Midwest for several of her books. And this she did.

The reader of West's Hoosier fiction notices that she uses an abundance of authentic detail covering not merely the flora and fauna of her ancestral region but its folkways and language, the latter being rich in colloquialisms, dialect, archaisms, and figurative expressions.[1] It is a land of corn and timothy and tobacco. Indiana forests are not just trees in the aggregate but oaks and willows, gums and sycamores, catalpas and redbuds, shagbark hickories and dogwoods. And the sassafras too, from whose roots Eliza in *Friendly Persuasion* makes her cups of aromatic tea. In May the locust blossoms shower the wood paths like summer snow. Twining about the branches of these trees and bushes grow the luscious fox grapes that adorn Venese's bower (see *Witch Diggers*). Overhead fly occasional buzzards and wild turkeys. Native flowers are plentiful too, including phlox and lilacs, goldenrod and snowball bushes, Johnny-jump-ups and spice pinks, while later in the year the fields are purple with ironweed and farewell summer. The intense fragrance of lilies-of-the-valley perfumes Jess Birdwell's house in *Friendly Persuasion* when he returns home from a trip.

Jess's nursery is a cornucopia of luscious fruits: He grows and sells many varieties of old-fashioned apples that include Rambo, Grimes Golden (his favorite), Maiden Blush, Summer Sweeting, Rome Beauty, Early Harvest, and Northern Spy. And crab apples for making preserves. And May Duke cherries. And gooseberries. And Lucretia dewberries. One of his peaches is the white-fleshed Stump of the World. Jess even grows the Flemish Beauty – "A pear whose taste is summer in the mouth." In the woods a visitor can sample the wild flavors of sarvice berries and pawpaws and persimmons.

Jess in one story feels *bodacious* because of the wen – or *rising* – at the base of his skull. If he chances to be impatient, he is said to fall into a *swivet*; if he acts sick, then he looks *peaked*. As an industrious and successful nurseryman peddling his stock about the country he is what a Hoosier of that day would call *work-brickel*, meaning good at labor and able to get a *mort* (quite a bit) of work done before nightfall. Some of his less productive neighbors are likely to spend too much time at the *switchel jug* (liquor jug) and *fash* themselves and, if they are not thrifty and foresighted, are likely to have a *hardscrabble* life of it. A kind and helpful person like Jess's wife would be called *clever*, and when summer arrives this happy woman might go *fluting and flying* about the house as she does her chores. It is a land where the good old Puritan work ethic is alive and well. The undertaker in *Witch Diggers* advises Christie Fraser to have big plans but act humble (*meechin*) if he is to get on in the world.

Figurative language is abundant too. When the heroine of *Leafy Rivers* is riding behind her brother on a horse and holding onto him, she learns that "His thin waist, beneath her hands, tingled like a pump handle when the water begins to rise." The admiring landlady Mrs. Culligan in *The Massacre at Fall Creek* believed that the hand-some Charlie Fort "could charm a bird out of a tree"; he seemed to excrete "something like birdlime to catch the unwary." And so Mrs. Culligan caters to his every need, in one scene feeding him a dish of cool "tender-grained clabber dusted with brown sugar," and, in the privacy of her bedroom, treating him to hotter dishes. After Hannah peeks and finds Charlie naked with Mrs. Culligan, the distraught girl "crippled home like a string-haltered horse." We are told that Hannah, fortunately, is not a "notionate flyaway girl"; nor is she a bit *feisty* (quarrelsome or aggressive), in spite of being red-haired.

The prose, so limpid and musical in many places, abounds in poetic touches. For instance, in *Friendly Persuasion* the "Apple trees bloomed into the dusk, the last of daylight seemingly sucked up into their white petals"; an early forenoon in May becomes "The morning of a piecemeal flicker-light day."[2]

A reader new to the *Friendly Persuasion* stories perhaps imag-ines the author as a little lady of churchmouse meekness attired in gray bonnet and First Day shawl, and as loyal as a DAR matron to her ancestral township of North Vernon, Indiana, near which music-loving Jess Birdwell enacts his adventures. Such a genteel interpreta-tion is, however, essentially untrue.

West did, though, revisit both Vernon and North Vernon at the time *Friendly Persuasion* was published and also while working on *Witch Diggers*. "I was tremulous about Southern Indiana for two reasons," she confided to me about the first visit. "It was the father-land. . . . And it was the place I really knew nothing about, yet had written about. It was like – going back there that first time [1945], having staked your existence on the truth of a dream" (22 May 1966 letter).

This return was apparently a pleasant one, for she was en route to New York to be honored at a reception by Harcourt, Brace publishers who were bringing out her first book. Later, while constructing *Witch Diggers*, she returned for a much longer sojourn to check on some nature descriptions she needed. At the railroad station she asked a porter whether she could take a taxi to the hotel. The porter replied, "Lady, if you take a taxi, you're gonna plumb overshoot the town."[3] The porter did not exaggerate much, for

North Vernon, although having been over many generations the railroad and highway center for Jennings County, had at the end of World War II fewer than 3,500 residents, while the older community of Vernon across the Muscatatuck River had less than a tenth of that number. Confronting the shocked author was a plain country hamlet with crudely dressed people and with manners to match; probably typical of Midwestern communities of this size, a latter day Gopher Prairie. So this was the town that Grace West had missed! But it was not so ugly that beautiful souls could not dwell there, at least in the daughter's imagination.

Though Vernon too had fallen on neglected days, West could reflect that here once lay the headquarters of General Lew Wallace of *Ben Hur* fame during Morgan's raid of 1863, the site of a station on the Underground Railroad (see West's "Neighbors"), a courthouse where Henry Ward Beecher once spoke, the home of the now deceased author Phyllis Jackson (*Victorian Cinderella*), and the Rush Branch Church District near which Joshua Milhous had his nursery. Various buildings still standing here and across the river may have reminded her of the flour and woolen mills, the sawmills, the quarries, and the pork-packing companies that enjoyed no little prosperity in the 1800s. Probably she knew that flatboats had once docked at the forks of the river on the east side of Vernon.

She tried the hotel briefly – train smoke blew in through the window – and then shifted her quarters to Rosa Toole Gordon's rooming house on 106 Jennings in North Vernon, where the Irish landlady fascinated her with her racy and verbally rich talk. Most of the time West holed up in her room upstairs, wrestling with the novel and living on oranges, crackers, cheese, and milk, except when she strolled out for dinner in some restaurant (West's 7 May 1966 letter to me). She must have struck the other boarders as odd, a well-dressed out-of-towner arriving alone, keeping to herself, and not looking for a job. Just taking notes, notes, notes. This rooming house yielded materials for at least two of her works. One of the boarders furnished the model for the drunken ex-jockey in *Witch Diggers*, and the rooms themselves inspired the story "Breach of Promise" (West's 22 May 1966 letter to me). It was not the hamlet of Vernon, however, but the rolling suburbs that provided West with settings for *Friendly Persuasion* and *Witch Diggers*, companion pieces that are markedly different in approach.

Friendly Persuasion

About 1939, when her first stories were being published in "little magazines" – she had not yet dared to try writing a novel – West began a series containing the idealistic nurseryman Jess Millhouse. It was lucky for her that John Woodburn, of Harcourt, Brace, saw the possibility of preparing a Quaker collection and talked her into the idea (West's 27 January 1966 letter to me). Once convinced, she persisted in the plan. Not even a certain editor at Doubleday could dampen her hopes when he rejected her plan outright in 1941.[4] And not even Thomas Wolfe's editor, Edward Aswell of Harper & Brothers, could budge her two years later or thereabouts, when he suggested assimilating into a novel some of the stories he had seen, for a novel was far, far more salable for a new author than a collection would be. But West thought such a conversion quite beyond her powers (West's 7 May 1966 letter to me). Besides, was she not already convinced that the stories had sufficient merit as they stood?

Protests arose against the book even before it reached the press. A cousin, Olive Marshburn, who took offense at the frank language in the magazine versions of the stories – *pa, ain't, duck dung* – and who also thought the fictional Millhouse family seemed right out of the Milhous family album, indicated that the stories should be linguistically deodorized, scrubbed, and dressed in such proper attire as would befit a genteel family tradition. She even felt that Jess Birdwell degraded the Quaker faith in one of the stories by praying more loudly than necessary (Jess was actually trying to cover up the sounds of the "heathenish" organ in the loft). What is more, the cousin wrote to Grace West and to an English professor at Whittier urging them to use their influence in bowdlerizing the stories, as letters allegedly possessed by Jessamyn West testify. Outraged at the attempted censorship, more so since it occurred behind her back, West pointedly signified that the characters were *her* fictions – and not family history, either – by changing Millhouse into the now Birdwell family. Too, she proudly clung to the offending words.

When the book *Friendly Persuasion* received a favorable acceptance, despite the retained "vulgarities," the cousin Olive Marshburn then donned Quaker costume and gave readings from it. Marshburn now claimed that the Millhouses, newly become Birdwells, were actually Milhouses in disguise and therefore respectable members of the speaker's own family. According to West, who was furious at the intrusion, Marshburn's attitude stood for everything that had to be overcome in her life before it was possible to write honestly; in fact, she said, it accounted somewhat for the long delay in at last getting started.[5] In brief, she would have to overcome the tendency to be agreeable or decent at the expense of being truthful, to be polite at the expense of being vivid, to be pretty at the expense of being honest. There was always the family to think of, or the Joneses next door – a sure route to a writer's frustration.[6]

Following many migraine headaches and the ever threatening return of TB if she overexerted herself, West at last made the Birdwell collection a published fact – the first edition appearing in America shortly after the surrender of Japan, on November 8, 1945, and the book was issued in England the next year. West called it her "love poem to Indiana." Almost without exception the reviews were favorable; in many instances they were cordial and glowing. Nathan L. Rothman in *Saturday Review* admired the style: "Miss West," he said, "wields a prose of a most friendly persuasion. It is as soft and musical as the speech of her Quakers, as sensitive to every manifestation of nature as they." Nor did he fail to mention the "sly wit" hiding hither and yon in the stories, and the "many passages of simple loftiness."[7] *New Mexico Quarterly*, in whose pages some of West's early endeavors were first manifest, loyally championed its former contributor as a "finely original, sensitive talent." "The flavor of Quaker speech, the Quaker humor [a characteristically gentle one] and balance and tolerance are in its every sentence," the reviewer, Katherine Simons noted, "seldom does an author achieve such harmony of expression and subject matter."[8]

The reception that had a special significance for West was that of the Quaker press, which was not quite so friendly. True, Richmond P. Miller in the *Friends Intelligencer* had nothing but praise for the new work,[9] and the English journal *Friend* carried a pleasant if brief notice.[10] But *Friends Journal* bore then and at the time of the motion picture some letters of adverse criticism. One 1956 letter accused the author of being "disrespectful" toward the Society of Friends by using the "commonest of words"[11] – amusingly ironic, coming from a member of a religious group that has always advocated plain and forthright language proper to a common folk. Of course, everyone knows that common folk never use *ain't* and *pa*! It

just so happens that West's Quaker ancestors actually did employ
such words, as she herself knew (West's 25 January 1966 letter to
me). Anyone refusing to admit such vocabulary into period fiction is
being overly fastidious and unrealistic, especially today.

Perhaps West did not plan any larger pattern for the stories
when she started out, yet one can discern in the book collection a
slight pattern – familial, chronological, and thematic. The narratives
are all told from the point of view of some Birdwell figure. The
father, Jess, has seven stories; Eliza and her children Josh and Mattie
have two each; and the granddaughter Elspeth, one. They follow a
rough chronology: The first one shows Jess as a young Quaker
husband operating the Maple Grove Nursery on the banks of the
Muscatatuck before the Civil War (about 1852), and the last one ends
with him at a brave 80, rich in children and happiness. In between
the stories children are born, such as Stephen, Jane (first mentioned
in "The Illumination"), and Little Jess (first mentioned in "The
Buried Leaf"). At some unspecified time between the first and
second stories the tiny daughter Sarah is born and dies after a
pathetically brief youth.

"Music on the Muscatatuck," the earliest of the items published,
begins as sheer poetry. It is superbly fashioned to introduce the
series.[12] Its rhythmic opening paragraph is also a model of
condensed narration, giving the setting, a clapboard house along the
river; the main figure in the series to follow, Jess; his ancestry, Irish;
his religion, Quaker; his reading matter, the works of William Penn,
John Woolman, and George Fox; the two dominant aesthetic tastes in
this man, music (represented by the starling in the cage) and floral
beauty; and even a hint at his occupation. We are surprised to learn
that he has a good-looking Quaker minister for a wife, Eliza. Here, a
dream removed from the ugliness and stark monotony of the
Midwest as depicted in literature by E. W. Howe (*Story of a Country
Town*) and Hamlin Garland (*Main-Travelled Roads*), is a quaint and
generally happy land of horse racing, trout fishing, roses, and fruits;
in this land poverty, drabness, and boredom are as scarce as Egyp-
tians in an Israeli heaven.

Jess loyally lives up to the spirit of his religion, but he is too
human to go along with all its austerities. The beauties of this world
are too much with him. Still hungering for music during a train trip,
he permits the organ salesman "Professor" Quigley to talk him into

buying one. The conversation between Quigley and Jess is delightfully amusing, and, as usual, the author underplays the whole dialogue; she is wary of saying too much, of being sentimental about
this Quaker with whom she obviously sympathizes. Nor does she
pass judgment. Here is Quigley baiting his victim with lachrymal lures
as he expounds on the virtues of the Payson and Clarke instrument:

> "The throat of an angel. It cries, it sighs, it sings. You can hear the voice of
> your lost child in it. Did you ever lose a child, Brother Birdwell?"
>   "No," said Jess shortly.
>   "You can hear the voice of your old mother calling to you from the further
> shore."
> "Ma lives in Germantown," said Jess. (*Persuasion*, 8)

The reader is satisfied by this stage that Quigley's foxiness carries
no harm and that what he is beguiling Jess into buying is wanted,
even hungered for, by this music-starved Hoosier in the first place;
hence the reader figuratively leans back in a Pullman seat and enjoys
the folksy humor played out before him or her.

Later, back at the nursery, all smiles stop when Eliza refuses to
permit the instrument in the house, believing it might seduce the
family with its sensuous, ear-flattering charms. After all, there are the
neighbors and the Grove Meeting to consider. (She embodies the
Quaker's historical prejudice against music.) To appease her and to
make a concession to appearances, Jess hauls the organ into the
attic, to which heaven he and his daughter Mattie learn to repair
whenever the secular spirit of song moves them. In the climax of this
story the ministry and oversight committee calls unexpectedly, and
embarrassed Jess is desperate to drown out his daughter's upstairs
playing. He delivers for that purpose a long, extempore prayer
before the assembled elders, his voice booming out at each fortis-
simo pause until Mattie has run through "The Old Musician and His
Harp" five times. After the elders hobble out, impressed with this
strange outburst of piety, there occurs a final touch of humor when
Jess again hears the song resume from upstairs and unrepentantly
taps out the beat with his foot.

"Shivaree before Breakfast" gains effectiveness by being told
from the point of view of the Birdwell boys Joshua and Labe, ages 13
and 10, respectively. Like the other Quakers in the stories, they
speak in the now quaint "thees" and "thous" that, together with

occasional dialect words found in and out of the dialogue, lend to
the book some of its realistic flavor. These boys set out on foot one
morning to shivaree a neighbor, Old Alf, whom they suspect of
having secretly married, for Labe had overheard the old man
addressing endearments to a certain Molly in the house. But no wife
trips to the window to see them, only the bachelor. Invited inside,
they are surprised to learn that Old Alf has invented, out of sheer
loneliness, an imaginary woman so that he can talk to someone.

Joshua, older and more conventional than his little brother,
though less sympathetically responsive, feels that here is something
dreadfully amiss in the adult sphere; therefore, when he assails Old
Alf with "Thee's crazy," he unwittingly fights back the recognition
that adulthood, which meant to him "not being worried or scared
anymore," can, like childhood, have its burden of sadness. Unwilling
to admit the truth openly, he asserts that the old man is simply
demented. Joshua has been used to interpreting life according to
codes laid down by others, codes making for orderliness and regu-
larity. Meanwhile Labe, with a more flexible and imaginative personality, is unaware of such behavior standards and enters sympathetically into Alf's fantasy, even elaborating on it.[13] Unlike his stiff-
backed brother, Labe sees Alf not as odd but as companionable and
fanciful, and he even promises to come back and visit him. The two
brothers are finely differentiated characters.

No tragic lesson occurs in "The Pacing Goose," in which Eliza,
who has a weakness for geese, sets out eight goose eggs to hatch.
Jess, wanting no troublesome fowl underfoot, privily tells the hired
man to secretly pierce the shells with a darning needle. But Enoch
bungles somehow and spares an egg; one goose named Samantha is
born, and rapidly grows under Eliza's feeding into a "full-rounded
convexity" – "Emphasis on the vexity," complains Jess.[14] The pet
gives short shrift to Jess's pansies, and it even intimidates him by
extending its reptilian neck and blowing icy hisses at him. Additional
rustic humor occurs after Samantha gets mixed up with geese on a
neighboring farm and Eliza has to go to court to recover her. After
Eliza had won her case, Jess, alone with his hired man, informs him
that the trial had taught him three things, two of which were
woman's dependability and her efficiency at mastering the law; and
the third thing was: Never employ a hired man without first learning
if he can count to eight (*Persuasion*, 45).

As with some of the other stories, the reading pleasure resides especially in the *manner* of telling. There is a smiling literary allusiveness when Enoch, a reader of Emerson, thinks that some general information on women "might have a more than transcendental value." Besides enjoying a sensuous description of backcountry cooking, we also appreciate Eliza's sly wit when, after hearing her husband complain that no one in the house has written any poetry though spring is in the air, and then seeing him sniff the pies laid out for cooling, tells him that he is like all men in wanting to have their poetry and eat it too.

There is no more thistledown delicacy of treatment in all the book than "Lead Her like a Pigeon," in which Mattie reaches the nubile state and experiences her first maidenly uneasiness at having to leave home someday. The theme of approaching marriage, announced cumulatively, begins with the girl's spotting the pair of doves (symbolizing Venus) in the clearing near the empty house; her planning to care for the flowers growing untended in the yard (the flowers symbolic of children); Jud Bent's references to her as Persephone and to Gard Bent, the new boyfriend and future husband, as Pluto, who in mythology takes the goddess into the underworld as his wife; the song beginning "Lead her like a pigeon," which she very much wants the boy with the horn to complete; and the still more conventional emblem of the wedding ring: "They [her maidenly hands washing dishes] could not play the tune she envied, the tinkling bell-like sound of her mother's wedding ring against the china. . . . [T]hat said, I'm a lady grown and mistress of dishes and cupboards" (*Persuasion*, 53-54). The author's daughter told me that West found the idea for one of her stories, possibly this one, in the sound of Grace's wedding ring tinkling on the dishes while they were being washed.

Since West once admitted that Mattie was drawn after what she thought her mother might have been like as a girl living in that time (West's 18 August 1965 letter to me), it is natural to suspect that Gard Bent reflects Eldo West. As evidence of this source, we find that Gard has Indian blood and shares with Eldo West a farming background and an interest in schoolteaching.

In July 1863 the Confederate raider John Hunt Morgan led a force of about 2,460 soldiers from Kentucky to Vernon and, finding an armed militia lying in wait for him across the river, decided to bypass the town. This is the historical background of "The Battle of Finney's Ford," against which are played some moral decisions among the Birdwells as to whether a Quaker should forego the creed of nonviolence when safety demands a call to arms. Josh, moved by the state governor's appeal for militia, goes against his religious tradition and parental advice to join a local ragtag force. Although he never fires a shot against the enemy and although he ends up wounded from an inglorious fall off a cliff, he does have the satisfaction of overcoming fear and of proving himself a warrior. In putting aside the Quaker ideal, however, and rendering exclusively to Caesar, Josh foreshadows the increasing outer-directedness of the Friends that one finds culminating in the mixed-faith marriage at the end of *Friendly Persuasion* and in the spiritually impoverished community of *A Matter of Time*. Yet Josh is not the only physically brave member of his family: Labe actually loves to fight, and his bravery therefore takes the form of self-control. We are led to believe that the author's heart is with Labe.

West, no exponent of heroics and physical violence, believed that courage can be shown just as easily without physical violence as with it. Unquestionably, a natural aversion to the games of war as well as a predictable Quaker quietism, to say nothing of hewing to a historical account in which no battle even occurred at Vernon, conspired to debar her from the subject of physical conflict. Another explanation is that she had early taken up a personal interest in stoicism as a philosophy to live by, such a belief making her lot as an invalid endurable. The philosophy carries over into the portrayal of her literary figures.[15] The present Birdwell story is, consequently, not likely to satisfy the reader who demands some raw action in spicing up scenes of moral decision, especially as the author does build up to a battle scene and then defeats expectation.

In contrast, "The Buried Leaf" is a quiet interlude among the selections. At the outset Mattie is vexed at her father's refusal to let her change her name to something she thinks is elegant. After sulking, she and Little Jess unearth in an abandoned cellar a box containing a leaf from the Bible that sets a new value on her name. From an anecdote told her by her father, she learns how heroic her ancestors had been in the wilderness.

"A Likely Exchange" and "First Day Finish" are companion pieces about horses, and they are so vividly wrought that some of the

author's relatives believe – despite the almost totally fictional basis
– that such happenings did occur. In the first piece Jess, alone on a
business trip in rural Kentucky, skillfully trades his own slow carriage
horse for an unsightly quadruped whose only good point is in
refusing to be passed on the road. This neatly satisfies the injunction
that his wife had given him on parting – that he get rid of their
"racy-looking animal" – and at the same time gratifies his own lurking desire for a beast that can outrace the Black Prince, owned by
the sleek Methodist preacher. It just so happens that the owner, a
Mrs. Hudspeth, wants a slow pacer, one slow enough to be no
obstacle in marrying off her four big, beefy, pipe-smoking daughters.
As she phrases it, "Men ain't got any heart for courting a girl they
can't pass – let alone catch up with" (*Persuasion*, 114). And so they
make a trade.

In the second story the now successful horse trader drives his
ungainly animal to victory the Sunday after he returns home; aston-
ishes Eliza, who had not planned to rip off to church in a cloud of
dust; and frustrates the smug Reverend Godley, who had expected to
tear past them as usual on his way to harangue his congregation.
Although none of the participants had intended it, the race becomes
an interdenominational contest, and its outcome even satisfies the
otherwise silent Quaker congregation.

There are various ways of creating the verisimilitude of a horse
race, such as by using a series of long, sustained sentences that gallop along breathlessly, flinging the lather of rhetoric into the air.
Twain shows early in *Roughing It* how it is done with the pony
express rider, and later with the dog chasing a jackrabbit. West does
not use this method; her effects stem largely from a suspense carefully built up, from subtlety of phrase rather than power of large
units of rhetoric, and from a confident knowledge of horseflesh.

Like the two selections just examined, " 'Yes, We'll Gather at the
River' " contains a strain of frontier humor in the tradition of such
early practitioners as George Washington Harris, Augustus B.
Longstreet, and Johnson J. Hooper. As evidence of this similarity,
one finds plenty of local color, including an interest in rural speech
extending here to the Quakers' "thees" and "thous"; a faint coarse-
ness that is, however, appropriate to the life of rustics; a crude and
decidedly comic figure; and, finally, a bit of roughhouse giving rise to
hearty laughter.

The unclean hayseed Lafe Millspaugh, afraid for 30 years of touching bathwater, is hired to build Jess a bathhouse on the porch – the first chamber of its kind west of the Ohio. Conservative Eliza opposes the project for fear the neighbors will talk, for, after all, this was an age when all but the rich used sponge baths. First it was music, then horse racing, and now a tub for bathing (and for singing in too?) – a luxury too indulgent, too epicurean for the church! The carpenter Lafe disapproves too, and takes it upon himself to omit building a door to the otherwise completed "carnal room," whereupon Jess gets revenge by dunking this presumptuous peckerwood in the tub. As usual with West's technique, she does not report the physical struggle directly as it happens but through the senses of a nonparticipant, Eliza. Actually the tiff turns out to be quite funny this way. Such an auctorial withdrawal from anything approaching violence reminds us of the practice of another Midwestern writer, Willa Cather, as in *Death Comes for the Archbishop*.

Now past middle age, Jess in the following story is initially worried about an enormous wen on his neck. "The Meeting House" opens symbolically with him at the fireside extending his fingers as if to gather warmth in them. Although he had planned to take a sentimental trip to a distant meetinghouse where his parents had worshiped, he never gets there; instead, he has some encounters along the route that remind him of the threat of death that faces even the young. In the house of one of his customers tiny, seven-year-old Jasper Rice lies dying in a bed far too big for him. "A poor peaked little grain of Rice for such a big conveyance" is Jess's metaphysical observation, this last being about as close to sentimentality as the story ever gets (*Persuasion*, 149). An equally pathetic case is Mrs. Rivers, a dying young woman deserted by her husband who, unable to bear the presence of sickness, finds consolation in a mistress. True here to the practice throughout *Friendly Persuasion*, West forebears to judge the morals or indiscretions of her people and presents everything objectively. The readers are left to judge for themselves.

The upshot of Jess's trip is that when he gets home and compares his anxiety over the wen with the suffering he has found in other people, he thinks himself fortunate indeed; he signals his renewed delight in the simple and beautiful things of this world by sniffing the rich fragrance of some newly opened lilies-of-the-valley.

Kept indoors by rain one day, Jess in "The Vase" shows an idle interest in a vase that Eliza has left half-finished years before. Here in this intensely domestic story the viewpoint shifts easily and unobtrusively to that of Eliza, for whom the vase, made from a cracked lamp shade, holds sentimental associations. To her the object recalls the enthusiasm, the bouquet, of her early married days when before her gleamed, as it so often does in youth, an ideal future whose chance sorrows are mercifully veiled for the time being. The swan, accordingly, symbolizes that dream, the swan being painted on a shade whose crack is hidden with decoration. We are told in flashback that shortly after the infant Sarah died, Eliza had begun work upon the companion swan on the shade but was understandably interrupted by Jess one wintry day when he came in to lament the snowflakes that were then covering up Sarah's grave. The second swan consequently remained "gray and shadowy . . . reminding her of so much, the dream before sunup" (*Persuasion*, 170), meaning the imperfectly fulfilled future as represented in the early vision. The theme here includes the life cycle with its attendant joys and sorrows.

Admittedly, the ostensible event in "The Illumination" is a gathering of neighbors in Jess's house to celebrate the advent of his gas lighting, but the essential interest, as with so many of the narratives, lies in character revelation. A sharp moral contrast is implicit in Jess, a humanist more than pleased to spend his money for the sensuous satisfaction of gas light, and in the miser Whitcomb, who refuses to buy for himself any luxuries at all. Part of the success in sketching Whitcomb lies in making him no stock figure, no ordinary miser. The author probes far enough into his makeup to enable the reader to pity him as a human being. Both men are sadly aware of time's winged chariot hovering near, the dust that waits for all; still, they strive in their markedly different ways to preserve something of value from the Heracleitan flux. Jess, at least, has a cheerful light to fend off the existential darkness, much as the old customer does in Hemingway's "A Clean, Well-lighted Place." Another, equally valid interpretation of the story is that Jess, a progressive, has to contend with the narrow-mindedness and backwardness of some of his midwestern neighbors.

West has injected into her hero some of the sensibility and responsiveness of one of her favorite literary figures, Henry David Thoreau. Though Jess's sensitivity to natural beauty was mentioned earlier, it is necessary to add that he, like many Friends in history, keeps a journal of spiritual observations (whimsically signing his sentences with names of famous men). Once he puts down a Thoreau-like "Eternity's the depth you go" and consents at last to sign his own name. When Eliza tells him that he ought to prepare his soul for the hereafter, he replies, while looking admiringly at the sky, "This is preparing," reminding us of Thoreau's confident death-bed declaration "One world at a time." Like the famous inspector of snowstorms, he too is a high-minded epicurean who believes in getting a good taste of this world's pudding before turning to the next world's ambrosia.

By the time we reach "Pictures from a Clapboard House," Mattie and Gard have long married. The Quaker family has been changing, becoming more worldly: Not only do the Birdwells have gas lighting and a bathtub, but the once-banned organ now rests respectably in the sitting room. Stephen, like members of the author's own family, has moved to California. Now he is back for a brief visit and, in defiance of the family, wed to a non-Quaker, the wild and none-too-faithful Lydia Cinnamond, who had been dating another man during the fiance's absence. But Stephen is no stickler about damaged goods, for he likes a bit of wildness in a girl. Just as we experience the second story in the book from the viewpoint of a youngster participating in an abortive shivaree, we see the child Elspeth in this antepenultimate idyll witnessing a successful shivaree during Christmas at the Maple Grove Nursery. Here again much of the delicacy and effectiveness depend on the narrative point of view, which in this case is Elspeth's. To the uncritical child the talk of infidelity in the household is innocently one with the glitter of snowfall, the Christmas tree shine, the untying of presents, and the shivaree; her child vision has the cinematic flow of pictures that shimmer in a radiance best known to one in the morning of life. The wondering and trusting innocence of Elspeth contrasts with the catlike softness and inconstancy of experienced Lydia. Thus the author uses the child as a lens through which we may discern all the more memorably the patterns of adult behavior.

Elspeth, representing the third generation of Birdwells in the book, is a link in the chain of eternity. Ever so sensitively West sketches at the outset the image of the child seated in the parlor stringing a popcorn harness for the Christmas tree: Elspeth thinks of her absent mother (second generation) as the clock ticks slowly "Forever . . . forever"; under this spell she understandably feels lonely, with her mother gone and with the ticktock of everlastingness insinuating itself in her ear, and, feeling a need for human affection as a hedge against a chilling eternity, she asks her grandmother if she loves her. "Better than I did my own," Eliza was used to replying to such a question, for "Then I was too young . . . to know childhood wasn't enduring" (*Persuasion*, 187). Though too much for the child to comprehend – and this immaturity is what makes the situation poignant – the granddaughter unreflectingly occupies her own place in the long procession of generations that move from the cradle to the casket. Even so, the story's tone remains cheerful, partly because the serious parts of the story are balanced by happy ones, and all are filtered to us through the frosted glass of innocence.

The account of Homer Perkins in "Homer and the Lilies" is perhaps the most touching narrative in *Friendly Persuasion*. An adopted 12-year-old lad, he is as curious as the once-youthful Jess had been concerning all that is strange and beautiful in the world about him, but Homer's misfortune is that the kindly old couple he lives with are dead to speech and to wonder. In Homer's eyes the ordinary can undergo transfiguration into something rich and strange. He questions eagerly about natural phenomena – whether a mouse can run backward – and listens with breathless delight to the whispery fall of first snowflakes on the roof just above his attic bed. In this lovable boy, and lovable twice over because readers can see in him the best part of their own real or imagined youth, Jess recovers the boyhood he had once known. We accomplish this seeing without the slightest intrusion of the sentimental.

One day in the woods Homer makes friends with the nurseryman, who is a match for him in Wordsworthian sensitivity. In an unconscious farewell gesture to this world – managed with the author's usual understatement – Homer one day pulls up and clutches to him an armful of Eliza's lilies simply because they ravish him with their scent and loveliness. Jess's reproof on that occasion is poignant when we look back on it, for not long afterward, during a winter storm, the boy passes away. By means of allusive wording, West succeeds in conveying the impression, ever so gently, that Jess himself has not many winters to go. In a symbolic sense he has died vicariously through Homer. On the literal level the sad imminence of his own demise is postponed yet awhile, enabling the group of stories to end on just the right bittersweet note. And the already wise Jess is wiser still.

It takes no great insight to learn that the plots in these stories are usually slight, for the focus is on some revealing incident or epiphany in the life of one or more of the principal characters. The book has three serious themes. The first concerns the adolescent confronted with the problems of adulthood. We can see this theme in "Shivaree" and in "The Battle of Finney's Ford," where the Quaker conscience is at odds with the demands of adulthood and patriotism. The second theme is about the eternal procession of humankind enacted by the various Birdwells and their acquaintances who either pass through the normal life cycle or, as with Jess and especially Elspeth, represent links in the long human chain. Several stories here are the more affecting for being bathed in the light of eternity. The second theme is closely related to the third one, that of illumination, as in "The Meeting House" and "Homer and the Lilies." In the former story contact with the dying young acts reflexively to produce in Jess a heightened aesthetic sense; in the latter story Homer's demise effects a spiritual change in the nurseryman, one more fitting now that Jess is presumably at the ripe age for wisdom and for meeting his Maker. As suggested earlier, the reader cannot help thinking that the constant threat of death in the author's own life conditioned her to create literature in which human beings are, as Victor Hugo said, under a glorious reprieve from the sentence of death. A German proverb runs, "A heart that has never suffered is a heart that will never sing."

As for the book's sources, West accounts for them summarily in *To See the Dream*: "*The Friendly Persuasion*, insofar as it is anyone's experience, is the experience of my great-grandparents as remembered by my mother from tales told her by her parents. . . . The facts are very few (*Dream*, 132-33). Among these facts are that Jess is modeled upon her great-grandfather Joshua Vickers Milhous, a nurseryman near Vernon.[16] Joshua had such a passion for music that on one of his visits to Indianapolis he bought a $260 Mason and Hamlin organ, and, of course, his Quaker minister wife, Elizabeth, objected, as did the congregation. Even though the Quaker neighbors never became accustomed to the instrument, the Milhous children were delighted, as was their mother in time. Nevertheless, the whole affair of Quigley and the church elders in "Music on the Muscatatuck" is fiction.[17]

Like Jess, Joshua had a love for flowers and birds and was enthusiastic about stargazing. He was supposed to have enjoyed fast horses, but the races in the book are pure inventions. The same applies to the Kentucky trip. " 'Yes, We'll Gather at the River' " derives partly from an experience Joshua had in building a bathroom; he had a tiff with the carpenter, who had refused to install a door because the specifications did not call for it. And "The Illumination" draws on Joshua's successful installation of manufactured gas in his home. Left out of the story is the unpleasant fact that fumes began to rise into the house from a storage tank underneath and necessitated removing the equipment – much to Elizabeth's relief.

The personality and appearance of Eliza are indebted to the Mary Frances McManaman mentioned earlier, a black-haired Irishwoman who made vases from lamp chimneys. The names Eliza, Mattie, Jess, and Josh are all derived from West's ancestors. There was no shivaree at a bachelor's house. West wrote to me that her mother had heard about an old man near the Maple Grove Nursery who used to talk to an imaginary spouse. As said before, Grace forms the basis, however slight, for Mattie's characterization: For instance, West wrote me of her mother's memories of "riding a white horse . . . [and carrying] cookies in a reversed footstool to an ailing woman in the woods." Grace also remembered a neighboring orphan boy of 16 or 17 named Homer who, in spite of good health, was found one morning dead in bed – with no evidence of foul play. Grace saw him in the coffin in his front yard with white tube roses in his hand. West said that "[t]he whole story came from the wonder in her voice at this sight . . ."(26 January 1966 letter to me).

"The Buried Leaf" owes its being to the author's own childhood when she saw in the cellar of an abandoned house a Bible left to molder. "Pictures from a Clapboard House" has a similarly faint origin in the author's experience, in this case from hearing over the telephone in the grandmother's house the clock ticking in her own house. And "The Battle of Finney's Ford" is all fiction except for Morgan's raid (West's 25 January 1966 letter to me).

One can see, then, that the facts are indeed skimpy. Far from being family history or even an attempt at it, *Friendly Persuasion* is almost totally a product of the imagination. To claim otherwise, as

some of West's relatives have wanted to do, is to grossly underesti-
mate what is entailed in converting a "germ," as Henry James calls it,
into an artistically wrought story. Despite all of West's efforts to
downplay this book, for fear that she would be labeled a one-book
author or a "sweet old Quaker lady," *Friendly Persuasion* is as
exquisitely wrought as anything else that she did.

Inasmuch as West left Indiana very early, apparently before she
gained any unfortunate impressions of the region, she could well
afford to look back with romantic nostalgia. Naturally, one wonders
what kind of Birdwell collection would have resulted had West
revisited North Vernon *before* the writing began. An earlier Quaker
author, James Baldwin (1841-1945), spent his entire youth in central
Indiana in the area around Westfield. His highly autobiographical
narrative *In My Youth* was later reissued with the significant subtitle
"An Intimate Personal Record of Life and Manners in the Middle
Ages of the Middle West."[18] This novel furnishes quite a different
view of pioneer life during the period that corresponds to the young
manhood of Jess Birdwell. It is the viewpoint of an insider. Jess and
his family, we will remember, seem to be somewhat isolated but not
lonely, have a simple yet not drab environment, and soon come to
know the beauty of music and the luxury of a bathtub and gas lighting. *In My Youth*, by contrast, shows a shy, sensitive boy starved for
beauty and oppressed by the harsh realities of a pioneer Quaker
settlement. Mercifully, he escapes into a world of fantasy where he
has imaginary playmates to keep him company and somehow make
life bearable. Still, the lad takes a cheerful view of Quaker life on the
frontier, despite the numberless privations – yes, including that of
music. Probably there is no more heart-wrenching, realistic contrast
with West's books to be found anywhere in the limited body of
Hoosier-Quaker literature.

Widely translated abroad (Dutch, French, German, Spanish, and
Italian editions appeared in 1945), *Friendly Persuasion* soon established Jessamyn West as the most accomplished Quaker writer of the
age; moreover the reputation of this book overshadowed most if not
all of her later work. And no doubt the successful 1956 motion
picture starring the popular Gary Cooper in the role of Jess Birdwell,
as well as the catchy theme song from it, "Thee I Love," heard over
the radio even a decade later, helped create this imbalance. The film,
though not a faithful rendition of the story, contains enough resem-

blances to remind the readers of their adventures with the text without constituting a repetition. A broad, folksy, sometimes sexy humor replaces wit for the most part. Unfortunately, the camera eye shows us little of the aesthetic and philosophical side of the remarkable nurseryman of the book.[19]

Further Persuasion

In the spring of 1969, almost a quarter century after the publication of *Friendly Persuasion*, West's second and final installment of the Birdwell pieces appeared in the form of *Except for Me and Thee*.[20] More than half of these stories had never been printed before and were written expressly for the book – an unprecedented method for West, whose motive was clearly to fill in gaps in the previous collection. Sarah and Gard had had roles that were barely sketched; now these figures are enlarged. Perhaps owing to the scriptwriting influence, both Little Jess and the Civil War take on increased significance. In the first collection the reader was left curious about Jess's bachelor days, but the new collection more than satisfies these needs. And for the first time a Jessamyn West book handles that infamous contradiction in the land of freedom and egalitarianism, black slavery.

By midsummer this new assemblage had the ephemeral distinction of being on several best-seller lists. Unquestionably West's family relationship to the newly elected president of the United States, Richard Nixon, drove up the sales, especially after her appearance on the NBC's televised "Today" show. Even more potent as advertising must have been the longtime popularity of *Friendly Persuasion* both as a book and as a film. Moreover, the new book fortunately came out at a time when the reading public was jaded with a superfluity of raw stories about sex, perversion, and brutality; consequently, it found a welcome, not only because it was a well-written book about a wholesome and quite believable family whose members clung to traditional moral values but also because it satisfied a desire for a more normal, peaceful, quaint, even charming mode of existence.

The character types, the main locale, the backcountry Quaker diction, the rustic drollery and high jinks, and even the situations are agreeably consistent with those of the 1945 collection. The book is warmhearted but unsentimental; kindly, folksy, comfortable; and, in those stories about slavery and war, compassionate toward the victims. It contains a dark seriousness only hinted at in the first edition. Thus the reader finds here and there a reaction against the idealized material of *Friendly Persuasion*, a reaction consisting of increased realism and a critical awareness that Quakers must somehow, short of violence, come to grips with and maybe alleviate the social evils of their age. There is less poetry now, and the style is not so light and graceful as in 1945. On the other hand, we find more wisdom and humaneness, together with what Matthew Arnold would have called the ability to see life whole.

"The Wooing," the first of the new set, shows Jess as a restless swain who rebels, albeit briefly, against the Quaker tradition of marrying only within the sect; for "He intended to live, not to repeat a pattern" (*Except*, 8). His wildest fling consists of letting himself get intoxicated in the company of a husband-hungry girl, acceding to her proposal, and the next day getting betrothed to still another girl. Some light comedy develops when the two prospective brides, having learned of each other's troth, walk sorrowfully up to the Birdwell dinner table together and require Jess to make a choice. He turns them both down, for by this time he has fallen in love with the preacher Eliza Cope. At the opening of the next story he and Eliza have been married for five years and are chafing at having to live in father-in-law Birdwell's house. Jess now takes a long trip West to look for a suitable homesite, and he picks a fertile and beautiful spot in Indiana, which becomes the Maple Grove Nursery. "The New Home," third in the group of stories about Jess's early life and his settling near Vernon, is chiefly memorable for the figure of the lightning rod salesman Herman Leutweiler, who has all the glib cunning and racy speech of Professor Quigley, and then some. Naturally, Jess must safeguard his new house against not only chain and sheet but ball lightning as well.

"First Loss" deals with the death of their firstborn, Sarah, victim of scarlet fever at age five. The coffin symbolism here is eerily effective. Following this sad episode comes the relatively inconsequential "Mother of Three," whose only excuse for being seems to be that it represents for the first and only time in the whole series the everyday trial of a young mother in rearing an obstreperous brood of children who sometimes get into mischief. The happenings are as commonplace as buckwheat pancakes. But aside from the occasional "inner light," Indian raids, wars, and the founding of homesteads and communities, how much of the daily living on the nineteenth-century American frontier could not be considered commonplace? The marvel is that West could, at least in the other stories, make intriguing these sober, God-fearing, orderly, practical, and artistically starved Quakers whose actual counterparts in history (the Milhouses) were mostly cut out of the same unexciting roll of provincial homespun. West put it even more starkly when she observed, "I don't believe the *true* stories about the Milhous family *could* be written, except in the ironic vein of Flannery O'Connor" [italics hers] (25 January 1966 letter to me).

"Neighbors," by far the longest episode in the book, ranks as one of the best. The setting is 1856. Despite the tone of calculated understatement and domesticity conveyed by the title, we find physical excitement and suspense as Eliza and her neighbors save a black slave couple from recapture. The turning point in the drama comes when Eliza is forced to admit, in the face of her conservatism and respect for legal authority, that there is a higher moral law to which the cruel Fugitive Slave Law must submit. The author makes her, rather than Jess, the focus of narration, perhaps because Eliza had not earlier committed herself to any serious social problems or experienced any danger. *Except for Me and Thee* might be subtitled "Eliza's Coming Out." A later adventure in which she again involves herself in the alleviation of human misery is "After the Battle," the battle being Morgan's raid, in which she binds the wound of a young Rebel trooper.

Jess in "Fast Horseflesh" gets his warmup for the race against Godley's Black Prince, whose defeat was covered in *Friendly Persuasion*. A newspaper editor named Arkell wins over him, evidently because Eliza, who wanted to teach her husband a lesson, prayed for the opponent's horse.

The weakness of using Jess exclusively as the focus of narration keeps "Growing Up" from being as funny or at least as satisfying as it might otherwise be. Some comic possibilities were lost in not permitting the reader to follow young Labe to his birthday party at Louella's, where, for all we know, the amorous seamstress might have given Labe some awkward moments. It stands to reason too that the emotional impact of growing up, of a lad's being pursued by an older woman, is something that the participant ought to feel more keenly than the parents. West would have solved this problem admirably had she not decided to restrict the focus of narration throughout the book to either Jess or his wife. "Shivaree before Breakfast," in the other collection, shows movingly how West can present the direct initiatory experience in the young without needing the consciousness of the Birdwell parents to provide interpretation. There, Josh and Labe are constantly before the reader; the main interest resides in their feelings, rather than the parents' response to the adventure with Old Alf.

It might as well be observed at this juncture that one of the biggest differences between the volumes of 1945 and 1969 is just this striving after a consistent focus of narration by showing every adventure as it impinges on Jess or Eliza, or both. (As hinted earlier, this focus is sometimes gained at a loss in dramatic power.) *Friendly Persuasion* had deviated from this "ideal" at least four times. But *Except for Me and Thee*, which was devised after many years of teaching creative writing in the universities (where correct mode of narration is sanctified), of building novels, and of contriving coherent motion picture scripts, demonstrates a tighter method of unifying an episodic story line. That West wrote so many of the new stories expressly for a collection in itself promoted unity, whereas the separate parts of *Friendly Persuasion*, designed for scattered magazines over the years, ranged at large by focusing on three generations of Birdwells.

"A Family Argument" reveals Jess as a wise patriarch who holds his family together in time of dissension by virtue of his firm will and fairmindedness. Like the nation still smarting from the trials of the Civil War just ended, the Birdwells have their internal quarrels too. And the years have brought changes: Mattie has married, alas, a Methodist; her Gard is now a farmer; Little Jess has grown into a pert youngster who likes to interrupt discussions; and Josh attends school in Philadelphia. Compared with Jess, all the young people present to celebrate his birthday seem foolish; they are like puppies growling over a rag and tearing it apart. Still, he refuses to wax bitter and complain: "The world suits me to a T, Mattie. That's my trouble. Why, sometimes I think the Lord made it especially for me. I like its colors. I don't see how the flavor of spring water can be improved on. I'd hate to have to try to invent a better fruit than a Grimes

Golden. Yellow lamplight on white snow. Thee ever seen anything prettier?" (*Except*, 283).

The moral of the final story serves to confirm Jess in his contentment. Two related plots operate, one inside the other, to treat the theme of family love. "Home for Christmas" finds Jess resisting Mattie's desire to put up a Christmas tree (Methodist bauble) – Quaker tradition did not provide for this modernism. "The bigger the celebration in the world, Jess feared, the less chance the heart had for its celebration" (*Except*, 294). We can almost hear him say, if we use our imagination, "For heaven's sake! If thee lets the tree in, thee will next have to drag in Christmas stockings and presents, other gimcracks having nothing to do with true Christmas spirit!" But the tree, Jess knew, would make Mattie and her little Elspeth happy. At this juncture the alcoholic Jasper Clark arrives to ask for a loan with which to buy his family some Christmas presents. He gets it: Jess thus makes his first hazardous step toward modernism. Not long afterward Clarence Clark, Jasper's son, clatters up to ask Jess to help deal with Jasper who, drunk now, has been shooting wildly from his upstairs window. It looks like a sordid affair.

The true situation in the Clark family gradually unfolds for Jess after he reaches the scene. He learns that Jasper did not spend the borrowed money on liquor (someone gave him the jug), and that he had first remembered to buy presents for the whole family. Jasper had gotten drunk because he learned that his daughter Jenny was pregnant out of wedlock; he was shooting to drive off the seducer should he come. Despite these misfortunes, the Clarks love and care for one another. But no sentimentality intrudes to mar the perfect dignity and restraint of those passages in which Jess and Clara converse about familial matters.

Back home, warmed by this example of domestic love, Jess permits the Christmas tree to go up, although he does so against his better judgment. "People are getting more worldly every day," he laments with the expected conservatism of a grandfather. "Except for me and thee, Jess" (*Except*, 309), Eliza puts in, evidently speaking for the author and herself, and incidentally providing the title for the book.

The only Birdwell story published earlier that was not included in the volume is "Little Jess and the Outrider."[21] Not only is it inferior to "After the Battle" in bringing home to the Birdwell clan the reality of war, but its inclusion would be repetitive, inasmuch as the theme of aiding a wounded trooper appears in both episodes. Besides, the focus in the omitted story is on Little Jess; *Except for Me and Thee*, as stated earlier, mistakenly limits the focus to Jess and Eliza.

As a best-seller, *Except for Me and Thee* obviously found some partisan reviewers. S. L. Steen wrote that the "characters are well portrayed, the prose poetic and charming with the Quaker idioms and touches of humor."[22] Zena Sutherland noted the "vibrant authenticity of the characters . . . [and the] practiced ease and resilience of style."[23] Perhaps it was Carlos Baker who gave the most thoughtful and sympathetic coverage of the book: He opined that readers will learn more about the Birdwells but have "a certain mild regret that [this] is not the equal of its predecessor. . . . What if this sequel is a little paler than 'The Friendly Persuasion'? . . . It will be a welcome accession to those (like myself) who are always eager to begin a new book by Jessamyn West."[24]

The two collections ought to be combined into one in order to keep the chronology straight. An examination of all the stories shows clearly that a suitable order can be followed in such a gathering if "Music on the Muscatatuck" is allowed to come first, as a beautifully seductive invitation to the series. The newcomer to the now-separate books might find the following sequence helpful:

1. Music on the Muscatatuck
2. First Loss
3. Mother of Three
4. Neighbors
5. Shivaree before Breakfast
6. The Pacing Goose
7. Lead Her like a Pigeon
8. Growing Up
9. The Battle of Finney's Ford
10. After the Battle
11. The Buried Leaf
12. Fast Horseflesh
13. A Likely Exchange
14. First Day Finish
15. "Yes, We'll Gather at the River"

The Buried Word

An early unpublished story called "Footprints beneath the Snow"[25] represents a first attempt to get at the materials of *The Witch Diggers* (1951). In this 22-page manuscript nubile Lovetta Lewis, spending the Christmas holidays with her grandparents at the Jennings County poor farm, which the grandparents manage, so doubts that her lover Gardiner Bent will come to get her that she despairs. Actually he delays because he had heard a false report that she was spending Christmas with his rival. But when in the dead of night Gardiner at last arrives in his sleigh, she leaps out to him through the snow and they ride off to a joyous reconciliation. The juxtaposition of youth with age; warm and passionate love with midwinter iciness; the lover arriving unexpectedly on one of the few nights of the year commonly devoted to celebration and hope (Christmas Eve); the maiden's sight of her future husband; the elopement from the bedroom; the old grandmother left behind to greet the chill of a winter morning – all these qualities are singularly evocative of Keats's tale of medieval elopement in "The Eve of St. Agnes." Regardless, *The Witch Diggers* will show far fewer resemblances to the poem and must be considered completely original.

We may observe in this abortive story the poor farm of great-grandfather James McManaman's day, but it is suitably fictionalized even in this period when West tended to be too transparently familial. There is a Jud Macmanaman as a carousing and bookish precursor to the serious and thoughtful Link Conboy of the novel. To their dissatisfied wives both men represent an image of failure for having chosen the wrong line of work. The love situation about the ineligible suitor perhaps echoes Grace Milhous and Eldo West, who did some of their courting at the farm.

"Footsteps beneath the Snow" contains some of the materials that eventually were used in "Lead Her like a Pigeon" and in "Pictures from a Clapboard House," a fact showing that originally the substance of *Friendly Persuasion* and *Witch Diggers* was hardly separable in the artist's mind. But creating Jess Birdwell and placing him at another ancestral location nearby no doubt cleared the way and left the poor farm with its figure of the waiting girl as a nucleus for a new, much longer story someday. The waiting girl became Cate Conboy.

A glimpse at the actual setting of *Witch Diggers* may prove a diverting introduction to the plot summary that follows.[26] Not more than five miles of rolling country south of Vernon on Highway 7 in the direction of Madison, the visitor today sees on the left the prominent landmark of the Freedom Church, while on his right, a few hundred feet farther, the entrance to a gravel road. If the visitor turns onto the road and winds with it awhile through meager farmland and around a bend, he or she presently arrives at a two-storey red-brick edifice, shaped like an L, that sprawls at the far end of the road. Alongside the front are some evergreen trees. These acres, known as the County Farm, contain the only red-brick building for miles around; the structure is old, dilapidated, mysterious, and lonely. In front, down a weedy declivity, Graham Creek winds its peaceful course through underbrush and among scraggly trees.

Walking to the back of the building, the visitor finds the place in sad disrepair, unless the current owner has succeeded in making his promised renovations. Farther back across the red clay fields lies a small plot of land that the plowman always cuts around. Here among the weeds and briars, as if to be neglected until Judgment Day, some dead have markers; others, lying under sunken ground covered with thorn and weed, have not a slab to identify them as the pauper inmates of the County Farm. These dead are not kin to the self-sustaining, admirable peasants of Thomas Gray's famous churchyard; still, if they could tell their stories, the listener would doubtless hear the simple annals of the needy and forlorn, the crippled and blind, the feeble-minded and mad. These are the kinds of people Grace West had known or heard about when she visited the farm.

In the narrative of *Witch Diggers*, which opens in Indianapolis during the Christmas season of 1899, Christian (Christie) Fraser, a salesman at 22, boards a train headed south to visit Cate Conboy, his new girl, at the poor farm. She has invited him. While en route to the poor farm, Christie recalls in a flashback sequence his first meeting with Cate at a party in the home of his cousin Sylvy Cope (the surname reappears in two other books) at Stony Creek. Foreshadowings of Christie's death begin early: In his reflections, in his morbid talk with the cousin, and some months later in a coffin episode; moreover, the coffin reappears several times. Christie, an outsider bringing in his fresh point of view, is a good choice of a character to introduce for us the oddities of the poor farm.

Christie's special weakness, as the bluff Uncle Wesley Cope once told him, is that he cannot resist saying yes. The young man fully illustrates this weakness soon enough, when he slips into bed with the Uncle's daughter, who is eager to marry him. The purpose of the bedroom scene is to establish Christie, unlike his later rival Ferris Thompson, and unlike Cate herself, as a normal and passionate lover.

Cate, four years Christie's junior, is second to her mother in being the best realized character in the novel. She is an egocentric, proud, boyish-looking (Conboy) girl with a superb figure, short curly hair, and dark flashing eyes. But given her mother's indoctrination in backcountry fears about sex, Cate suffers from a common hangup in West's books: A belief that sex leads invariably to pain and suffering. She cannot accept woman's sexuality as a normal part of her makeup. Lib yells at her for bathing naked in the presence of her little sister; she orders Cate to cover herself with a towel, else she will be giving the sister bad thoughts. Lib says there is too much passion in the family as it is: Distrust those awful sexual impulses. And Cate, who wants dearly to please her mother, hearkens and obeys.

By contrast, Christie is an ardent lover. Arriving at the junction, he takes a macabre wagon ride out to the County Farm with the undertaker Korby, a vulgar social climber who is known for ostentatiously planting a kiss on the forehead of each and every corpse before closing the coffin. A chilling confrontation occurs when Christie is left holding a child's casket at the door of the main building, Korby having raced off suddenly, and Dandie Conboy opens the door angrily to snatch the casket out of his hands.

We learn that Dandie, who insists on finding his own happiness without the aid of his altruistic father, has fallen in love with and will soon marry the softly feminine Nory Tate, a girl who has been raped and made pregnant by her uncle. Part of the story's suspense is whether or not Dandie will succeed in wringing from her the ravager's identity and what revenge he will then exact (in chapter 10 he castrates the old man).

Another rebel is Cate's precocious little sister, Em, who pertly announces to Christie at their first meeting that she was probably adopted since she is so unlike the other Conboys. This amusing Em feels out of place at the house, for "she missed . . . those daily draughts of envy, admiration, and hate with which she was customarily refreshed at school. At school she was somebody, a person to be reckoned with."[27] Her innocent exhibitionism – drawing pubic hairs on herself with burned matches in order to seem grown up and displaying herself naked to a Peeping Tom in an honest endeavor to cure him of his obsession – is, of course, sensational yet still consistent with what we might expect of a well-meaning little flaunter living in such surroundings and developing, unlike her sister Cate, an uninhibited interest in sex. As with some other figures in the story, Em stumbles about searching for happiness, and her search is made all the more difficult because of her bizarre methods and the shocked disapproval of the family. Soon enough learning that she gets people into trouble by telling secrets, she learns to keep the important ones to herself, including the news that insane Mary Abel plans to destroy the pigs belonging to the poor farm. No wonder that in the latter part of the novel she has lost her charming spontaneity.

Christie meets the parents as well. Lib, modeled after the West's mother,[28] is a handsome woman who enjoys being the poor farm's matron because of the social distinction. In the course of the narrative she develops from a benevolent shrew, quick to belittle her husband, to a wifely companion who shows him genuine respect, and from the unaffectionate mother of Cate she becomes a creature of sorrow who pities her daughter and even kisses her for the first time – for Lib needs to feel superior to and have pity for others before she can ever show them affection. There is simply not space enough here to do justice to this provocative woman, to her pride and aloofness, her wrongheadedness, her vulgarity and slovenliness in keeping house, her capacity for insult, and her dexterity in putting presumptuous people in their place.

The problem with her husband, Link, is that he cannot get close to the souls of the inmates, though he tries and tries. He has waited all his life to meet someone to whom he can open his heart. But his children are largely uncommunicative with him, Lib is too proud and distant (when not merely condescending), and most of the poor house inmates are lame conversationalists. The only inmate with whom Link can communicate is John Manlief, an intelligent mute who miraculously regains his powers of speech from having bestowed love on a nursling pig – that's right, a pig – that he has kept hidden in his room.

Among the grotesques cared for at the County Farm, Christie finds the cultists James and Mary Abel, brother and sister, who are obsessed that the Devil has long ago buried Truth somewhere in the earth and that it is now necessary to dig it up so that humankind can again be happy. For this digging they try to recruit the young sales-man who, unfortunately for them, has settled for the lesser happiness of making love to Cate whenever he can get her alone; never-theless, they do manage to enlist the adventurer Em for their mad diggings. The activities of the witch diggers provide a symbolic parallel to the misguided and sometimes frantic efforts of the so-called normal person, such as Cate, to reach happiness. After we read about foolish Cate getting married, the Abels no longer seem so demented.

The main plot pertains to the courting and betrothal of Christie and Cate; her sudden renunciation of Christie, who is for her "that old darkness" she feels she has to master and deny before she can enter safely, like a desexed nun, into the platonic bosom of the Thompson family; and her decision to marry the sensible, unexciting, and hypocritically delicate-minded Ferris Thompson, a man who does not even arouse her. She believes that if he is above such a dirty thing as sex, then she can master her own libidinous impulses and thus live a "mysteriously better life."[29] Ferris, she thinks, repre-sents the antithesis of the loose and terrible sexual behavior that she is alarmed to find around her and even in her own ardent lovemak-ing (she once let Christie play with her breasts). Being almost sexless, Ferris would, consequently, be "good." In due course she marries him, despite intelligent advice to the contrary, and she goes to live in the prissily inane household of domineering Mother Thompson, "a small, bow-legged woman who looked . . . a good deal like an anxious hen searching for a spot to drop an overdue egg" (*Diggers*, 136), and whose notion of housekeeping includes blowing dust from corners by means of a midget bellows.

Shocked at hearing of Cate's nuptials, the salesman gets drunk, he is taken in by Sylvy, and the two are soon betrothed. Now that Cate has made a mess of her life she at last realizes that she hates her husband and wants Christie instead. And so she lures Christie to her with a letter. The plan almost works, except that he chances to visit Link at the poor farm first, where he loses his life trying to rescue livestock from the barn set afire by Mary Abel. His death leaves a guilt-stricken Cate, who somehow has to apportion the blame and perhaps learn from wise John Manlief the right way to love.

The story is clearly a tragedy about an admirable young woman who refuses to trust the honest dictates of her heart because of a mistaken notion about virtue – her "tragic flaw" is an error of judgment – and who consequently brings calamity on herself and her true love. As in Emily Brontë's equally strange *Wuthering Heights*, a passionate girl learns too late that she has married the wrong man. Here in *The Witch Diggers* is perhaps the most tightly knitted and carefully worked-out tragedy that West gave us. From the death symbols at the beginning, all the way through to the conflagration, we feel a dark inevitability at work. The high point of mischief is the mistaken marriage, the death of love, aptly symbolized by the cooking of the goose named Eros. It is only a step further to the death of the lover himself. The witch diggers, who are on one level simply bizarre symbols of the mad quest for happiness in which Cate and Christie are to suffer, become in this intricately plotted novel agents of the catastrophe at the end.

The sources of *The Witch Diggers* are interesting mainly insofar as they demonstrate how little of actuality West chose to work with.[30] She made no interviews in or near North Vernon, she said, and she studied the administrations of none of the poor farm superintendents following MacManaman (she had never even heard of his immediate successors, O. M. Amick and Albert Ochs, until I told her about them). She admits having examined, during a visit at the poor farm, some nineteenth-century account books and having copied from them a few things such as "prices, items bought . . . whiskey, horse collars, rag carpets, etc.," along with some names of people associated with the asylum. On page 50 of the notebook used at the time, there is a list of the inmates' names; comparison with the list on page 169 of the novel shows that West used three of them in altered form and three in unaltered form. Of these characters only one, Lily Bias, is engaged in any significant role. And where did the Conboy name come from? Although listed on the same page of the notebook as the other names − "Conboy for threshing 406 bu wheat 18.27" − the surname in the book derives from the author's childhood when she heard her mother speak of going shopping at the "Conboy's," a country store in the Butlerville area.

Equally tenuous are other "facts" from the external world:

1. Grace West told her there were "witch diggers" in Jennings County somewhere, but she did not know why they dug or whether the diggers themselves knew.
2. A tobacco-chewing and promiscuous hired woman named Mag Ross worked for James MacManaman; unlike the jovially earthy Mag Creagan in the story, the original was old and unattractive.
3. Grace West also told her about the castration of a man in the county who was accused of incestuous relations with his daughter; nevertheless, this incident has no known connection with the poor farm.
4. Of the poor house inmates, Miss West did learn from her mother about "Old Bob," or "Big Bob" as he was known during Ochs's administration, a giant black man of dangerous temper and childish mentality, at whose death a coffin had to be specially made to be long enough for him. He figures several times in the novel.
5. Great-grandmother MacManaman played Santa Claus to the paupers at Christmastime.
6. A North Vernon drunk, mentioned earlier, was the model for the ex-jockey Neddy Oates.[31]

All else in the novel was imagined − but this means practically everything.

And what an imagination! It runs into a riot of low comedy at times, as at the funeral service in the cemetery when the venereal Hoxie Fifield, tricked by an inmate into daubing his loins with turpentine, races toward the group while doing awesome aerial stunts. Some may object to this mixture of the comic and the macabre. Shakespeare, however, found humor in a graveyard, and theater audiences have been praising the scene in *Hamlet* ever since. William Faulkner's novels, praised by just about everybody these days, show several instances of grim humor. In general, West's humor succeeds well when she handles low types (she never treats of upperclass life anyway), almost as if remembering the advice of Henry Fielding in *Tom Jones*, who says that "the highest life is much the dullest" and that "the various callings in lower spheres produce the great variety of humorous characters."

Even though the story never flags in human interest, never descends into mere sentimentality, and has merits beyond what this brief study reports, it does not move the reader to the pitch of emotional involvement that the greatest literature does, as for instance Charles Dickens's *Little Dorrit* and Honoré de Balzac's *La Cousine Bette*. But most of the superior novels we read in a lifetime also do not reach that level. *Witch Diggers* is a first novel, and it is a superbly structured one at that; the first novels of several authors far more famous than West do not even come close to her achievement here.

The search for happiness theme is about as universal as any found among the acknowledged classics. Granting that West stops short of offering neat answers, the reader never doubts that what she is describing is a moral universe in which there is some kind of intelligent answer to human problems, though the answer may be as difficult to find as if the Devil himself had buried it in the bowels of the earth. With Jessamyn West, love is the divining rod for finding such answers.

She wrote *Witch Diggers*, she claims, "in an effort to become an 'honest woman,' " for she believed that *Friendly Persuasion* was not sufficiently realistic – not typical of the impoverished and backward region of southern Indiana. Hence the novel, a better book as far as she was concerned, would balance the account.[32]

That great dame of American letters, Eudora Welty, in one of the warmest of the predominantly favorable reviews of *Witch Diggers*, remarked that the fault of each character lies in his inarticulateness – "from whence stems his fate and his disaster." This observation makes a good deal of sense if it is limited to the Conboy family. Welty also mentioned that West created characters that are "alive and vividly struggling, explained fully"; nonetheless, the touch of mystery remains that surrounds real-life persons.[33] W. E. Wilson thought that the author fell a little short of the high mark set by her previous book, and this statement is about as severe as any of the critics made.[34] As could be expected, the Quaker press, in fact Quakers in general, tended to ignore the novel; maybe they felt that, if they looked the other way long enough, West might reconsider this new direction her craft was taking and come out with another quaint, innocuous, clean, untroubled idyll about the Quaker past – and she did, almost two decades later. Meanwhile, some of her other work would become increasingly realistic.

Witch Diggers did not sell well, and the reason is not easy to find. Surely the reason is not simply that it "wasn't dirty enough," as West explained with facetious bitterness.[35] It could be that she had already created too indelibly the image of herself as the graceful, poetic Quaker who writes with a Constable-like lovingness only of the beautiful nineteenth-century past, of childhood, of racehorses, and of other pleasant things.

An Experiment in Operetta

Hardly had *Friendly Persuasion* begun to grace the bookstores in 1945 when Raoul Péne duBois read a few pages of it and decided that this Californian would be the very person to write the words and lyrics to a musical he had in mind about Jean Jacques (John James) Audubon. West accepted his commission to do the work, for the artist-naturalist in her felt a kinship with the Haitian ornithologist whose portraits of American birds are among the nonpareils of rustic art. Her interests in this figure and in Thoreau would merge in the study of nature and the love of freedom and life in the rough. DuBois arranged for the music to be written by Pulitzer Prize winner Gail Kubik.

By July of the following year West's labor was mostly done.[36] DuBois, as an independent New York theatrical producer, doubtless had in mind the spatial resources of the large Broadway stage: "He told me not to hold back," West explained years later on the eve of the world premiere, "because he would handle anything scenically."[37] His expansive instruction probably harmed the work by ignoring that need, evident now, to compress certain huge scenes and instill unity, yet with orders to restrain herself, she might very well have refused the commission. The canvases turned out to be big – wagon train, river flatboat, forests – and the story embraced several ingredients of the Hollywood formula film. The operetta interested a film company enough for it to invest $100,000 in attempting its production, but the company finally abandoned the project because of formidable production problems.[38] The piece as brought out in 1948 by West's usual publisher, Harcourt, Brace, contained illustrations by duBois himself and carried the title *A Mirror for the Sky*.[39] Although the subtitle carries the word *opera*, the work was delivered at its first performance under the label of "musical drama." A purist, however, might insist that *Mirror for the Sky* is properly an "operetta" because it is an amusing if somewhat sentimental play stressing spectacle and a happy ending, delivered with spoken dialogue, loose plot, arias, choruses, and dances.

Mirror for the Sky conveys a romantic story in 15 scenes that depict the love life and artistic struggle of Audubon against a background of the American wilderness from 1808 to 1841. The work treats his courtship of Lucy Blakewell (historically, Bakewell), daughter of well-to-do parents, of which the father seems to like Audubon but cannot forgive him his poverty, whereas the mother treats him with unqualified disdain; the almost incredible faith and patience of Lucy following their marriage as she endures frontier hardships and defends her husband against charges of idleness and nonsupport; Audubon's refusal to compromise and become a well-paid portrait painter in Philadelphia; and, last, his belated recognition and fame.

It should come as no surprise that book reviewers disagreed about the merits of this work, for being unable to listen to or read the music or see the stage spectacle poses special difficulties. A sensitive critic would surely enjoy reading some of the songs even though he or she did not know the tunes. A good example is the witty song in act 1, scene 5 sung by Wayland Platter.

The stage production came about practically by accident. Horace W. Robinson, the director of the University Theater at the University of Oregon, chanced on a copy of the play in a second-hand bookstore and wrote to Gail Kubik to learn about the music. About six years later Robinson and his committee decided to present a mammoth public performance on 23 and 24 May 1958, in the large field house called McArthur Court on the university campus. This would be not only the biggest stage show in the history of Eugene, Oregon, but the first time the university had tried a work never before presented on the stage. McArthur Court could seat an audience of 5,000 and have room for the 250-voice University Chorus, the 62-member University-Eugene Symphony Orchestra, and a cast of 32 actors and 69 extras, not to mention dozens of production and business personnel along with a profusion of stage properties.

Chosen to play Audubon was a graduate student named Phil Green, a baritone who had experience in dozens of musical comedies and operettas and who had also sung with the Robert Shaw Chorale and the American Opera Society. An undergraduate with experience in summer theater work, Josephine Verri, would play Lucy.

Despite insufficient time for rehearsals, the operetta opened on the evening of 23 May as planned. The extensive publicity and promotion of this work in the local newspaper, on television and radio, and by fliers and letters brought in about 3,000 customers for the opening performance; also seated in the audience were Jessamyn West and Gail Kubik.

Perhaps it was just as well that no professional dramatic critic was present. After the intermission, vacant seats were "very obvious," according to one customer who was shocked at how the *Eugene* (Oregon) *Register-Guard* in its review the next day played down the shortcomings of the entertainment.[40] One person there, supposedly exceedingly knowledgeable about dramas, had this to say: "It was a bomb. It was ill-fated because of the place (McArthur Court . . . where it was staged). The extraordinary nature of the production tended to de-emphasize the story and emphasize the spectacle."[41]

To Horace Robinson, one of the principal criticisms offered by patrons was the difficulty in following the story, in keeping the characters straight, and in understanding their relationships. He adds that the music was "magnificent," but, being quite modern and sophisticated, it was not especially suited to the rustic quality of the libretto, which is surely a period piece. Moreover, in the production the music and libretto tried to "out do each other in terms of time and in terms of consequence." Having watched the premiere, West allegedly confessed to Robinson that she, too, was dissatisfied with her piece and knew some ways to improve it.[42] Insofar as is known to me, the operetta has never been repeated elsewhere, although the Roger Wagner Chorale has employed some of the songs in its programs.

One criticism of Robinson's is particularly valid: The lack of continuity. Any reader of the book can see that Audubon and Lucy are quickly swallowed up by the spectacle of the great American wilderness, its colorful humor, its singing, its restless movement of flatboat and wagon train. Not all of the scenes are essential; and taken as a whole the scenes do not contribute toward any single dramatic action but instead relate to a whole lifetime of artistic perseverance and wifely fidelity. It is the kind of story best suited for a novel or motion picture.

Circe at Whitewater

West's novel *Leafy Rivers*[43] is alluded to in the writing notebook as an entry written down some 15 or 20 years before. The entry reads simply: "A story in the past – the woman who drove the pigs." Even before she had completed the manuscript, West was placing less value on it than on, say, *A Matter of Time*,[44] which is covered later in connection with the California items. In *Leafy Rivers* Indiana provides the main setting, but Ohio figures in the opening and closing scenes.

Using the omniscient point of view for her narrative, the author tells us that buxom young Leafy is about to give birth to her first child at her mother's home in Blue Grass, Ohio, where she is visiting for a few weeks before returning home with her husband to their Indiana homestead. Only Leafy knows that the father of the child is not her husband.

While waiting and waiting for Leafy's "wood colt" to get born – it will be a difficult birth – we slip back into 1816 and follow Leafy and her husband, Reno Rivers, into the Hoosier state where they run a pig farm for a year while endeavoring to make the place pay for itself. Their Whitewater landlord, the widower-sheriff Simon Yanders, falls in love with Leafy and dares to kiss her one day, and when a debt becomes overdue and the sheriff tries to enforce payment by seizing their livestock, she locks him in the barn, steals his horse, and sets out alone to drive the pigs to Cincinnati, where she will sell them to pay off their debt.

Along the trail the herd roots out a nest of snakes, the old Edenic symbol of sin. Like the stolen kiss, the snakes represent an appropriate foreshadowing of fallen virtue. A storm soon makes Leafy take shelter in a fancy covered wagon, actually a boudoir on wheels, owned by a drover named Cashie Wade, whose mistress she soon becomes. As controller of pigs Leafy now takes on the role of Circe. Hanging just beneath the wagon is a wire-enclosed pen for carrying sick pigs: it is no accident in this thickly symbolic story that the bed of adultery lies just a squeal away from the bed of swine.[45]

Through the sexual embraces of this backwoods Lothario, Leafy gets sexually awakened; we are supposed to believe that all this rutting along the pig traces satisfies her need for variety – especially after she gets pregnant for her efforts – and enables her to become more loving as a wife. Leafy learns from her mistakes, however, that the sexual act does not constitute love in the true sense and that, if Cashie can embrace her so readily, he can do so with almost any woman.

Having thus compromised her heroine, the author now begins to keep a balance sheet as if determined that Yanders, who had shoplifted a kiss from the girl, and Cashie, who had robbed the store, must each pay a penalty. The cuckolded Reno, back at Whitewater, at last shows his enterprise by galloping out to search for his wife despite his dangerously infected foot. The lame foot suggests the crippled god Vulcan, whose wife, Venus, betrayed him continually. Reno almost kills himself in the derring-do but is rescued by Sheriff Yanders, whom Leafy's little brother Offie had freed from the barn, and then rides to Cincinnati stretched out in Cashie's own wagon – ironically, even lying in the very same feathered bed his wife had warmed more than once in dalliance.

While we learn these adventures, the baby continues to show a Tristram Shandy-like reluctance in getting born. And Leafy's brother Chancellor discovers that his life's calling is to be a preacher (reminding us of Orpha's brother in *The Life I Really Lived*).

Chancellor's voluptuous girlfriend, Venese, is the most luridly drawn of all the characters; just as Cashie tempts Leafy into adultery,

Venese tempts Chancellor into fornication. This young woman whets her appetite for meeting her lover by encouraging delayed absences, by putting up temporary barriers to their love, by deliberately arousing his jealousy. And Chancellor enjoys the "chanceyness" (the author's word)[46] of these sylvan encounters – that is, until she takes what is for us the unbelievable step of arranging to be caught naked in the presence of another suitor just so that she can pique her boyfriend's appetite. One gets the feeling that Venese's function is mainly to spice up the Blue Grass phase of the story and make the erring Leafy seem by comparison the soul of abstinence.

Venese, who likes to woo secluded in a bower of fox grapes, with the fruit "hanging down for the taking . . . sweet and tangy once you got past their skins" (*Leafy*, 13), clearly suggests by name, by her rendezvous, and by her mode of pleasure the role of Venus. By every endowment she is well fitted to keep a love affair, or a marriage, from growing monotonous. Of all the West heroines she comes closest to deserving the tribute that Shakespeare's Enobarbus pays to Cleopatra: "Age cannot wither her, nor custom stale / Her infinite variety." Still, Venese is no deceiving adventuress but a faithful backwoods belle. That she is attracted to a fellow about to don the sober garb of the ministry may make some readers skeptical. But ever since Hawthorne's Arthur Dimmesdale of *The Scarlet Letter*, the reading public has been discovering that preachers are also human. Bernard De Voto in his *Mark Twain's America* tells of the sexual freedom on the frontier and of the correlation between camp meetings and the rush of marriages that followed for the next three months. In the light of history Venese and Chancellor are not, then, unusual in their behavior.

West evidently wanted us not to compare Chancellor to Sinclair Lewis's Elmer Gantry – the lad is too goodhearted and too serious for that – but instead to find him uninhibited and virile, in contrast with his colorless brother-in-law, Reno. Chancellor's religious profession should come as no surprise to anyone, for the frontier church in early America offered one of the few opportunities a young man *could* have for the exercise of power and influence. We are led to believe that he and his girlfriend will soon abandon their little prayer meetings in the grape bower, for he tells her that she will have to get herself "saved" just as he did.

In one intriguingly symbolic scene Chancellor happens on Venese lying on the school ground one day in the midst of students; her dress is being used as a tablecloth; and she, playing out a game, allows the students to "set" her body with victuals from lunch baskets as if she were a table. Unconsciously aware of erotic significance here – her body, so to speak, a banquet spread out for the generality – Chancellor jerks her to her feet. After all, her last name is Lucey (loosey).

When the child is born, jealous Reno mistakenly believes that Yanders is the father. This is one of several ironies in the final chapters. Cashie is actually the father, no doubt about it. But because the truth about the paternity is not so explicitly set forth as some readers might desire (some reviewers surely misunderstood), the following bit of interior monologue from Leafy might help: "Everybody here tonight but Reno himself, who said the words that I [Leafy] had to hear, ready to claim the credit for what those October nights [with Cashie] along the trace produced" (*Leafy*, 302). Translated, this means that various people mistakenly believe that *they* helped the most in the safe delivery of the child, but Leafy knows that the major help came when Reno assured her that he would stay devoted despite her fall from grace.

Among the arresting features of the novel must be counted the double names and name changes. Cashie Wade is also known as Olin; he is dissatisfied with both names; by extension, he is dissatisfied with both of his selves; and he wants to get a new name. Leafy, who turns over a new leaf at the end of the story, is for once able to make up her mind and demands to be known as Mary Pratt. Offie matures enough to want to be called Howard. Prill, the mother, who also undergoes changes in the story, is sometimes called by her girlhood name, Aprilla. Even Dr. Daubenheyer, who delivers our heroine's baby, has another name, June. Reno and Bass neither look for a change in themselves nor make one; their names, accordingly, are fixed. Chancellor, more so the master of himself than the other figures, has no desire to be called anything else.[47]

West takes realism to greater lengths in *Leafy Rivers* than is usual for her. It is almost as if she were trying harder than ever to purge herself of the reputation of being the author of a sweet, charming, innocent Quakerism of the "theeing" and "thouing" variety. For instance, Leafy's Quaker family, aptly named the Converses, are of quite another variety than the Birdwells. They have no characteristic manner of speech or dress, voice no pacifist convictions, avoid no physical conflict, and undergo no persecutions as a religious group or even speak of them. Like the Baptists, they attend evangelist camp meetings of the Holy Roller vintage. Protestant groups on the early American frontier often became fundamentalist and revivalist, no matter what their original denomination; one reason for this similarity is owing to their common use of meeting facilities, which happens to be the case in *Leafy Rivers*.

West could hardly claim originality for the theme of a wife's sexual awakening by proxy, especially since Kate Chopin used it earlier in her novel *The Awakening*, and pulp novels and films have exploited it for so long that by now it is a cliché. Even the sensational subject matter did not prevent the sales from being disappointing (Farmer, 31).

Regrettably, the writer did not endow Leafy with that richness of humanity making Lib Conboy and Cress Delahanty so alive in their books that one truly cares what happens to them. It is true that West did not have to admire her figures in order to portray them well; still, such admiration did seem to help, at least with the leading females.

John T. Flanagan, writing around 1971 before *Massacre at Fall Creek* came along, was correct in saying that *Leafy Rivers* is Jessamyn West's "most successful book structurally [up to that time], but it . . . is complicated by the intentional alternations of place and time" (Flanagan, 305) that might cause the reader to lose patience. Flanagan here goes on to admit, however, that the author achieves "a magnificent sense of place" in the vividly selected details about the woods and farm life in Indiana (306). What one also notices in this novel is the technical skill: the clever symbols, the parallelisms, and the multiple and interlocking plots, all of which are smoothly resolved. The novel gives the effect of a tour de force, calculated and brilliant, cerebral rather than emotionally appealing.

The ending is so "professional," as Joan Joffe Hall objects, that it suggests the influence of formula writing, though Hall does not go so far as to say that. "It's 'professional' in a bad sense too," she continues, "for she strains to tie up loose threads in a tidy ending."[48] The ragged edges of life should have been left intact.

One is tempted to blame West's stints in Hollywood for the clichés and slick writing that turn up in *Leafy Rivers*. Indeed, some of the characteristics of the formula film are only too evident here: Each of the major characters has a problem that is resolved at the end; the setting is interestingly different; there is wilderness adventure; there is even some violence, which goes counter to West's usual practice. Sex rears its head in two parallel love plots, one (Chancellor-Venese) to satisfy those looking for the storm-tossed adventures of fornication leading safely into the harbor of marriage, and the other (Cashie-Leafy) to satisfy those looking for the thrills of hell-raising adultery in which the deceived husband, mirabile dictu, forgives all at the end. Of course, the "villains" are finally made to pay or to reform a little, and the values of the unbroken marriage are reaffirmed at last.

Frontier Justice

In 1975 appeared *The Massacre at Fall Creek*, a narrative dealing with the currently popular subject of the white man's treatment of the Indian on the American frontier.[49] No doubt West's claim to having Indian blood made the topic appealing to her. The place in this, her only historical novel, is once again Indiana. Nearly two decades earlier West had found in Oliver Hampton Smith's *Early Indiana Trials and Sketches*[50] a little-known reference to a back-woods massacre wherein five white men had murdered nine Indians who were camped along Fall Creek. Unfortunately for West the researcher (she never enjoyed doing research anyway), fire had long ago destroyed the scene of the trial, namely the Pendleton court-house, together with its official records. As she reports in an epilogue to the novel, she was able to find only "some [few] scanty [eyewitness] accounts of the trials and executions," some of these contradictory, published by public figures long after the main incident was over. Of the five historic figures referred to in the story, only three of them make an appearance, and briefly at that: James Brown Ray, the governor of Indiana; Colonel John Johnston, the Indian agent for the Northwest Territory; and James Noble, the prosecuting lawyer. All the principal figures in the story are imaginary.

What West learned was that in 1824 an amazing "first" happened in American law. Four white men were actually brought to trial on a charge of first-degree murder for the slaughter of nine Indians, most of them women and children. The Indians had posed no threat; nor had they committed any crime. The trial would not, however, have taken place had not Colonel Johnston insisted on it, pointing out that the surrounding Indian tribes threatened mass reprisals if justice were not done. One ticklish matter is that the accused whites were being tried for doing what had hitherto come naturally to them for generations as part of their Manifest Destiny – sweeping the Senecas steadily westward, grabbing their lands, and killing them, much as one would kill rattlesnakes or wolves. Moreover, for these other killings the whites came to be admired in their circles as brave Indian fighters making the frontier safe for the settlers, heroic defenders of the Christian faith against the heathenish redskin. John Wood, one of the accused in the novel, exemplifies the problem: "From his cradle to now, the old man [Wood] had heard talk of moving west. Presidents had talked about it. Jefferson had sent Lewis and Clark to open the way. . . . Preachers spoke of the West as if it was the Promised Land. But there was no way to go west and live without killing Indians" (*Massacre*, 347). And this bloody practice would continue long after the Pendleton trial was over, until in 1890 the U.S. Cavalry outdid itself in brutality by murdering more than 200 unresisting men, women, and children at Wounded Knee, South Dakota.[51]

Although the main emphasis in *The Massacre at Fall Creek* is on the trial followed by the hanging of the guilty, the central character, 17-year-old Hannah Cape, provides us, as Kay Kinsella Rout observes, with an "excellent focus" for the moral issues. We see much of the action from her point of view, while "her youthfulness and her awkward indecisiveness about her sexuality serve as analogues for a new country's attempts to reconcile its opposing values of Christianity and Indian hating."[52] Other parts of the story are told through the letters that Hannah's lover, the lawyer Charlie Fort, sends back to his father for publication in the Cincinnati *Western Spy*, just as the historical Oliver Hampton Smith sent his account of the trial off to the *Indianapolis Daily Journal*.

Hannah, the tall, sturdy, redheaded daughter of a preacher, has a crush on a sensitive but psychotic neighbor boy called Johnny Wood, who, driven by his sneering stepmother to prove his manliness, joins his father and three other bigots in shooting Indians camped out on Fall Creek. Their object is to prevent further encroachment on the white settlements. As Johnny confesses later in court, the half-breed squaw Wide Eyes pleaded with him for her life by ripping open her dress and showing him her breasts in order to prove that she was as white as he was, but the crazy boy thinks this melodramatic gesture is obscene and threatening and so shoots her once in each breast. As Rout tells us, Johnny's "fervent religiosity is his shield against his vulnerability to women, as was [*sic*] his indifference to all reality outside the cover of a book" (8). Johnny's confederates do equally atrocious things such as swinging a helpless child around and splintering his head against a tree. Clasby, the ringleader of these marauders, escapes capture until the end of the story.

Thanks to the instigation of the Indian agent, Colonel Johnston, all the murderers save Clasby are rounded up and jailed to await trial. The passionate young lawyer Charlie Fort is chosen to head the defense; his insensitive and social-climbing rival for the hand of Hannah, one O. A. Dilk, will aid in the prosecution. Meanwhile leaders from various Indian tribes in the region assemble at Pendleton to see whether the whites will punish the offenders. Their implied threat of retaliation looms like a red cloud over the remainder of the story and helps add suspense. West is careful to individualize these Indian leaders, not only by tribe, dress, and name but by attitude toward capital punishment. Her Indian hero Black Antler, for instance, opposes the death penalty under any circumstances; as a result, many of the whites and most of the Indians shun him. Nevertheless, he remains one of the most admirable even if not well developed figures in the story.

The whites too are not of one mind about punishing their own but realize that unless they try the killers and mete out justice, they stand to forfeit their own lives in the thinly defended settlements. It is a measure of white justice in those days that had the massacre occurred in the settled and safe region of Indianapolis, the accused would never have been brought to trial, or at least never convicted.

This story contains no true heroes and heroines, because, as Farmer writes, "courage and cowardice, love and hate, guilt and innocence are too closely entwined in each of the characters, just as they are in life" (Farmer, 32). Nor are there any out-and-out villains. This is true not merely because the author found it difficult (as she says) to portray genuine evil but also because she went to some trouble to create a balanced point of view consistent with the way our pioneer forebears actually thought and behaved in the crude new society being built on the fringe of the wilderness. In so doing West creates humanized people who differ in their personalities, their religious beliefs, and, most of all, their conditioning by the habits and perils of the frontier. She tries to show us all sides of what we would now call criminal behavior, how justice can be ambiguous (more on this later), and how in this mixed-up world so full of cruelty we should at least practice mercy.

Among the accused now in jail, the fiery and blasphemous George Benson has killed Indians by habit rather than malice, sees absolutely no wrong in what he has done, and rages indignant that the cowering townspeople will not break him out of jail. John Wood, Sr., outwardly a hypocrite for taking refuge in the Bible after his bloody deeds, at least admits his guilt. His life story serves as an epitome of what must have happened to many a frontiersman in that day: At last he recognizes that he was heading toward the gallows all along, since he first bought New York State land swindled from the Indians; headed into the West for easy money and free land (nothing to do, everyone said, but clear it and kill Indians); and married his hate-filled wife, Reba, whom he could not handle and who finally corrupted him and his son, now in jail too.

The most sympathetically drawn villain is the former Indian fighter and now loving family man Luther Bemis, who could have avoided arrest after he had cut the throat of Red Cloud, but who follows his code of honor by turning himself in to the sheriff. Although he confesses his guilt and repents, the wonder is that his so-called Christian principles had allowed him to murder in the first place. Later on he escapes from jail to visit his newborn son, fully intending to return after he accomplishes this. Clasby, the least sympathetic figure, is the ringleader and moral coward of the group; he alone steals from his slain victims and takes off into the wilderness rather than face the consequences of his acts. We are told that the Indians finally catch up with Clasby and will wreak on him their own type of horrific revenge that is as natural to them as the white man's hanging is peculiar: They will eat Clasby.

Rout remarks that the novel contains several moral ambiguities. Perhaps the greatest of these lies in what happens to young Johnny Wood, who was found guilty of first-degree murder and sentenced to be hanged. It is easy to see justice in the hanging of the family men, Bemis, Benson, and the senior Wood, because they had the power to

act freely and then abused that power. But the case is quite otherwise with Johnny. His fellow prisoners had already been hanged and
his turn is next. But at the last minute the Indiana governor rides in,
as he did in history, and pardons Johnny. Obviously, the governor
believes him to be mentally incompetent and therefore not responsible; even the Indians are satisfied with the atonement already
exacted; and we, who read about this unfortunate lad, know he was
the victim of his stepmother's lust for land and power. As Rout
reminds us, however, this was not an age of mental hospitals; consequently, the boy's release marks a flaw in the code of justice based
on compassion (Rout, 9). Johnny will now go out into the world
unprovided for (unless his wicked stepmother takes him in, God
forbid) and be free to commit another atrocity, if not on a harlot
who invites him to bed, then on a coquette who displays too much
of her leg or decolletage.

Incidentally, West agonized over writing the execution scene.
Mary Ganz in her review of the novel quotes the author: " 'I thought
I couldn't write it,' she said. 'It would be all over, and they would
have been hanged. Then I decided I had to.' "[53]

Another moral ambiguity turns up in Hannah's relationship with
Charlie Fort. After having sex with him she feels guilty and makes him
promise to postpone any more such indulgence until after they are
married; she concludes, paradoxically, that making love is not sinful
but having a "woods colt" is. Charlie has violated the prohibitions of
parents and society in debauching a 17-year-old girl, an act that the
author does not ordinarily approve of even though many girls were
supposed to have reached sexual maturity by that age, as witness the
early marriages in those days. Apparently we are supposed to agree
with Hannah that her fornication is forgivable because she and
Charlie are going to be married. This is admittedly specious reasoning but it is not at all strange to the millions of young couples in
America today who think nothing of engaging in premarital sex. In
thus resolving the dilemma of what to do when the flesh will not
wait, West manages to preserve the values of both premarital intercourse and a respectable social order following marriage (Rout, 6-7).

Certain improbabilities are likely to nag the reader. The main
ones concern Luther Bemis, who, though suffering horribly from
ruined knees and from gangrene brought on by freezing his feet, and
doped up with draughts of opium, manages to have sex with his wife

in a crowded jail cell. Why sex now? He is actually bent on the pleasure of impregnating her with still another child, a little girl this time
(he hopes), although they already have an infant boy whom this
widow of a convicted murderer will have to support after he is dead.
How she will manage financially or any other way after he is gone is
a matter that neither one of them bothers to figure out. In this final
reckless act of his, Bemis at least remains true to his essential wildness in not planning for the welfare of others.

Not only is the theme of the novel important, the characters
vividly drawn for the most part, and the suspense admirably maintained from beginning to end, but we find here in abundance the
flavor of rough and rugged frontier life. The author maintains a good
balance between the two stories, Hannah's love life versus the trial
and hanging, neither one getting too much emphasis; moreover, she
weaves the stories into a seamless whole by having Hannah and her
lover take key roles in both of them. It is no wonder that Elisabeth
Fisher, P. S. Prescott, and Joseph Marie Anderson all gave the novel
highly favorable reviews.[54] Amid this chorus of praise the review in
the *New Yorker* sounds imperceptive and perverse – there we read,
oddly, that *Massacre at Fall Creek* is "heavy handed," that the
author should have written nonfiction instead, and that the heroine
was "intended for the very young"[55] The book became a best-seller
and was chosen as a Reader's Digest Book Club selection and a
Literary Guild main selection (Farmer 33).

West sold the film rights for $250,000 and the reprint rights for
another $250,000 (Ganz, 28; my interview with Dr. McPherson).

Chapter Three

Southern California

The second and equally important regional background for Jessamyn West's literary development is California of the twentieth century, and is represented for the most part by some science fiction; by two collections of short stories, *Love Death and the Ladies' Drill Team* and *Crimson Ramblers of the World, Farewell*; by a unified collection of short stories, *Cress Delahanty*; and by four novels, *South of the Angels*, *A Matter of Time*, *The Life I Really Lived*, and *The State of Stony Lonesome*.

After finishing temporarily with the ancestral accounts that had led to her first book, West moved in the 1950s to the time and experiences commensurate with her own youth in California. For the most part this brought an increased realism to her work, although every now and then she went back to those early days, as in *Leafy Rivers*, *Except for Me and Thee*, *The Massacre at Fall Creek*, and the first half of *The Life I Really Lived*.

Just as we found that *Friendly Persuasion* had its "corrective" in *Witch Diggers*, so *Cress Delahanty*, whose chaste adolescent heroine is only beginning to be aware of sex, is followed by the earthy and even bawdy *South of the Angels*, using the same region and time period. Further, the Quaker meetinghouse has a diminishing role in the moral life of the people, even less than in *Leafy Rivers*.

John Flanagan notes that in the novels about California,

the . . . occupations differ somewhat [from those in the Indiana books] but the social level and the economic focus show no substantial change. Citrus ranches . . . substitute for the Ohio Valley homesteads. . . . The subsistence farmer is still common although he is not so labeled; . . . the children find school a location for peripheral activities, picnics, and dramatic and musical events; the women attend PTA meetings and supervise bake sales and raffles. Instead of backwoods hired hands there are itinerant fruit pickers, largely

Mexicans . . . textbook salesmen, seaside resort fry cooks, fish peddlers, and
piano tuners. (Flanagan, 307-8)

And contrary to the case with many novels and motion pictures
coming out of California, the stories of Jessamyn West show no interest in the crime or violence or even sophistication of the big city;
very few of her characters even get into Los Angeles, despite its
tempting proximity. And when they do visit there, it is not for long.

The southern California of West's stories is a land of eternal
summer, boasting as much floral abundance as even Indiana and
Kentucky: in flowerpots and yards grow poppies and iris, mariposa
lilies and poinsettias, geraniums and iris, while the fields blossom
with lupines and mustard and milkweed and Indian paintbrushes.
Warm winds send tumbleweed rolling through the dusty streets. As
for trees, one finds the manzanita, the yucca, the bay, the smoke
tree, the acacia, the jacaranda, and the evergreen toyon with its clusters of white flowers and bright red berries. Palm and eucalyptus are
still more common, as is the pepper tree with its dry, papery rustle.
Among the shrubs number the carpenteria and the oleander with
their clusters of fragrant blooms. Instead of nurseries we have entire
groves of oranges, lemons, apricots, peaches, olives, dates, and
English walnuts. Here the industrious Jess Birdwell would no doubt
have become a rich orchardist with miles on miles of irrigated land.

The Education of the Heart

West's 1979 novel *The Life I Really Lived* is the only one of her
works to employ both regions and is therefore suitable for intro-
ducing the California phase to the reader. One of the quotations
West used to preface her novel comes from the often paradoxical
Oscar Wilde and has a pointed application to the story: "One's real
life is the life one does not lead." In her interview with Carolyn Doty,
West restricted the interpretation by saying, "[I]t is my real life in
Wilde's sense" (Doty, 158). At any rate, she seems to mean that what
is most important to her is not the external world of happenings but
what goes on in the writer's imagination with all its interesting possibilities. For the first time in her major work West narrated in the first
person, thereby giving a feeling of authenticity to her story. She
gained more such feeling by making the life of the heroine superfi-

cially like her own: Thus Orpha Chase is left-handed and suffers from migraines, was born in a small community back East, has an adorable brother, and has one paternal ancestor who manages a poor farm and another who runs a plant nursery. Moreover, as a teenager she marries a school principal (except that the adult West married a man who soon became one); teaches happily in a rural, one-room school; moves to Orange County, California, when she is still young; keeps a writer's notebook (Orpha's is called "Book of Unspoken Thoughts") whose contents shock those who peek into it,[1] writes at first pious stories and then a successful novel; and even helps prepare the motion picture version of the novel. And then there is the Quaker faith. The writer Ann Farmer tells us that some of Orpha's cats bear the same names that West's cats did. "As does West herself," Farmer adds, "Orpha loves to see the soaring of turkey buzzards and feel the raging of a Santa Ana." The differences between the two are impor-tant, however, as West indicated to Farmer. West said that if her heroine's life did parallel her own, she would have taken the precau-tion of writing in the third person in order to prevent people from thinking that *she* had done a lot of bed hopping. She could have added that her Orpha, unlike herself, never went to the university and that her books are all novels.[2] Because the time span ranges from the turn of the century up to the early days of World War II, we get a good deal of social history through references to Theodore Roosevelt, World War I, Charles Lindbergh, the Scopes trial, the Great Depression, the New Deal administration of Franklin Roose-velt, and the Oakies flooding into California.

This novel about the education of the heart is told in retrospect by a religious and happily married woman with an admirable, 40-year public reputation of successful fiction writing. Such is her public image. But she decides to expose for the first time the "true" story of her flawed life, to tell about the "dark and bloody ground" that lay in years past. She does this not to learn her identity, as the current cliché has it, but to make a confession.[3] In her background lie lots of sensational things like dog poisoning, incest, adultery, fornication, seduction, illegitimacy, child abandonment, homosexuality, suicide, and murder.

Early on the sexually ignorant Orpha Chase wed her school principal, the bookish Lon Dudley, who is a secret pederast. We learn that Lon has been buggering the male student studying at their

house, and when the boy's father learns of this outrage he storms
over with the intention of informing Orpha. But Lon shoots the
father to prevent the disclosure, and then shoots himself. Surprisingly to the reader, Orpha then allows this same boy who had been
her rival-in-love to live there and take care of her farm. As if this
ménage were not odd enough, she then adopts an illegitimate baby
girl left there by the heartless mother. Soon she gets fired by the
school board when its members learn that she is now living with a
teenage boy and raising an infant who might, for all they know, be
the fruit of this union. Thus far she is the helpless, good-hearted,
naive victim that we can sympathize with.

Having met disaster in her first marriage, Orpha resolves that she
will follow her mind instead of her heart in marrying the next time.
No more romance. Now we see her going to the altar with a much
older man, the shoe salesman Jake Hesse. Jake is as sexually
squeamish as Lon was degenerate, and lives in what Orpha calls a
"fig leaf world." A former mama's boy, he had chosen as his first wife
a woman to substitute for his mother, and after that wife left him he
chose Orpha because she looked like the first one. Thus in his eyes
he keeps repeating acts of incest: No wonder he has psychological
troubles. He spends the honeymoon in his house, he strongly
objects to calling the family cat Pussy (his wife's pet name for the
animal), and when he wants sex he cups his wife's breasts in his
hands and says, "Bedtime, Orpha!" Horrified by her book on socialism – considered a radical subject around the turn of the century –
he burns it; he orders Orpha to burn her notebooks too, but by this
time she has enough spunk to say no.

Orpha rebels still more after she meets the philanderer Tom
O'Hara. The language describing this coupling is low key. Not only
do we find no graphic details about bodies and actual intercourse,
but nothing about those seductive glances and hothouse innuendos
and passionate foreplay that modern sophisticated readers, even if
they are not literary voyeurs, would feel natural in a novel of
intrigue. Tom, by the way, is not just a conventional skirtchaser; the
author goes to some trouble to flesh out his characterization. Thus
we learn that Tom is basically kindhearted and affectionate toward
his wife (faithful after his fashion). And when Orpha decides to leave
him and travel to California, he generously supplies her with rail
money. His wife turns out to be still another person with a sexual

problem; she fears that if she indulges in sex she will conceive another child with a birth defect.

Halfway through the book the sluggish, episodic structure gives way to a strong plot development. The shift takes place when Orpha's older brother, Joe, a sterling character gone to California for his health, summons his sister to join him. At this point the story of Joe's legal trial overshadows the story of Orpha's continuing affairs. But West manages to unify the two plots.

Joe Chase has become a charismatic Quaker evangelist noted for his faith-healing powers, his spectacular career rivaling that of the historical Aimee Semple McPherson. The crippled and the ill flock by the thousands to his services in Los Angeles. But the author fails to show Joe performing any dramatic examples of healing; it is miracle enough, she seems to think, that he has recovered his own health with the aid of religion. Joe never assumes credit for his cures; he claims that God alone is responsible; and he always takes care to refer the sick to regular medical doctors if no improvement occurs. But this precaution is not enough to save him from trouble with the law.

Joe's fall begins when young Marie Griswold asks him to cure her of breast cancer. She seeks this method of cure, rather than surgery, solely to please her husband, who cannot tolerate the unsightly and defeminizing effects of mastectomy. And when her tumor shows no improvement, she hides this fact from Joe because she does not want this man whom she admires to lose faith in his work. God intends for some of us to suffer, she thinks. Orpha, her confidante, advises surgery – but in vain. Joe even makes another appointment for her with the doctor. But she dies. Then her angry father brings suit against the preacher on a charge that he willfully and criminally kept the woman from seeking medical help. But the Reverend Joe Chase is found innocent. By now, however, the famed faith healer is dying of a resurgence of his old enemy, TB. The end of the novel finds him mustering enough strength to deliver one last sermon just before he dies by the altar. Unfortunately, Joe Chase remains one of the least believable characters in the book.

During the trial Orpha had been working as technical consultant on the film being made of her novel *Talbot Ware*, based on her brother's life. She and the leading actor, a handsome man 10 years her junior, have an affair; although it is all love with Orpha, Greg

McGovern is interested in using her only for his pleasure and career. He proves unfaithful; moreover, he has the arrogance to assure her that until he actually "repudiates her," she retains an important role in his emotional life. Does this treatment make Orpha break off her relationship with this cad? Not really. Her final indignity comes when Greg begins to date her starstruck daughter, the teenage Wanda – the "woods colt" that Orpha had adopted back in Kentucky – and actually marries her. Yes, Wanda knows about his loose habits. We are left with the bittersweet thought that since Wanda entered the marriage with eyes wide open, she will suffer less in the long run. The story ends in a hurried and somewhat implausible manner, with Orpha now married to the defense lawyer and settling down in Hawaii.

One of the curious features of *The Life I Really Lived* is the amiable, clublike feeling that exists among the various wronged women who are rivals in love. One would expect fur to fly when these women meet, but there is hardly a scratch. When Orpha goes out of curiosity to see Jake Hesse's former wife, Rosa, the latter feels sorry for her visitor but otherwise shows no resentment. And when Orpha visits Nora, the wife of her lover Tom O'Hara, the wife gratefully accepts her as a surrogate bed partner for Tom, as if saying: *Better that you get pregnant than I do. Just send him back when you're finished.* How humiliating! And when our heroine discovers in Greg's apartment one of his other mistresses, the two of them talk without ever raising their voices or engaging in name calling. Nor is there any acrimonious confrontation between Orpha and her adopted daughter when the latter announces her marriage. Initial heartbreak, yes. But no hard words. Not even any warnings to Wanda about the kind of egotistic heel she is chained to.

Mostly it had been a learning experience for Orpha Chase. She finally learned, as she said, the difference between love and "being in love." Apparently she got herself informed about sex too finally. From Jake Hesse she learned that "the mind should not be trusted with decisions that involve the body" (*Life*, 400). But in this story where Orpha has several husbands and lovers, we miss especially the voice of authentic passion. We are told that Orpha is fond of Tom and Greg and goes to bed with them, but we never experience the exhilarating joy of romance – or the heat of lust either, for that matter. It is one thing to avoid being a literary voyeur, it is another to give enough of the picture so that the reader will be convinced. West was surely too coy in *The Life I Really Lived*. Having committed herself to portraying the life of a tainted woman, she should have striven for a commensurate degree of frankness and realism.

The reader is told that Orpha's Indian summer marriage with Ralph Navarro, the lawyer, brings fulfillment at last. Orpha tells us, incongruously, that this Navarro strikes her as being like "an older Lon" (her first husband). We are even told, implausibly, that he and Lon would have liked each other because they are individualists. It is obvious that she had enjoyed an active sex life with Tom O'Hara and Greg McGovern, but in the case of her last love, Navarro, whom she feels perfectly content to be with, amorous details never appear. Not so much as even a hug or a kiss. One is tempted to blame this quiescence on West's advanced age – until we recall those lusty scenes in *Massacre at Fall Creek* penned just four years earlier.

But it is true that potentially dramatic moments – especially the sensational ones – slip by unremarked or muted. Sometimes the shocking event is reported after the fact, as if to distance the reader (or the author?) from the event. Take, for instance, the moment when Orpha learns for the first time that her husband Lon had been a bisexual. Here is the relevant dialogue spoken by Orpha and Ebon, the seduced boy:

> "Lon dead, your father dead, for nothing?"
> "Not for nothing. It was about Lon and me."
> There was no way, at that time and at my age, I could take that in.

And three pages later we read:

> "Did Lon ever kiss you?" [Orpha asked]
> "Yes."
> That was as far as I could go. I didn't want to imagine any more, and, as a matter of fact, I didn't know how to imagine more. But they had touched, mouth to mouth.
> For a minute or two I thought, The one you should have shot, Lon, was me (*Life*, 111, 114).

The average wife would have been furious. But these quoted passages carry the entire burden of the surprise and anguish for Orpha Chase. Does she throw up? faint? destroy Lon's photograph?

smash dishes? curse? run out of the house? Nothing of the sort. This oddly passive woman might have at least recalled that the Bible, which she studies nightly, contains fiery condemnations of sodomy and other perversions. Further, she never seems to consider Ebon guilty or abnormal in any way. One might think that Orpha would be offended by the boy, especially since he had been her rival in love. But no, she welcomes him into the household as a grieving little brother and lets him work the farm and babysit with the infant Wanda. It is no wonder that the reviewer Nancy Hale said many questions are left unanswered.[4]

The novel consists essentially of two stories, one about Orpha's love life and the other about Joe's trial. True, the author tries to unify the stories by having Orpha and Navarro serve as links between the two, but the linkage occurs only in the second half of the book and there our heroine's romantic adventures pale in interest, largely because her two California lovers are not sufficiently individualized.

Navarro, for instance, is so unremarkable among the large cast of characters in the book that his creation seems almost an afterthought. Greg McGovern also seems two-dimensional. We are told, for instance, that Greg is a rising movie star, a playboy with a harem of complaisant young women at his call, and his life – style well epitomizes the falsity and shallowness of Hollywood, a place excoriated in the novels of Nathaniel West. But what is missing in *The Life I Really Lived* is more of the atmosphere associated with this actor or his fellows: The glamorous women, the acres of Beverly Hills real estate, the servants, the chauffeurs, the Rolls Royces, the posh parties, the oceans of liquor, the Gucci clothes, the jewels, the bodyguards, the adoring crowds, the press agents, the paparazzi, the newspaper and radio interviewers – at least give us a goodly portion of the dizzying, cynical, dollar-mad, hot-house extravaganza of Tinseltown such as Jackie Collins portrays, however crudely, in *Hollywood Husbands* and *Hollywood Wives*.

The reviews of *The Life I Really Lived* were generally favorable. About the only important negative reaction came from Nancy Hale, mentioned earlier, and from Lucille de View, who objected to West's assumption that happiness for a woman depends on her finding a satisfying love relationship: "Is the answer to finding joy always (or only) through romance?"[5] At the other pole lies the more sympathetic judgment by Jean Strouse that ended with these words: "West makes you laugh and cry. She strikes a few false notes, forces some contrivances of plot. But when Orpha says, at the end, that 'after all the pain and stupidity and cruelty in my life, I found that love sanctifies,' I believe her."[6] It is not a great novel. It is not among West's better works.

Fantasies

She does better work with her California fantasies, especially *The Pismire Plan* (1948).[7] The latter is unusual for science fiction in being a brilliant satire about the tastelessness and vulgarity of twentieth-century American civilization. What is offered is a brave new world of the absurd.

George Pismire, whose offensive name suggests antlike efficiency, is a successful eastern businessman. Driving along the cluttered and overly huckstered California highways, he has shocking encounters: a store that inflicts on each customer a singing commercial, a motel that insists on supplying chargeable items, a Nubian goat raiser who will not sell even a sip of milk unless it be in a vessel made by his crony next door, a café catering to luxury dogs, and other places only too reminiscent of actuality. The step-by-step narration of how Pismire arrives at his plan for recompensing the distressed consumer of such vendibles and services – not the dogs, of course, but the human beings – is drolly suspenseful.

Among the profusion of targets for satire are foolish Americans who repeat slogans and follow the ratings of this and that product, fancy cemeteries (Isle of the Departed being an open dig at the notorious Forest Lawn), radio and billboard advertising with all its sex madness and grotesquerie, wildly exotic products ("Tasty Rattlesnake Tenderloins"), soap operas, insufferably infantile motion pictures, and do-it-yourself establishments. When Pismire sees a long column of motionless people clinging to a copper wire, some of them throwing a fit once in a while, he is told they are receiving the Hosmer Ripples, which are supposed to be beneficial emanations originating in the mysterious Hosmer Wright, who is to be found in a bungalow at the far other end of the wire. The people do not have to pay for the Ripples, for that would be illegal; instead, they make "love gifts." Out of curiosity Pismire visits the bungalow and finds the wire tied to nothing more than a stove.

Pismire would recompense the helpless and gullible consumers. Since advertising and commerce are so hopelessly bad, the merciful thing is to create people who will not mind them. In due course he establishes a vast new business called Rent-a-Patron Service, whereby selected groups of people, instead of having to endure and be victimized by such things as stupefying motion pictures, insipid café meals, and mindless commercials, are *paid* to test these beforehand. This way, no matter how wretched the product, there will always be some customers for it, if only the testers, and, regardless of how much these customers suffer, they will at least be paid for their trouble. The ultimate goal in this mock-serious story is that human genes are made to undergo a mutation to ensure the birth of the ideal (that is, undemanding and uncritical) consumer.

The next story to be considered is more fantastic still. What cataclysmic changes would occur if we awakened some morning and found that children had suddenly grown to adult size and that adults, except for a favored few, had all shrunk to the helplessness of dolls? Would the children, by virtue of their now superior stature, obey a natural impulse to dominate their elders and rule humankind? They certainly do dominate – and with astonishing results – in *The Chilekings* (1967), which depicts a utopia influenced by Wordsworthian views about the innate goodness of children.[8]

An imaginary editor annotates the report of a long-winded, utterly conventional army tank officer named Captain Phipps, a report frequently digressive because it was written by a doddering old codger 60 years after the principal events had taken place. In doleful disillusionment he writes that children have destroyed war munitions everywhere because they had been horrified by the sight of bloodshed, and then they enthroned a reign of peace; moreover, they extirpated the profit system of economics, they distributed the goods of the earth equitably, and they eliminated universal education, thus reversing the usual sequence whereby the first part of life is spent in study and the last part in work. Freudianism entered too in the form of publicized meetings for child-sex activities – both innocent and not so innocent libidinal play.

Through the use of fantasy, the pacifism of *Friendly Persuasion* and the adolescent insight of *Cress Delahanty* are brought to bear on far-ranging issues of world significance. But West sometimes tempers these solemn ideas with bursts of wholesome laughter.

Chilekings, however, lacks something of the insouciance and exuberance of *Pismire;* for the whole scheme is more consciously worked out, more sophisticated; and for the purpose of achieving greater psychological realism, the narration is modeled to the tedious thought patterns of Captain Phipps. *The Chilekings* represents a technical advance over *Pismire*, but there must be some readers who prefer the other fantasy if only for its freshness and outrageous mirth.

Mysteries of Life Made Orderly

Some of West's finest writing occurs in the collection called *Love Death and the Ladies' Drill Team*, which came out in 1955.[9]

In the first story, "A Time of Learning," the young house painter Emmett Macguire learns what it is like to suffer from unrequited love. One painting of his in the barn at home symbolizes what will happen to him after he goes off to work at the farm where pretty Ivy Lish dwells. At the Lish place the youth is put to work painting the barn. Soon he has fallen in love with the daughter, Ivy, and is inspired to create a portrait of her that far outshines anything to be expected of a mere barn painter. But little does he know that all his depth of feeling and power of expression are lost on the fickle girl, who thoughtlessly gives the portrait as a gift to one of her suitors. In this type of story that reveals the heartbreak accompanying growing up – tender young love laying its sacrifice on the altar of indifference – the author almost invariably succeeds – and succeeds memorably.

As the book title indicates, many of the stories deal with love or death in some manner. Among the preponderantly favorable reviews of this first West collection of unrelated stories was one by Carlos Baker in the *New York Times Book Review*, wherein Baker praises West for combining so well the ironic, the pathetic, and the curious, and avers that "The Mysteries of Life in an Orderly Manner" is the one story in the group that best describes West's aims in writing.[10] This story resembles many being written today by the "minimalist" school, treating a revelation of character or the exploration of a situation as its main goal, rather than a physical adventure or a problem to be solved. When Mr. Cooper drives his wife, Emily, into the California hill town on initiation night so that she can at last join the

Pocahontas Lodge, he subjects her reverence for ceremony and rule to a dose of good-natured levity. For instance, as they wait in the parked car, Emily speaks disapprovingly of some passing members who are carrying candles to the meeting; this is wrong, she says in the approved parlance of the true follower, because "The Lodge treats of the mysteries of life in an orderly manner," and to her the candles are not part of that order. To which Mr. Cooper wittily responds, "Maybe they are part of the mystery" (*Love Death*, 27).

He is the norm in the story, for he can see the joiner instinct in its absurd aspect and yet remain sufficiently tolerant. Emily's weakness, like that of many converts to secret organizations, is that she lacks a sense of humor that might enable her to see the arcana of titles, rituals, rules, and regalia from the viewpoint of the skeptical outsider. She takes everything too seriously. "Don't joke about serious things," she tells him angrily (*Love Death*, 29).

But the meaning runs still deeper. Various passages in the dialogue suggest that the real reason Emily is joining the lodge is her lack of self-confidence. We know that her husband will not supply it to her, whereas the close fellowship the organization provides might be just what she needs, or make her think it does so if only by supplying a factitious sense of order among the mysteries of her world. The success of the story is partly achieved by the fine balance maintained between Emily's viewpoint and that of her husband; there is some justice on both sides. The Coopers seem to have a poor marriage, and Emily accordingly needs something with which her husband, the self-sufficient and self-confident one, cannot or will not provide her.

"Love, Death, and the Ladies' Drill Team" is a still better story. In it we see again Emily Cooper, this time on a September day within the Pocahontas circle and looking out on what she has somehow missed. Specifically, the scene is an upstairs room, Burnham Hall, that is used by the lodge members for weight-reducing, figure-enhancing exercises. Emily is now 36, her children are in school, and her empty house has spoken to her of middle-aged loneliness; hence the lodge is now a drillmaster enabling her to endure, in a kind of passionless stoicism, the long and loveless glide into liniment and old age and death. For all the overweight, bored, unloved, and unloving women, the lodge is a substitute husband.

As Emily sits by a window in the hall waiting for Mrs. Rotunda (delightful name!) to get the drill started, she and the other matrons notice below in a vacant lot a female called Imola standing in the wind, shortly to be joined by her lover, Ramos. The two below, described in sensual terms, represent the very freedom and passion and love that the individual females in the drill hall lack. Imola, in contrast with the other women, is obviously happy. Therefore, when the righteous Mrs. Tetford looks out the window and openly pities Imola, she is unconsciously ironic, but Emily knows that *pity* is the wrong word.

The wind, as Christopher G. Katope points out in an explication of the story,[11] is definitely important in unifying the structure; nevertheless, contrary to what he says it does not signalize any "renewed vitality" in the protagonist. If Emily goes beyond the observing stage, we do not learn about it. To be sure, she imagines that she is "the one responsive and harmonious harp" that feels the full warmth and power of the September wind, yet Katope's interpretation notwithstanding, she does not turn this feeling into resolve and action. In Percy B. Shelley's "Ode to the West Wind," the romantic analogue to which Katope refers, the persona wishes to become an active agent and spread a message around the world. Instead, West hints at the analogue for the purpose of irony. The warm wind, symbolic of passion, blows everywhere, around the spindly legs of merchants on the street and among blue dust flowers in the lot and around the bodies of the lovers – but not among Emily's companions in the hall.

Images of love and death abound in the work. The sensual aspects of love show in the description of Imola, whose dress blows suggestively against her thighs; who wears no brassiere; who is said to sunbathe in the nude with guitar-playing Ramos. Their kisses down in the lot are enough to throw all the staring women into bemused silence. Death is suggested by Emily's thoughts on aging, the sight of the undertaker, the talk about funerals, the presence of a Miss Graves, and other things not quite so direct, such as the description of Mrs. Rotunda's gray hair "arranged with all the finality of marble."

"Home-Coming" studies the problem a newly released sanatorium patient has in trying to adjust his own enfeebled constitution to the robust pace of his wife. Having been drained of his strength by trying to please the selfish woman, he gropes his way back to the sanatorium within just a few hours, lucky to still be alive. The setting much resembles La Vina Sanatorium. Compared with the other pieces in the book, "Home-Coming" is, however, a tour de force.

Doubtless the author's actual experience as a teacher and as the wife of a teacher and school administrator accounts for much of the realistic school atmosphere in "The Battle of the Suits." Harry "Senator" Whitehall, the 15-year-old brat in this story, should be evidence enough for anyone that West invented at least a few unsavory people. The story about the pompous little Senator (as the troublemaker student calls himself) is told from the point of view of a janitor named Joe Ortiz, employed in the Temple Home for Boys. Ortiz makes the mistake of buying for himself a double-breasted, pin-striped suit identical to the one purchased by the Senator. Naturally, the feelings of the self-important youngster are too important for him to permit a mere janitor to be seen about the area with such a suit on: He protests to the superintendent. But Joe, under fire, refuses to take his garments back to the store for a refund. We catch a glimpse here of the all-too-familiar atmosphere of the "progressive" school that caters heavily to student egos.

The humor in the story is delicious. For instance, Joe reflects on the claim that his little tormentor once saved his life by eating diluted honey: "[Joe] had studied classic myths at San Miguel High School, and he had an unpleasant picture now of the Senator, a big, fat, black-haired baby, being suckled by an oversized hairy-legged bee. Maybe there would be a statue of it on the courthouse lawn some-day" (*Love Death*, 62). And again, when Joe counters the superin-tendent's claim that the Senator has had a "rough life . . . underpriv-ileged up to now": " 'I know,' Joe said. 'He was brought up by the bees' " (*Love Death*, 66).

For a long time Mr. Sterling, in "Tom Wolfe's My Name," has derived pleasure from pretending to townspeople to be the veritable Thomas Wolfe, now secluded on a California grape vineyard in order to escape publicity. There the reputed author does all of his "writing" of the Wolfe books into big ledgers that are kept for visi-tors to see. A textbook salesman named Madden, who had always doubted Sterling's story, chances to read in a newspaper about Wolfe's death in Baltimore and decides that now would be just the time to pay the pretender a call. This would expose the impostor. At this suspenseful juncture we begin to wonder how the grape man will explain his still being alive.

Of course, the main interest for the reader, if not for the salesman, does not consist in proving Sterling a charlatan; the reader has been made dubious enough from the outset. What remains – if this story is to be truly meaningful – is to discover some clue to the hitherto hidden life of the impostor. Sterling's ordinarily empty eyes, which change and come to a focus when he introduces himself as Thomas Wolfe, let us know that he has an obsession that gives him a principal reason for living. This clue is, unfortunately, the only one given about his inner life.

Madden finds the study on the ranch to be a jumble of papers, pans, dirty laundry, books, and milk bottles – all the paraphernalia to fit the Wolfe legend. But he is amazed to find Sterling dead on the couch, and next to him is the ledger into which he had been copying Wolfe's *The Story of a Novel*. But nowhere does Madden find a newspaper reporting the death of the novelist. We are supposed to believe, evidently, that Sterling had so completely identified himself with his idol over the years (maybe the liar ultimately believing his own lie?) that his very heartbeat is coexistent with Wolfe's. This trick ending falls a bit flat, despite the interesting story line throughout. The lack of pervasive supernatural foreshadowing, or hint of fate, or other means of reinforcing the idea of the bizarre, makes us wait in vain to hear the other shoe drop. The death should have been rationally or supernaturally explained; either one or a combination of these. We might argue that Wolfe's *The Story of a Novel* is fairly short, is only a pamphlet, and that its publication two years before the author's demise would have allowed an enterprising fraud like Sterling to have copied it earlier. Another minor flaw in this story is that Wolfe's use of ledgers for producing manuscripts was restricted to the *Wanderjahre* period when the first draft of *Look Homeward Angel* was written, and was abandoned after that except for keeping notes and travel jottings.[12] Maybe West was appealing to the popular conception then held by the public, or was indicating that Sterling was ignorant about this one point. In any case, "Tom Wolfe's My Name" is one of her infrequent stories of the fantastic. Her skill in this genre was not a mean one, as we have noted in discussing her science fiction.

According to what West's husband told me, "Learn to Say Good-bye" is based on an experience the couple had witnessed at the county fair back when they were teaching at Hemet. A boy who had just won the prize for raising his pet bull broke into tears when he had to hand the lead rope over to the auctioneer. The future U.S. President Ronald Reagan produced and acted in a television version of this story aired on the "General Electric Hour" in 1960.

The version of "A Little Collar for the Monkey" in this collection is an improvement over the one published in *Woman's Home Companion* in February 1948; it contains additional concrete, descriptive details, and the imagery is more vivid. As a rule, West improved her short stories before publishing them in collections if there was a long time lapse.

Mrs. Prosper of "A Little Collar for the Monkey" is afflicted with Dr. Chooney's sin, a perverted intelligence seeking power over a helpless female. She wants to control her marriageable daughter Lily. One of Mrs. Prosper's recreations had been to keep a sturdy apricot tree in her yard from bearing fruit by pinching off all the buds each spring. Maybe she will continue to keep Lily sterile too, she thinks, by driving away all suitors. But on the morning the story opens, a fish peddler intends to outwit the mother and to elope with the long-suffering Lily. On the way to discovering the denouement, the reader discovers one of the richest West stories as regards to character contrast.

"Public Address System" begins in a manner unusual for West – at the end of the story. Then, after capturing the reader's interest about why Bill Hare is currently unpopular in town, she reverts to his first association with the potential lunatic, Leonard Hobart, and starts to work forward. The opening of "Public Address System" contains the slickness of the popular magazine where formulas are rampant. But as soon as we break past the opening and become acquainted with Leonard Hobart's incipient irrationality, the cause of his long silence over the years, and finally his emergence into verbal thunder as a sports announcer, we find it difficult to lay the story down.

"Foot-Shaped Shoes" recalls the idyllic early period of the author in Hemet just after graduation from Whittier. Its hero is a big, strapping adolescent named Rusty who is modeled after the writer's brother Merle West (the book's dedication reads: "For Merle –

Rusty grown up"). Such predisposition being a fact, it is no wonder that Rusty's sister is a young newlywed who adores her brother about as much as she does her husband. The best-drawn figure in the story is the heartless whore, Mrs. Campos, who is a far cry from the endearing strumpets of another California author, John Steinbeck of *Sweet Thursday*. The existence of Mrs. Campos proves that West could portray evil in its repellent aspects when she so desired. For the most part the story is iridescent with happy sentiment about the newlyweds' adoption of the Campos boy.

Harrison Smith's review of *Love Death and the Ladies' Drill Team* in *Saturday Review* completely misunderstood one of the best sketched of all the West villains, "Horace Chooney, M.D." Contrary to the reviewer's statement, Chooney is not "an elderly and humane doctor," is not suffering from an ailment soon to kill him, and does not have a benign attitude toward his female patient, who in turn is not an adolescent but a young woman of 22 or 23.[13] The story of Chooney is really about a cultivated but cruel, sensual physician, who, having had an affair in the city with a female patient who had died (though she was normal at the outset of the treatment), finds it suddenly necessary to abscond to the country and to set up practice under a new name in order to escape notoriety.

Miss Chester, his most recent prey, whom he finds physically attractive – something of the lamb for the tiger in him to victimize, because he delights in testing his power to hurt and wound – has no serious ailment aside from mere loneliness. Without giving a fig for the Hippocratic oath, Chooney makes her case seem serious, deludes her with a few photographs of the woman he has ruined, and discreetly makes an appointment to commence his diabolic treatment. Chooney, in short, is a sadistic sensualist, an emotional vampire of a particularly dangerous species.[14]

"Dr. Chooney, M.D." is as carefully wrought as any of the short stories of Faulkner or Hemingway. It is full of irony, that Holy Grail sought after by today's literary explicators, especially in the scene where Chooney manipulates the photographs. Not the least of the ironies is, as West herself observed, that *Mademoiselle* magazine first brought to light the malpractices of this medical bluebeard. (I cover the origin of this story in chapter 1.)

Every now and then some author writes a wonderfully heartwarming narrative that is seemingly right out of some Wordsworthian remembered experience, or maybe imagined in some state of inspired euphoria. Dylan Thomas's "A Child's Christmas in Wales" is a good example. And such a story is West's "The Singing Lesson," which contains the incomparable piano tuner, Wilbur Smiley, who one day appears at Miss McManaman's country school. On entering, he shocks her by making a vulgar simile. Clearly he is a raw, plain-spoken, straightforward redneck from a world very different from that of the genteel and decorous teacher. The following dialogue gives us an idea of his personality; it also illustrates a gift West had for originating colloquial speech of an amusing turn for her trades-people or lower-class figures:

> "Please," began Miss McManaman again. "To whom . . . ?"
>
> "Wilbur Smiley. Smiley is my name but damned melancholy by nature."
>
> " 'You mustn't swear, Mr. Smiley, before the dear little children.' "
>
> "Well, you mustn't," she said.
>
> "Paugh," said Mr. Smiley. "Where'd you learn the bad words you know, Miss? Right here," he said pointing.
>
> "In the boys. And the girls. . . . What's the worst you know, children?" A dozen hands went up.
>
> "Ta ta, children," he reproved them.
>
> "You see?" he asked Miss McManaman. "It's in 'em. Working like yeast in a barrel and frothing at the bunghole. Treat 'em like human beings," he advised. "Or cure 'em if you're a mind to. Make 'em spend a day writing bad words on the blackboard. That'll take the brimstone out of them." (*Love Death*, 238-39)

The confession of being naturally melancholy arouses our suspense. Having delivered himself of these startling observations, he humbles her by saying that tuning the school piano would be a sheer waste of money since only she, the teacher, ever plays it. The school woodbox, with its pet ground owl, semidrowned squirrels, and family of field mice, provokes another jocularity from him: "What's this? . . . Furbearing wood[?]" (*Love Death*, 240).

The classroom, besieged outside by steadily falling rain, is saved from the regular lesson by this vital rough who has come among them to judge everything from his own fresh perspective. It seems a warm and homey place now. Learning that he had interrupted their singing lesson – though the poor teacher has no talent for singing anyway (reminding us of the author's confessed failure to play the piano well, as she tells us in *Hide and Seek*) – he suddenly decides that he will perform for them himself. From this sad-faced little man with the peaked head and deep-sunken eyes pours a stream of delicious melody that wafts Miss McManaman off into a rapture of bliss and pain: "As if all the things of which she had dreamed and for which she had waited, without having a name for them, were now spread before her, named, shining, and palpable. But at this very moment of knowing and naming, she saw also that they would vanish: melt, run away, be lost forever. And that was pain" (*Love Death*, 241). As ironic counterpoint, Smiley has his own love sorrow, and this sorrow explains why his song turns out to be poignant: Smiley, the poor man's nightingale, with a thorn in his throat. By means of such seemingly unpromising materials as a profane piano tuner and a genteel teacher of a country school, West has woven a spell about us so that we too yearn to hear that music.

At the close, when Smiley leaves, it is as if some never-to-be-recovered enchantment goes with him into the sullen day and over whatever rainbow bridge supposedly connects the mundane world with the aerial reaches of art. Smiley reminds us a trifle of Professor Quigley with respect to his musical talent and crisp readiness of tongue, yet he is assuredly a unique, fully realized personality.

Beautiful Youth

Judging from current tastes, a way for a piece of adolescent fiction to survive is to use the child to comment on the adult world, as in Mark Twain's *The Adventures of Huckleberry Finn*, J. D. Salinger's *The Catcher in the Rye*, and William Golding's *Lord of the Flies*, for it appears that interest in childhood for its own sake is not enough to please readers in the long run. Such thoughtful books enjoy today a somewhat greater popularity than Booth Tarkington's *Seventeen* and Gene Stratton-Porter's *A Girl of the Limberlost*, which had immense sales in their day but are largely devoid of serious overtones. West's *Cress Delahanty*, as we shall see later in this study, does have a few serious overtones that reflect not so much on adult life, however, as on the universal problems of growing up. The book has enjoyed considerable popularity: It was selected for Book-of-the-Month Club distribution, and various of its stories were anthologized in textbooks for the public schools.

Just as her beloved Thoreau had done in *Walden*, West organized her book by means of an obvious chronology; she used the seasons to mark time, and she treated only of a limited period in the youth of the principal figure. But otherwise there is, of course, little correlation between their methods. The five parts of the story collection – too loosely constructed to be a novel – handle Cress's years from 12 to 16; within these parts the chapters are titled by the various seasons: "Summer I," "Summer II," and so forth. Partly because of the close attention paid to chronology, the process of unifying the once disparate stories into a whole is more successful than it is in *Friendly Persuasion*.

The earliest magazine story, thus assimilated and renamed, constitutes the opening. This was "The Child's Day" (1940), which starred the elfin figure Minta Eilertson. A few years later Cress Delahanty showed up in serial print along with Chapple Norby. In the late 1940s and 1950s diminutive heroines for other parts of the future book appeared as Kate Kinsman, Connie Malloy, and Virginia Hanrahan, Irish lasses most of them. Somehow the author selected the tall, big-boned, towheaded Cress Delahanty to embody all their separate personalities and adventures in growing up, whether idealized ones from biography or purely invented ones.

In the book Cress Delahanty is first disclosed as a quaintly dreamy adolescent who is attitudinizing poetically all alone one October day when her parents, John and Gertrude, have gone for a drive. As subsequent descriptions show, the ranch and the nearby town of Tenant (a mythical town recurring in several West books) much resemble Yorba Linda, and Cress herself seems a young Jessamyn West. The exquisiteness of the opening section is difficult to translate into plot summary, for it is a series of smoothly shifting impressions of what it is like to be a 12-year-old girl, sensitive, lovable, and boy-crazy. But Cress is also intelligent. She enjoys being alone with her notebook of Shelleyan phrases, her book of private poems, her plain nourishing lunch of cocoa-sugar-milk paste, the wind murmuring without, and the cheerful flames crackling in the fireplace: An atmosphere delightfully cozy.

In Cress's ingenuous comments to herself we see the first hints of puberty. And true to the condition of childhood, feeling and wondering, not reasoning, are the paramount states of mind. We see her standing almost nude before the mirror, attired in nothing but her mother's black lace shawl, daydreaming deliciously about the femme fatale she imagines herself to be in the glass: " 'There is something evil and wanton there,' she thought . . . and trembled with pity for that dark one who loved her so dearly." Despite Cress's fascination with vocabulary, she is yet unable to articulate the special word that describes her imagined personality. Consequently, she dances the word: "She danced it until she trembled and leaning on bent elbows looked deep into the mirror and said, 'There is nothing I will not touch. I am Cress. I will know everything.' "[15] Here we can see not only the fantasy life that occupies so much of adolescence but the incomparable power of dancing to express feelings incommunicable in words. At the risk of indulging in biographical fallacy, I suspect that on one level of interpretation Cress can be considered the persona for the novice writer in West at this early stage in her career (around 1940), whose vow might have been: "I will not be denied any insight into human nature. In the sphere of writing I will attempt everything someday, even the sordid and evil, and will not be a Play-It-Safe Compromiser afraid of what neighbors and friends may say of my books. Let the Grundys and the Quakers take their chances, too." Here West is also articulating that theory of hers announced earlier, namely that the fiction writer locates in the successive layers of her own personality the creatures imagined for her books. Cress herself, however, does not aspire to authorship; nor does she do anything that would shock today's readers, even though she certainly dares enough to keep them interested.

Next Cress is at high school evincing her interest in boys by befriending, a little too vigorously, the shy and bespectacled Edwin Kibbler. At that time she unintentionally shatters an olla, the falling fragments of which knock out some of the poor boy's teeth. But all ends well, for she becomes Edwin's girlfriend. (In *South of the Angels* a love affair begins in a similar way.)

After her beloved Grandmother dies, Cress goes to cook for and comfort Grandfather. At first she believes that his drinking and his arguing with his crony, Mr. Powers, prove that he lacks feeling for his dead wife. The wise Powers takes her aside and assures her that appearances are deceiving, that the old man is hurt too profoundly to give his sorrow mere verbal expression. On being corrected Cress stiffens; nonetheless, the lesson sinks home, and she comes to a fuller understanding of human nature. A kitsch artist would perhaps

have Cress break down in tears or run off to Grandfather for forgive-
ness. But West believed in honing emotion to keenness by indirec-
tion and at the same time making it acceptable through restraint.
Further, here as elsewhere she avoids the "switcheroo" or reversal
technique that she condemned in *To See the Dream*, whereby the
fundamental makeup in a character is altered. What takes place in
Cress is development, "becoming more of the same," as the author
defines development. "All the best writing," West declared in *To See
the Dream*, "has been of those who become more and more themselves, of the discovery by the hero of himself" (*Dream*, 146). Cress
understands where she has erred.

In an adventure similar to one West had as a girl, Cress, at a
beach resort, drops her gorgeously colored hat into an aquarium
where the dyes, to her public embarrassment, so stain the water that
her father has to buy all the fish as restitution ("Where," 8).

To gain popularity at school Cress devises Delahanty's Law,
which means carrying her shoes to the bus in the morning and
putting them on there so that she can save dressing time. True to her
intent, this practice gets talked about. But her eccentricity backfires
when she applies for the post of freshman editor and finds that no
one thinks her serious and responsible enough for the job. Moral:
Do not try to be popular at the expense of the solid virtues.

In "Winter II" we meet Cress's friend Bernardine, the school's
most popular girl. Bernardine, anything but natural, insists on being
called Nedra on Fridays out of respect for a rich young man whom
she had said no to once just before he died and left her nothing.
Cress, now scheduled to perform in a folk dance, worries that her
awkwardness might cause her to make an embarrassing blunder.
While trying to cope with this fear, she finds herself unable to bear
any more of Bernardine's artificiality and snobbery. Cress learns to
know better the failings not only in her friend but in herself.

Another of her lessons in maturing deals with illicit sex. Mrs.
Charlesbois keeps the unwitting Cress around after piano lessons in
order to cover up an affair she is having with an accordion-playing
laborer. Suspense mounts after the girl discovers she is being used
and tries to enlighten Mr. Charlesbois, who unaccountably forestalls
her with evasive pleasantries and a "crooked Jack O'Lantern smile"
(symbolic of his moral character). The shocker arrives on the next-
to-the-last page, where the cuckolded husband discloses obliquely

that he knows about the intrigue, that he condones it, and that, as Cress had earlier sensed, he harbors an indecent interest in her too. The story is a masterpiece of innuendo and veiled allusion, whose contents are clear to the perceptive adult and yet discreetly inoffensive to the young reader. If there is a strained note anywhere, it has to do with Cress's sucking a lemon after her illumination: a too obvious symbol of the taste of this experience. Counterbalancing the Charlesbois story and offering an example of innocent young love is the episode about Edwin's rehearsing his Latin in the springtime arroyo while blond admirer Cress looks on.

"Spring II" finds Cress about to spend the night with Ina Wallenius in her home on the side of Kettle Hill, which in some ways resembles the Olinda of West's childhood. The "ratty little town," as her schoolmate Ina labels it, consists of small, uniform, company houses shaded by pepper trees from the sight of the many oil derricks rising like warts on the hillside. Added attractions are pumps that never cease throbbing and the ubiquitous fragrance of raw oil. Lurking in this unpleasant scene is the father, a Bible-reading sadist who keeps his daughter slaving at every household chore. He sometimes shows Ina his gratitude by openly arranging a little punishment for some peccadillo of hers. In the story's climax the ogre takes Cress for a walk and shows her what jolly sport it is to catch harmless gopher snakes and drown them in the oily sump holes. When one snake struggles in vain to stay afloat, Cress protests that it will die. "Maybe so, maybe not," he deliberates coolly. "It's too early to say. Sink – swim; sink – swim" (*Cress*, 181-82). More so than with the depiction of the odious Mrs. Prosper, another household tyrant, the present one seems to be taken right out of life. But the illusion of actuality can be the measure of art.

"Early Summer," a little concerto on the theme of loneliness, begins with a sparkling arpeggio speaking of *tempus edax rerum* and ends with an organlike diminuendo telling of the hopelessness of unrequited love. Calvin Dean, the star of the school debating squad, does not even know that wistful Cress, now all of 14, has a crush on him. West's sensitive prose style, attuned to every nuance of her lovesick adolescent, once more shows what it can accomplish:

> She had more feelings than she knew what to do with, more emotions than her tranquil life permitted her to discharge. She had to invent sorrows and

concoct dramas. She would stoop down to rejoice with a daffodil that pushed a stone aside in its upward thrust, or would loosen a butterfly from a spider web with wailings that brought her no sympathy from any listener. As if she cared for sympathy! She was capable emotionally of a woman's tragedies and, up to now, she had been unable to overtake any of these. Now, however, she loved and was not loved in return. (*Cress*, 188)

This passage has the authentic ring of youth's emotional plight. Youth *is* a tortured emotional chaos for many people; at best it is a checkered existence. And where unreciprocated love is concerned, the sorrow is perhaps impossible to articulate in all its knife-edge sharpness save by the uncommon writer who has suffered through it all and remembers. Ames, near the end of Theodore Dreiser's novel *Sister Carrie*, tells Carrie Meeber: "Most people are not capable of voicing their feelings. They depend upon others. That is what genius is for." Most adults, in reviewing their childhood from the calm remove of middle age or later, tend to discount its pains and crown it with a golden halo. We tend to remember what we *want* to remember. But the true artist – for instance a Jessamyn West – leaps over the barrier that adults erect against their often anguished youth, where self-doubt, humiliation, grudge, and deprivation conspire to make a brief hell on earth, and tells what those bittersweet days were really like. And, thanks to the magic of art, the expected pain is transfigured into a thing of beauty.

I suspect that this whole section of the book is especially autobiographical. Dr. Boyce says that Calvin Dean was a real boy, "of a good family in Fullerton attending the Fullerton schools in Jessamyn's day. Why did she use the real name . . . when all the other names are fictitious? Was she yielding to a long desire to tell Calvin that as a girl, she admired him very much?"[16] West, who read this explanation from her old teacher, had two answers: (a) that she had an unfortunate habit of using names of people she knew, and (b) that she was not trying to convey anything to Calvin Dean – although he had been the school hero, a "big football player" and president of the student body, a boy that all the freshman girls, including herself, "worshipped" (West's 28 March 1966 letter to me).

In "Summer I" Cress comes to know the poignancy of losing a childhood friend who grows up and is about to be married, about to enter that mystique of wifely interests so strangely excluding to the uninitiated maiden. "Summer II" shows her at a beach party where she loses favor with some vain, empty-headed, and stuffy school-mates whose unspoken desire is to be on the lookout for boys but who would never, never speak that thought aloud. Cress, however, manages to offend them by daring to ask some boys, one of whom had been following them on the pretense of getting a light for his cigarette, whether a light was what he *really* wanted. This is too much for the prudish girls. Well pictured are the boorish boy catcher, Yolanda, and the depressingly unoriginal twins, Avis and Mavis Davis. So is Aunt Iris, the unmarried lame biologist whose misfortune it is to be their chaperon. The description of Aunt Iris's bedroom filled with books, magazines, phonograph, and laboratory equipment aptly attests that this woman has been living a full and varied, even if unconventional, life despite her lameness – and the absence of a husband or boyfriend: "[I]t looked like a place where a person was living, not empty and bare as the girls' rooms were, places where they were only waiting" (*Cress*, 235). The chaperon's situation points up the hollowness that the girls endure, their utter dependence on external things, on coming events such as engage-ment or marriage, to give their lives fulfillment. This woman has not postponed living even if she did not find a mate.

Then there are pimples enough to make Cress draw all the shades in the house for the whole winter. As if this situation were not risible enough, her mother signs her up for a talent contest in which Cress presents a skit that puzzles everyone. Fortunately, she is mature enough to criticize herself objectively and to accept failure with such cheer as to mystify her parents all over again.

Cress's platonic love for the dying Mr. Cornelius is told in part through an extended interior monologue, the first and only instance of this technique in the book, but in its way it prepares for the method used later in *A Matter of Time*. Cress has such a selfless adoration for the 38-eight-year-old Cornelius that she asks the Lord to accept her in his place. This episode is one of those few used in her stories, states West, which have any basis in her own experience. It has its inspiration in the case of Harold Nixon, Richard Nixon's older brother, who, after considerable suffering, died of tuberculo-sis. As the author explains, "It somehow became my conviction [as a little girl] that I should offer the Lord my life in return for Harold's. And I did so, in all sincerity, I thought. The Lord, however, preferred Harold" (9 February 1966 letter to me).

Each passing day for Cornelius is, as for the doomed Mary Jessup in *South of the Angels*, bathed in the radiance of eternity. Now that he is about to leave the world, he is sharply sensitive to the delights of sensory impressions – "tipped the cup of seeing until he had the last drop" – almost as if he had perused and taken to heart Walter Pater's concluding advice in *The Renaissance* on the necessity to collect, treasure, and luxuriate in what Pater terms "this fruit of quickened, multiplied consciousness."

The two stories featuring Cornelius, particularly the second one, have all the quality of genuine tenderness, yet are fully controlled through the use of aesthetic distance. When the girl goes against the advice of conventional friends to tell the man to his face, but with his wife listening, that she loves him, had even planned to run away with him and nurse him back to health, the reader derives an unwonted pleasure and gratification at witnessing this kind of openness.

For the book's conclusion West rewrote an item she had published in 1946 in *Harper's* under the title "Grandpa Was Her Mirror." The story is about a girl's redemptive experience in confronting the fact of death and her emergence into womanhood. Probably no more rewarding study can be made of the growth of Jessamyn West as a craftswoman than comparing these two versions. Edwin is absent in the original. In lieu of the mother in that version is a much older sister, Myra, workworn but compassionate, whose role as mistress of the household entitles her to take charge of Chapple when Mr. Norby brings the latter home from Woolman College to be at the bedside of dying Grandpa. In both versions everyone expects the college girl to be cold and indifferent toward the old man, and she is at first. Having rejected the old gardener at Woolman, her initial attitude toward Grandpa comes as no surprise: Old men are uninteresting, repellent, burdensome.

For the book version Edwin is put on Woolman campus, partly to help round out the structure of the cycle, of course, yet also to point up early in the story how self-centered Cress has become at 16 and away from home. In this manner Edwin functions somewhat as the sardonic Myra did in the magazine story, only he loves the girl in the special way that only a boyfriend can and is therefore more effectual when he gives her advice. His advice prepares her for the ultimate moment of awareness at the bedside.

The last improvement appears in the passage beginning with Grandpa's remarks about the yellow violets. It is true that now the real Reservoir Hill is substituted for North Hill, yet this is no gain except for pleasing those few readers familiar with Yorba Linda landscape. More certain improvement comes with the elimination of the sentimentality in the original – "Tears filled his faded eyes and spread over the tight skin of his cheek bones."[17] And more still in altering the moral of the story and in making that moral unobtrusive. In the original Grandpa's farewell to the violets ("Now I have to leave them") causes Chapple to fear that death also can and will come to her, that she is consequently one with the old man as regards sad mortality. When she sobs, she sobs for herself, not especially for him. An ancient and much respected device is this use of fear of death to reform the living, but it hardly seems to fit a girl who does not deserve to die yet and is in no immediate danger.

The rewritten Cress changes in a more plausible way. She finds herself sharing something aesthetically and emotionally significant with the dying man, despite his age, and this something is their love for the yellow violets, which triggers her sympathy: "You were young [as I am now]," runs the final version as found in the book, "and you loved flowers. . . . And you still do. . . . Grandpa, just like me" (*Cress*, 311). Not their bond in death but their bond in the beauty of life unites them. Cress is lifted then into an awareness of the sympathies that properly unite youth with age. There is evidence to support Dr. Boyce when he says that *Cress Delahanty* is the "thinly disguised story of her [West's] girlhood."[18] Besides the parallels already indicated, the sensitive girl in each instance grows up in a new settlement among the citrus groves about 90 minutes by train from Woolman (patently Whittier), whose route passes through La Habre and then Brea; the seashore is only a short drive away; Saddle Back Mountain and Reservoir Hill are in view; the father is a citrus grower and an officer on the school board; the girl is a freckled towhead with literary tastes, who has a grandmother who dies; and, in addition to being fond of yellow violets, she attends a Quaker college fairly early and gets on the debating and basketball teams. To summarize, Cress has an environment very much like that which Jessamyn West had known, plus some tastes and experiences that are undeniably similar to the author's. But the book is not deliberate autobiography; on the other hand, the use of autobiographical details adds verisimilitude to the work.

The two years spent in reworking and assembling the magazine stories (Dempsey, 12) were well spent. Of 13 reviews of *Cress Delahanty* that could be located, not a single one was negative; on the contrary, the general feeling ran quite the other way. Such overwhelming approbation, I fear, is enough to make academia think the book assuredly deficient, for literary scholars almost take it for granted that greatness means neglect. And, as if to make matters worse, *Cress Delahanty* has sold well from the beginning.

West's friend Edward Weeks, in his review in *Atlantic*, compared her favorably with Booth Tarkington for peeking "so surely and so sunnily into the adolescent world."[19] Riley Hughes in the *Catholic World* dubbed the book "an exquisite work of art."[20] In the *New York Herald Tribune Book Review* Dan Wickenden, aside from profuse general praise, opined that West "illuminates even the most commonplace material with her own particular magic."[21] Frances Gaither's coverage in the *New York Times Book Review*, although too frothy to take seriously, does contain one astute observation: The book succeeds best in those scenes where the parents have the least to say and the reader can observe Cress directly without intermediary interpretation.[22] The cautious Eleanor Scott wrote in the *Saturday Review* that "these stories are very true and very good without attaining the highest distinction either in style or in content." Yet it would be quite a task to ascertain just how *Cress Delahanty* does fall short, if it does, of the "highest distinction" in content and style, and Scott omits giving the criteria.[23] The book most certainly contains much of the subtlety, depth, humor, and wisdom associated with great art. The essence of growing up, its quickenings, its high-minded enthusiasms, its dewy loves, its tremors of apprehension – all are here. Someone is entitled to add that it is a more beautiful childhood than most people have known. Incidentally, none of the reviewers seemed to question that the book is properly one for adults and children alike, which it is.

Cactus and Yellow Violets

Still more daringly sexual than *Witch Diggers*, but not markedly risqué as compared with many works of the present era, *South of the*

Angels was the most ambitious of the West stories up to 1960. To the older generation of Quakers back in Whittier, *South of the Angels* must have seemed south of the angels indeed! It is West's longest fictional work, contains more than 30 characters, most of whom are thoroughly developed; and is complex enough to make the average reader wish that the author had furnished a dramatis personae. This novel will rank for future generations as being among West's top three, the others being *Witch Diggers* and *Massacre at Fall Creek*.[24]

The time at the beginning of the story is 1916, and the locale is the Tract, as the new settlers call it, that is situated 25 miles southeast of Los Angeles and about half that distance from Whittier and the Olinda oil fields. Her childhood friend Gladys Gauldin, who knows the region, affirms that " 'South of the Angels' . . . describes Yorba Linda [as it was in their girlhood] very well" and that many of the incidents are taken from West's life. She then says that some Yorba Lindans "resented" portions of the book, feeling they could identify such and such characters from among the community.[25] Although West confirmed to Mock in her letter that the place resembles the Yorba Linda of history, the people involved are generally fictitious. She protested to him, "God forbid that anyone find any resemblances between the characters in *that* book [*South of the Angels*] and anybody, Milhous or non-Milhous, living or dead!" (letter to Mock).

Nonetheless, there remains the curious, but only curious, parallel that in 1914, just three years before a similar incident in the novel, a group of Yorba Linda stockholders brought a successful lawsuit against Janss Investment Company because of its handling of the incorporated water company.[26] As this suit went as far as the U.S. Supreme Court, it does seem inevitable that a certain 12-year-old girl in the township would hear about it – as stated earlier, Yorba Linda was extremely small, and West's own father was at one time the superintendent of the water company. What further correlations exist between the real and the fictional lawsuit are unknown to me.

The many ramifications of the story permit only a skeleton summary here. At least six separate families, some of them Quakers, plus a few bachelors move to the Tract, where they live in tents until permanent dwellings can be erected. The agricultural problem of securing water is matched by the emotional problems of loneliness, sexual frustration, and eagerness of the young to find sweethearts.

Among these sufferers are the Copes, consisting of the newspaper-man Lute; his wife, Indiana Rose (called Indy), who was formerly separated from him but returns in time to have an affair with the carpenter Tom Mount; and two daughters, one of whom, Press, is the story's beautiful heroine who has reached the dangerous age of 17. Press is in love with a neighborhood boy named Chat Lewis but withholds herself from him out of a guilty feeling that she owes her mother special attention. After she learns how faithless Indy has been, the filial bond is broken. Other love relationships, at least eight of them not counting the married ones, help tie together the dwellers of the Tract.

Several additional unifying features operate. First is the physical Tract itself, in which everyone has a not-too-clear title to a piece of land and where all share in a clamor for water rights. The lake that they meanwhile use in common is a gathering place for neighborly gossip. Then there is the "lucky" bed in the Lewis household, on which Pete and Rosa Ramos, and later Shel and Joicey Lewis, conceive their latest offspring. Other unifying elements consist of the two main themes running through the novel, the first of which is the love-fertility-death cycle, the love particulars of which have already been indicated. Although the lecherous Tom Mount beds down with several local women in fruitless fornication, the outcome is different with other human couples in the area who mate, as foreshadowed by the birth of a calf at one of the farms. When the essential water for the crops has arrived at the end of a nine-month wait, exactly the term for the human gestation period, some wives bear their first babies. And coinciding with the arrival of the babies, as part of the fertility pattern, the birth pains of the agrarian experiment subside and the crops and trees are at last growing.

Foreshadowing of death comes early in the story with the severe tubercular illness of Mrs. Waite, who is hardly expected to live. At the end of the novel, as if to offset the birth of the two children, is the awesome coincidence of two deaths that same night: Pete Ramos and the hopeless invalid Mary Jessup. And so death neatly balances out life, and the little world of the Tract goes on. As we can see, the novel is structurally interesting.

Possibly West, who was extremely well-read and the owner of an ample library of books in her house, had an acquaintance with such seminal works on the fertility myth as Sir James Frazer's *The Golden*

Bough and Jessie Weston's *From Ritual to Romance*. In any case, the
decades of farm life behind West – not to mention her gardener
husband's status as one of California's leading lily experts, with up to
a thousand flowering plants and shrubs and trees on the property –
must have illustrated many a time for her the great round of nature,
of budding leaf, of flower, of fruit, of fallen or barren branch, and
must have intimated to the symbol-conscious artist in her the
concept of nature as metaphor for human mortality. Of the almost
limitless possibilities for this kind of influence, not to be dismissed is
the author's own close brush with death and the record of family
calamity – a surprising amount of serious illness and death by
disease.[27]

In the second theme, that of ironic fulfillment, old Mary Jessup
has spent almost a lifetime believing she never loved her husband,
for she could not put out of her mind the loss of a certain Chester
Bannister who had once jilted her to run off with a widow. As Mary
is dying from some undisclosed ailment, she at last comprehends,
with Wendlin's help, that she had actually always loved him. The
relief she gains from this realization enables her to die in peace, and
she even forgets that she was contemplating suicide. Like Jess Birdwell and Mr. Cornelius, she gains from the prospect of death such a
heightened awareness of the beauties and pleasures of ordinary
living that she is positively radiant at the end.

Mary Jessup taught her friend Asa Brice that something crucial
was missing in the solitary bachelordom of raising a garden and
inspecting snowstorms and taking down nature notes; namely, affection in the form of a lover or wife. When he first arrived, he thought
that his individualistic approach to living would bring him happiness;
it never did. As every reader of the novel knows, this eloquent and
attractive young naturalist falls in love with Mount's former mistress
Eunice Frye. The author seems to believe that a young man in
possession of his freedom needs a good woman in order to make his
life complete.

Asa Brice is clearly modeled on Thoreau, who in real life was
hardly malleable material for intimate human relationships, although
several women took a romantic interest in this lifelong bachelor. For
the sake of a love plot the author humanizes Asa. But the resulting
Asa is no ordinary romantic hero; he has depth. He is content, like
his Concord model, to let the next world take care of itself, and he

dismisses the conventional Christian interpretation of the Divine Plan. We are not surprised to learn also that he is stiff and reserved, watches the weather diligently, keeps track of the season's first blooms, has a keen sense of smell, likes walks, observes woodchucks and ants with absorbed curiosity, keeps a notebook, prefers to rough it outdoors even after other settlers have retreated to living in houses, and dislikes war as well as he does organized society. To complete the nearly thorough portrait of the author of *Walden*, he is short and blond and has the big Emerson nose that Concord villagers said Thoreau was growing for himself. No wonder West was scanning the journals of Thoreau in her Hollywood motel room in 1955, during the time the novel was underway![28]

Even so, Asa emerges in the story as a distinct personality, aside from his attributes of the great American Transcendentalist; moreover, he utters some of the most puissant lines in all of West's oeuvre. The portrayal is more skillful than what Stratton-Porter did with her Thoreau figure in *The Harvester*, and it at least equals the handling of another such figure (Van Dorn) in Maxwell Anderson's much-neglected drama *High Tor*. Incidentally, Thoreau himself figures in West's ineffably touching short story "Like Visitant of Air."[29]

Indy is another character in *South of the Angels* who suffers loneliness, not for lacking a mate but for being married to the wrong one. Through adultery she has become a sexually rejuvenated woman, but by the time her carnal indiscretions have taught her what she has been missing at home, Lute learns of the affair, and, by appealing to her sense of pity for him, tricks her into becoming his willing prisoner. Their confrontation in book 4, chapter 4, is a masterful study in human psychology.

Lute, though having ensnared his wife again, still cannot win from her the love he desires. A psychologist would conclude that he has a sadomasochistic syndrome. Behind his mental illness lies his hatred for Tom Mount; thus he takes out this hatred on his wife in sexual aggression. All that this bedroom athlete knows to do whenever Indy is lonely is to give her his simplistic "cure" of more sex, a remedy that, even with her new passion gained from Mount, leaves her at best dutifully passive. This passivity tantalizes and spurs him on to virtual rapes as he tries to make his victim say whether her experience be pleasure or pain. Sphinxlike, she denies him ultimate gratification and thereby unwittingly urges him on to new violations and to ever new remorse because of them. As a result, he longs for some cleansing that will end his torment.

The roots of his problem are partly Freudian, extending back, as the Freudians reason, to the viper's nest of childhood where Lute's mother derived no pleasure from married sex, envisioned the wife's role as a stoic, and passed on to her son her own dreadful inhibitions. If one is to believe what West says elsewhere in her writings, a wholesome sex education in Lute's early years might have worked wonders for him. He is one of the most vivid and believable characters that she created.

When Indy does not fulfill her daughter's ideal of what a mother should be, Press, feeling free of her, runs off and gives herself to Chad in a wild gamble to gain happiness. The reader is told that Chad would make an unforgivable mistake if he rejected her now because Press might understand him in a cerebral way but her body would not understand, would never forgive him. As Press's own father had in his day turned Indy down in just such circumstances before they were married, we cannot doubt within the logic of the novel the emotional alienation that this rejection might have caused the daughter, morality or no morality. We note the irony of this girl, Press, restrained as a nun through many a chapter, now throwing herself at the suitor who had long but vainly solicited her love.

West assumed that a woman's emotional organization is so much more sensitive than a man's that women can suffer an erotic trauma if they are frustrated in gaining the sexual consummation that is their right. This theory of West's runs counter to traditional injunctions against premarital sex, as if implying that it is better for a woman or even a teenaged girl to give in to the man she loves rather than endure the lasting results of rejection. In *Love Is Not What You Think*, which among other things is an impassioned essay on the spiritual qualities associated with physical love, West furnishes a gloss on the problem at hand. Among various authorities on love she cites Albert Camus several times approvingly in her rationale for a romantic, intuitive approach. She could have had Press Cope on her mind when she wrote the following, for the essay and the novel were published only a year apart:

"All love is a meeting. It is sorrowful for a woman if she is not met in all the potentialities of her nature; sorrowful for anyone, *but most sorrowful for a woman* [italics mine], who needs to be encompassed by her lover. Still, a woman had better, if faced by that bitter predicament, go against her judgment than against her senses. A woman judges with her senses. There is no use telling her that something which she does not feel to be right is right."³⁰

This, then, is the guidance that Chad follows for the sake of his beloved in accepting her, body and all. It is the guidance that Cate Conboy in *Witch Diggers* and Orpha Chase in *Life I Really Lived* failed to follow – to their misery. We are led to believe that young Press will at least be able to avoid one of the greatest mistakes of her parents, for her heart offering is not turned down.

Not so with Crystal Raunce. In the Tract's newspaper office one day she confesses to Lute her innocent affection for him. Shocked, he rudely rejects her, for the Puritan in him is unable to disassociate love from sex, and he bluntly tells her to suppress her imagination. Plain-featured Crystal turns away brokenheartedly from Lute, who should have helped her with understanding and kindness, and she soon consorts with the local carpenter, Tom Mount, in her quest for affection. What Tom offers is not, however, the innocent love Crystal at first had in mind.

The theme of ironic fulfillment surfaces elsewhere as well. Crystal's vulgar father, LeRoy Raunce, whose theology told him that he was "saved" and therefore "sinless," had built a church with the expectation that he would naturally be chosen its minister; unfortunately, a false accusation of indecency destroys his chances for the post. Pete Ramos believed that having a son would represent for him the fullness of manhood; consequently, it is a bitter irony that on the night of his son's birth he should be slain defending the life of a friend who was trying to *evade* the responsibilities of paternity.

The case of Sylvester Perkins, developer of the Tract, represents the fall of an idealist, a man appropriately represented by the mountaintops toward which he habitually gazes from his office window. His aim from the beginning had been altruistic in wanting every one of the settlers to lead a good life in a beautiful place. He never saw a child at play in the Tract, or a housewife watering a flower, but he melted with pleasure. When he had settled his clients on the land, they then show their gratitude by suing him because he had secretly mortgaged the water company in order to raise the money needed for irrigation pipes. In short, Perkins was unlucky. Louella, his wife, undergoes an unexpected fulfillment too. From the beginning she had thought her scheming husband a fraud, and she had resolved that she would leave him someday whenever someone else would prove to her his guilt. When he loses his court trial, she surprises herself by not reacting at all as expected. Her discovery of how she truly feels about this rare man parallels to some extent the case of Mrs. Jessup and her husband.

South of the Angels exemplifies certain ways in which West treats her male figures. Open physical conflict is, as usual, underplayed, and the little there is of it is reported by a third party. The practice of having some of her men kneel before their women may strike the reader as old-fashioned chivalry right out of antebellum literature. Perkins thinks of dropping to his knees before Louella when she is ready to comfort him. Pete falls to his knees before Rosa after their child has arrived. And Lute kneels before Indy and covers his face with her skirts, squinting out slyly at times to see what effect his pleading might have.

Moreover, West's male characters are not especially aggressive as lovers, and even the supposedly coarse lovers are lacking in raw maleness. They do not have sweats of anticipation, or erections; nor do they ogle female buttocks, or peek into bosoms, or strip off panties even in the imagination; and even the crudest among them do not usually use offensive language when speaking of sex. Christie Fraser, as seen in an earlier novel, is a fair example of the type, a bit too tame, one would think, for a hot-blooded young man who frolics freely with the girls.

The lickerish Tom Mount, who wants to keep a good supply of women on hand even though he might never get around to using all of them, is at the other end of the libidinal spectrum. In his carnal acquisitiveness he reminds us of that collector of hearts Greg McGovern, the movie star in *The Life I Really Lived*. In addition to being selfish he is rather lazy and passive as a lover, like a sluggish python in a tree waiting for its chicken to pass beneath. In the Fort Collins seduction scene with Eunice the descriptions of him are not those of the passionate, impatient lover burning to consummate his lust. Oh, no. Tom undressed before his woman as if he were tired already, and lay down on the bed expecting *her* to initiate copulation, sending the silent message, "Help me, Baby."[31]

So cool is this lothario that, on seeing Indy bathing nude in her
yard, he, like a gentleman, turns his head the other way. Has he
become jaded by his repeated adventures in the boudoir? Doubtful,
especially since the bather in question is soon to become his
mistress. He seems almost effeminate. Anyone familiar with the
carousing, lusty, hot-breathing, bodice-ripping rakehells sweating
their way through many contemporary novels would easily find fault
with the way mild, easygoing Tom Mount is depicted. Nevertheless,
real life teaches us that the fellow who succeeds the most with
women is not always the swaggering and pushy libertine with his
blunt vocabulary and all-too-obvious intentions, but rather the quiet
and relaxed schemer who has the spider's patience to wait until the
fly bumbles into its web. Such is Tom Mount.

In the West books the truly aggressive people, the pursuers, the
sexy-talking ones, are the women. When it comes to sheer forward-
ness, Mount, for all his conquests – insofar as they are actually
shown in the novel – cannot hold a candle to Press and Medora.
Much less can shy Ortiz, for he has to be hunted down by his girl-
friend-in-heat, Medora, before he will consent to tamper with her
virginity. As for dirty expressions and vile four-lettered words, Opal
and this same Medora have all but cornered the market in *South of
the Angels*. But whether portraying men or women, West is relatively
delicate-minded as compared with many of her contemporary
authors; still, she is much franker than Henry James or Edith Whar-
ton ever tried to be.

The critical reception of *South of the Angels* left more than a
little to be desired. William Hogan, an avowed champion of the
novelist, complimented her in the *Saturday Review* on her skill, yet
urged unconvincingly that she ought not to have chosen a big canvas
– the "pageant" being too long and overpopulated.[32] Hogan seemed
to miss completely the cleverly arranged contrasts and parallels (ruin
of the orange trees, and, simultaneously, Mary's dying), the ironies,
the ingenious double entendres, the surprising verbal linkups
between chapters and scenes (see book 1, chapters 2-3), and the
thoroughness, let alone the complexity, of the numerous characterizations. Orville Prescott in the *San Francisco Chronicle* failed to
mention any unified pattern or patterns; still, he fretted that the
book is too concerned with sexual passion.[33] The *Atlantic* carried
Edward Weeks's brief but suave and appreciative views, including

one that the story contains "many gleaming moments."[34] The most unqualified praise of all came from R. T. Bresler in the *Library Journal*, who hailed it as a "beautifully written book" executed in "meticulously realized prose."[35]

To summarize, none of the reviewers recorded any significant structural unity, and several thought the work too long and the characters too many. John T. Flanagan, writing many years later, found considerable merit in the novel but also a lack of focus. "Almost any one of these persons," he said, "could have served the author as a central character; instead the narrative moves from one to another, from episode to episode, without sequence or apparent direction." He objects that the "narrative appeal is slight. The characters too often seem to get out of hand" (Flanagan, 304-5). But like all the other critics who have written about this book, he misses the numerous unifying techniques (already covered) that tie together this ingenious even if sprawling novel.

Possibly the assumption that repeatedly led some reviewers astray in the case of West's later books is that, since she had written some so-called simple, honest, and straightforward stories about Quakers and adolescents, she was not going to be complicated or clever in anything different. They were comfortable with the "sweet little old Quaker lady"; they had her figured out. Consequently, when she left her Quakers behind and began making excursions into symbolism, sex, complex thematic patterns, flashbacks, and other features of avant-garde or coterie literature, even showing the darker side of adolescence, her efforts were often either misunderstood or ignored.

South of the Angels contains much to admire. There is the naturalness of it all, with the story ending as an episode in life might, for a certain inconclusiveness lingers despite all the answers that are supplied. The story ends as it should end – in accord with the logical demands of character and situation. The lifecycle theme ensures that no neat ending is feasible.

Sister, Dear Sister

West set great store by her novel *A Matter of Time*, which was serialized in *Redbook* in 1966 and issued in the fall in hardcover. It was important for her in several ways, in being the first of her novels to

use flashbacks extensively, the first to be written in the first person,
and the first to be set in the present time. Another first lies in her use
of the subject matter, euthanasia, which was and still is highly
controversial. Also important, this is the most biographical of all her
works of fiction (Farmer, 39; Graham, 24), the original title of the
manuscript having been "Sister, Dear Sister."

The writing of *A Matter of Time* took two years, during which
period West placed a group of short stories in *Good Housekeeping,
Harper's,* and *Ladies' Home Journal.* The novel was to be a momen-
tous "breakthrough into present time and reality," whose story was
so sensational and so agonizing to write as to make her truly believe
that it would never be published. "[P]erhaps only this belief [that it
might not be published] permitted me to write it," she adds.[36]

The story proceeds on two levels. First, it follows events in the
present time in which beautiful Blix, dying in her desert home,
enlists the aid of her older sister, a librarian named Tasmania (called
Tassie), and her physician, Dr. Reyes, to poison herself when her
cancer becomes hopelessly enlarged and excruciating. Blix is now
middle-aged, and, like Tassie, she is in her second marriage; their
first marriages had been failures. Blix's latest husband is an auto
dealer who visits occasionally, at which time he grieves in the
manner now fashionable in novels and motion pictures – by
guzzling whiskey. As a personality he is a nonentity.

The second and by far more interesting level consists of the
flashbacks Tassie has of remembered experiences as she converses
with her dying sister. Consequently, the two women come to understand the whys and wherefores of much that they have gone through
and they clear up misunderstandings.

As sisters Blix and Tassie are sharply differentiated. Blix, the
family beauty, is hard to please; she is a rebel, generous to a fault, a
good dresser, and knowledgeable about where to eat and places to
go. Moreover, she attracts too many sexually active males for her
mother's peace of mind. But Blix never quite comes alive for the
reader even as a temptress, probably because she so often gets lost
in the flashbacks, sometimes in flashbacks-within-flashbacks, where
her adventures tend to be summarized rather than depicted in a
graphic and suspenseful manner. The author seems determined to
downplay the sexual element in particular, perhaps out of respect to

her dead sister, on whom Blix is modeled, but in doing so dilutes the realism that the modern reader expects.

Blix's plain sister, Tassie, unlucky in attracting men, takes pride in withdrawing and conforming, in being self-righteous and pure. And as she always remains above suspicion, it follows that she never gets any real adventure. Even in her childhood Tassie was eager, too eager, to please her sickly mother. She continually shrinks from committing herself to either optimism or joy. As a stoic she stands for a phase the author herself once passed through, therefore suggesting that Tassie is an alter ego acting out in good health the unfortunate withdrawal that helped keep the sickly author so long from the literary scene.

The failure of parents, church, and college to prepare Tassie for congenial mating (no sex education whatever) leads her to ignore the warning of friends and to go to the altar with a selfish prig named Everett. The impression generated is that, had she only let her body and her senses guide her, in accordance with the intuitive, trust-your-instincts philosophy in *Love Is Not What You Think*, she would never have wed this cold fish. Webster Schott points out in his perceptive review in *Life* that Tassie's first marriage is "the logical outcome of a Christian neurosis that said give but do not take."[37]

In addition to husband Everett's other defects, he is an all-around failure at making a living. Meanwhile lonely Tassie forms a habit of falling in love with various men, such as Manuel, the Mexican apricot picker, and never does anything about it. To her mind the secret desire is everything; the fulfillment, unnecessary.

Blix, too receptive to males and better informed about sex than her sister, has an affair with a handsome man named Vurl. When the mother discovers contraceptive devices in Blix's purses, she persuades Tassie to use dishonest methods to break up the union. "Mama's girl" Tassie readily hops to the task of trying to make her sister virtuous. The upshot is ironic. Long afterward, Tassie discovers during her sickroom conversations that Blix had learned her lesson only too well – that when she finally decided to get married, she chose to exact a price: "The first question I'm going to ask a boy is, 'What's your bank balance?' "[38] No more giving it away free, no more letting the heart rule the head.

In the narrator's reminiscences other members of the Murphy family are introduced, including the father, Orland, who was always too absorbed in tinkering with the radio to tune in to his children's problems. Then there are Blackie, the imaginative little redheaded brother, and Marmion, another brother, a dead weight as a personality, who had earlier set himself against anything so immature as showing enthusiasm. The only interesting brother is Le Cid, the oddest named of all the oddly named children, who openly scorns Christian orthodoxy and who alone of the offspring has the gumption to break away from the stultifying community and church to lead an enviable life among the thespians of London. "I was less at ease with Le Cid than with any of the others," Tassie admits about this apostate from the Pilgrim Church (clearly a counter for the Society of Friends). "Le Cid's number I didn't have" (*Matter of Time*, 51). Her admission is not surprising, for her brother is no timid, try-to-please-mama milksop like herself; he exhibits the defiant individualism that makes a few young people in every generation decide to be themselves, and to follow their dream even into bohemia. But Le Cid's flaw, and it is a large one, is that in his rush to be himself he has surrendered his religious heritage and found no other religion to replace it.

One of the gratifying things about the story is the close-knit, fun-loving, and exciting family circle. Yet when it comes to religion, the Murphys are content to ignore or be ignorant of primary religious experience. Like many so-called religious Americans in the twentieth century, their church attendance is perfunctory. Since their removal from Kentucky, where membership in the sect carried responsibilities, all but Tassie now lack any desire to do something as a sign of spiritual conviction. They never observe religious holidays or consider being charitable to the poor. The parents sometimes read the Bible aloud, but they grow silent when the children ask them questions about religion. *A Matter of Time* delineates through such passages the desuetude and worldliness that have befallen Protestant religions on the West Coast, particularly Quakerism, now that the pioneer stage has passed.

The father in the family is vaguely drawn and basically uninteresting. On the other hand, the mother, Maude, with her bloomer-girl prudishness, does come to life as a joint wrongdoer with her husband and as a personality who, despite her faults, richly stimulated Tassie's imagination. We see behind the winsome anecdotist Grace West, altered in some ways, maybe, but still there: "Listening to Mother, I learned to live where I wasn't. Compelled by her art, I had my most vivid life in her memories. I imagined those [Kentucky] hills and branches, those creeks and springs; the Aunt Libs and Uncle Steves, the Great-grandfather Amoses and Grandmother Elizas. And everything we imagine is, because it is a part of ourselves, more real than reality. It is the reality *we* have manufactured. We possess it, as God does the world *He* created. It is the dust into which we have blown the breath of life" (*Matter of Time*, 75-76). This passage illustrates a quality that is endearing in West's writings: A profound gratitude to those who have enriched her life.

Along with Everett and Le Cid, Dr. Reyes is one of the better developed adult male characterizations in the novel but even so remains two-dimensional. Many readers would probably label this doctor a criminal for condoning and winking at the practice of euthanasia, but West, who had a lot of experience with doctors in and out of sanatoriums, goes out of her way to make him a sympathetic figure. She is not, however, kind in the novel to the lesbian nurse with her "poisonous little fingers" roaming about Tassie's body (*Matter of Time*, 159-60).

In the climax of the story Blix, after learning from her doctor that her case is hopeless, plans to die with her sister's cooperation. Better, she thinks, to die alert and in full possession of her senses, not like a drugged animal lingering out her days uselessly. This is what the author calls, paradoxically, a "celebration of life." But let us try to give West all the credit due; she means here that Blix demonstrates her control over her own life, refuses to be a victim, and manages to keep to the end as much of her humanity as possible (Graham, 26). Tassie will help her save up a lethal dose of pills and arranges to be present so that the suicide will go off without a hitch. Dr. Reyes, knowing what the sisters have conspired to do, arranges to be out of town for a few days. The reader might object, however, that neither the doctor nor the two husbands, who are in on the plan, raise any arguments about the morality of euthanasia, especially since Tassie and the doctor could be prosecuted for being accessories to suicide.

A sybarite to the end, Blix attires herself in a green silk dress, symbolic of the abundant life to which she is bidding farewell and of the green earth she will soon join; anoints her body with perfume;

applies silver nail polish; and, as the final act of her ritual, takes a fatal handful of capsules from a gilt-edged toothpick holder.

The subject of euthanasia not only bothered some of West's readers at the time the novel came out but still lends itself to debate at the time that I am writing, when readers are presumably more open-minded or at least ambivalent. Many Occidentals consider suicides abnormal people, neurotics at best, who in their hurry to leave this "worthless" life might readily take an unwilling person or two with them on that journey to the undiscovered country. Not many people today are Roman enough to accept with either welcome or complacency the prospect of suicide, no matter how distressed the victim – but opinion is changing. It is curious, however, that West faults her characters for lacking fundamental Christian conscience and practice; on the other hand, she asks her readers to condone this act of suicide, itself rated as a sin by many Christians.

As Felicia Lamport correctly noted in *Book Week*, the imagery is often vivid, sometimes strikingly so.[39] West proved herself once again adept at sensuous nature description, as where, for example, she described a hot summer afternoon in California: "The valley smelled like a country kitchen, wood range fired up and jam kettle bubbling. Cherries, apricots, peaches, plums; all had come to a rolling boil. The ripening vegetables had a bland, starchy smell, a man smell, as contrasted with the female smell of the acid-sweet fruits" (*Matter of Time*, 164). Almost always she describes nature at the level of leaf and bud and fruit, with their attendant sensuousness and even domestic associations. It is typically a feminine slant. No big canvases. The passage about the dragonfly in book 12 is a splendid example of her method, and it fittingly symbolizes Blix's journey to a better world after death – if suicides get a ticket to that place. In a marsh some larva worms sadly discuss what has befallen one of their lost neighbors and misunderstand the glorious transformation that has taken place; meanwhile the mourned one, rid of its chrysalis shell, has soared off into an undreamed-of light. The inspiration for this was probably found in Alfred, Lord Tennyson's "The Two Voices," where he has the suicidal voice cite the newly transformed dragonfly as an example of freedom through death.

The novel is different from many of West's earlier works in containing a more frequent and at times a more sustained handling of poetic and rhetorical technique. Examples of the former have already been given. The sentences are often as finely etched and as stalwart as a damascene blade. Epigrams make their appearance, such as "A hospital by definition is a place where when they make tea, water results"; and "Cowards may die many deaths, the doomed experience many resurrections" (*Matter of Time*, 183, 206).

We should note that West selected her names patiently with due regard for connotations, and if they sound "awkward," then perhaps she was showing that the lives of the characters, like the Converses in *Leafy Rivers*, are out of kilter. Marmion, for example, seems to be a pun on *mar*; he likes to mar any joyous impulse that might perchance spring up in his breast. Le Cid connotes an adventurous, romantic figure, which is rather what he turns out to be finally. Tassie reminds us of *tassel*, a slight device without much inner strength and one that depends on some support, a meaning applicable to the character's emotional dependence, first on her mother and later on her sister. Vurl, the aggressive and athletic seducer, would dearly like to *curl* up with a woman, any woman, including Tassie, as one passionate scene reveals. The word also suggests *cur*. It has an unpleasant combination of consonants – as Tassie duly notes; for the animal growl of the *r* lurks between a soft, fricative *v* and the purling liquid of an *l* – a sound both voluptuous and repellent. And, as a final touch of eroticism, overdone in this instance, this lecher's surname is none other than Seaman. The names of Blix and Blackie convey ironic implications: Frank Norris's Blix comes to a happy ending in his novel by that name; Blackie has red hair. The name Murphy could have been chosen for its very commonness, in addition to being Irish – a favored race in West books.

The Hollywood writing experience had an indirect influence on the construction of *A Matter of Time*. So stimulating was the experience of being questioned on her methods by studio officials that West solicited similar challenging inquiries from her editor at Harcourt, Brace & World (since known as Harcourt Brace Jovanovich), and these were readily supplied. One wonders about the nature of these inquiries as well as the replies, and we can only speculate that the author was, among other things, trying hard to avoid conflict with the law (more on this later). After the manuscript of *A Matter of Time* had already undergone an enormous amount of cutting

before it left Napa for the first time, Julian Muller advised an additional cut of about 100 pages.[40]

Elaine Gottlieb in the *New York Times Book Review* observes a
certain "lack of depth" in the depiction of secondary characters. For
this reviewer, the portraits of Blix and Tassie were compelling
enough to make the others, however, seem unimportant. Most of the
reviews, including Gottlieb's, were mainly complimentary.[41] This
applies also to the one by Charles Poore in the daily edition of the
New York Times. Poore, nevertheless, objected to the "awkward"
naming of the characters[42] (prompted, perhaps by the fact that West
has her Tassie bring up this very peculiarity of naming). Rita Estok in
Library Journal was one of the few reviewers who objected openly
to the idea of euthanasia.[43] Several women wrote to the author that
they hoped she would rot in hell (Whittle, 54).

Despite the author's high hopes and the favorable critical reception, *A Matter of Time* did not catch on with the public, which continued to prefer – and expect – "pleasant" books on the order of
Friendly Persuasion and *Cress Delahanty.* The unpleasant subject of
suicide does not, of course, doom a book to obscurity, as several
modern classics such as Leo Tolstoy's *Anna Karenina* and Jack London's *Martin Eden* can well testify. But once that suicide is aided
and abetted by a sympathetically rendered second party, the story's
heroine, the situation is not only very different but evidently without
precedent. Suicide is made to appear so easy and attractive and
painless in Blix's case that the enlightened, progressive reader is
encouraged to approve and – who knows? – choose that way out
for himself or herself when life becomes too painful to bear. To that
extent the book is morbid – despite the author's intentions – and
for that reason must have lost some potential readers. West, however, in her interview with Lee Graham (published later) disavowed
advocating any general practice of euthanasia; she stated that Blix
had a right to decide for herself, that there could be no general rule
governing this matter. Nor did she think the book morbid: "This
didn't seem to me a nonaffirmative or a negative book. . . it seemed
to me a *celebration of life* [italics Graham's]. . . . A woman dies in it,
it is true, but she doesn't die as a victim, she dies as a person who is
in control of her life, who expresses courage, who is full of laughter
and gaiety and bravery. It is, in its last hundred pages, about death.

That is true. But we are all going to die, it's part of our living. . . . It seems to me to be facing the whole of life" (Graham, 26).

Insofar as the origin of *A Matter of Time* can be pieced together from details available, West's story "Reverdy" furnished some matter, the younger sister there assuming the role of the older, and vice versa.[44] Suggestive but not directly contributory is "Another Word Entirely," a work printed in the *New Mexico Quarterly* in 1947, about a pair of girls, one of whom has an abortion following an adulterous romance.[45]

The memory of three grandparents and both of her own parents afflicted with cancer, and, above all, Carmen, who suffered terribly from that disease, plus the thought that she herself might be afflicted someday, had moved West to explore in fiction what she thought she might do in a similar situation where the agony was increasing and nearly unrelievable.[46] In *A Matter of Time* lie numerous veiled connections with the author's familial background. Linda in the present story, for example, evokes Yorba Linda. The apricot orchard evokes memories of Hemet; Pilgrim College, a small, humdrum church school 25 miles from Los Angeles, is a dead ringer for Whittier College.[47] Tassie's serious illness parallels West's tuberculosis. The Pilgrim Church suggests West Coast Quakerism, although it could as easily refer to some long-established fundamentalist Protestant sects in America. In the Whittier district during the author's childhood there was little to distinguish the Methodists and the Baptists from the Quakers, save for communion and baptism, for they all sang in church, heard preaching, and attended revivals. In a letter to me dated 20 December 1966 West clinches the identification when she says that " 'A Matter of Time' was The Friendly Persuasion family *now*; the emptiness of much Quakerism *now*" [italics hers]. The identification of the heroine Blix with the author's sister, Carmen, is, however, even more pronounced, on the basis of both internal and external evidence. More on this later.

All through the book one can sense the affection West had for her immediate family,[48] but that did not keep her from exposing the heroine's own family for its irresponsibility and error and spiritual privation. The portrait of Mrs. Murphy owes much to the ailing Grace West of her later years; the unenthusiastic brother Marmion, who had decided "to make 'doing without' his life's glory" (*Time*, 11), is a reflection of Myron; Blackie (with his red hair) suggests brother

Merle; while Le Cid is pure invention, the kind of artistic-minded brother that the author, brought up in a culturally deprived family, perhaps wished for but never had.

Blix's soft beauty is of course borrowed from Carmen, a girl who, as an early photograph shows, was physically attractive in no small degree. West wrote to me cautiously on 28 March 1966 that this girl, who had the highest IQ in her eighth grade class, "had the problem of a lot [of] admirers." Translated, this means that Carmen became, like Blix, sexually active in her teens. She was "exquisite," "dainty," and a "sharp dresser," Dr. Maxwell McPherson remembers. But her role in the book goes far beyond mere surface details. Very shortly after my *Jessamyn West* appeared in 1972, Dr. McPherson, visiting in my home, confided to my wife and me that the suicide was not at all fiction. "That was Carmen. It really happened. Jessamyn helped her do it!" he exclaimed, evidently still amazed that his wife could participate in such a deed and then write about it. Although I already knew that Blix had a deeply biographical origin, the news that the author herself had collaborated in her sister's demise back in 1963 came as a profound shock.

Just a few years after her husband's disclosure, and after the legal statute of limitations had expired, West went public with the facts in her memoir *The Woman Said Yes*, which is about the lives of her mother and sister. Even though she was 74 at the time, at an age when a person might express regrets about crimes she had committed, West obviously regretted nothing about her complicity – and never did up to the day of her death. The dedication to the book reads, "With love for Grace and Carmen and to celebrate their courage" (*Woman*); and the subsequent text leaves no doubt in the reader's mind that West, if given the choice of reliving those days, would not flinch from helping her sister put an end to her hopeless battle with intestinal cancer. The first half of this memoir concentrates on the life of Grace West, who was born in a log cabin in Indiana and who, despite having battled illness, including cancer, much of her life, lived to the ripe age of 77. Through hearing this mother's recollections of days back East, the daughter found materials and inspiration for much of her art. It is worth noting, however, that in this memoir the author is so fascinated with Grace's contribution that she completely omits mentioning Maxwell McPherson, except as her teacher husband away somewhere earning financial support for her. She mentions none of the visits he made to her sick bed. Eldo West fares no better. At any rate, the Grace West we see here is such a charming and funny and life-affirming woman that we can only regret that no photographs were included with the text. No student of the author's life would want to miss this part of the book.

The second half of *The Woman Said Yes* shows the author herself helping Carmen accumulate enough capsules to make a lethal dose and then arranging matters so that no last-minute rescue can take place. The Dr. Reyes of the novel is here identified as Dr. Munger (no doubt another fictitious name, chosen to safeguard his professional reputation); otherwise their roles are similar. In general, many things in *The Woman Said Yes* correspond to those in the novel.

The author tells us that three special elements bound her to her sister: (a) Carmen's blond beauty and slanted eyes; (b) the need that the older and still-childless Jessamyn felt to mother someone (who in this case enjoyed being mothered); and (c) most important for the emotional and intellectual development of the author, the fact that Carmen alone in this family of nonreaders "understood the fever and excitement of words: reading them, writing them" (*Woman*, 146).

West tells us that on a trip to Europe with Carmen about 1961, after many years of lovingly catering to the whims and desires of this spoiled sister, she experienced an epiphany: "It was then the worm turned, and discovered in turning that it had lived with Carmen a wormlike life. Not a life that Carmen necessarily admired; but one adapts oneself to the nature of the creature with whom one finds oneself coupled." Carmen frankly admitted that she liked being waited on, even though she did not approve of the people who did the serving. The memoirist concludes, "Natures and temperaments differ and are largely unchangeable. It takes more grace to receive than to give. . . . I remember with pleasure the gifts I have made. Those I have received I forget. It may be more blessed to give than to receive, but there is more grace in receiving than giving. When you receive, whom do you love and praise? The giver. When you give, the same holds true. Carmen's grace in receiving had made me a lifelong lover of myself, happy in bringing happiness, I believed, to her" (*Woman*, 146-47). Earlier in the book West had remarked sagely about such people as her sister, "If there is any lesson for me to learn from my life so far, it is that love must not abate. It must not hinge upon reciprocity. If you have truly loved, love on, no matter what. Admit that this act or word in the loved one is undesired – but love on. Otherwise you build up for yourself great suffering" (*Woman*, 110).

Carmen, we are told, faced her end with stoic fortitude. She "did not talk of death; lament her fate; wonder about the possibility of life after death; cry for more; mourn over past mistakes" (*Woman*, 150). "My darling, you did it," the author concludes on an elegiac note that would please readers sympathetic to mercy killing. "You had the courage. It was a great gift to all of us. To depart like a courteous guest. You did not wear out your welcome. You did not linger to cause us all to suffer" (*Woman*, 178).

Crimson Ramblers

September 1970 brought the windfall of *Crimson Ramblers of the World, Farewell.*[49] One special advantage of this new harvest was to let the reader sample some of the very earliest items from West's pen, such as the TB asylum stories "99.6" and "The Day of the Hawk," hitherto accessible only in back issues of obscure periodicals. Still another asylum story is "I'll Have to Ask Him to Come Sooner." Here a not-so-ladylike patient waylays the husband of her fellow inmate with the intention, she piously tells herself, of upbraiding him for always being late to visit his distressed wife; instead, she ends up in his embraces because all along she had merely desired him for herself. Many selections in the book share in common a young female narrator or heroine, who is identified differently in each case, and who is troubled about or witness to some affair of the heart.

The title story, a new one, proves that West had not lost her knack for capturing those crucial, formative moments in the young when the soul is shaped for good or ill. In the story Mrs. Prescott catches her adolescent daughter Elizabeth at the knothole one morning as she accidentally stares down at her father, who is bathing in the nude in the kitchen; scolds her that this "spying" is evil and perverted; and tells her that she has tendencies to be guarded against most rigidly. Guilt-stricken because she feels that her mother must be right (echoes of the author's feelings about her own mother), the impressionable innocent plays traitor to her natural feelings the next day at school and rejects the love overtures of her new and promising boyfriend, the colorful Crimson Rambler. Hers is a mother-fixation aborning, reminding the reader of Sidney Howard's play *The Silver Cord*, also on the dangers of mother love.

"Night Piece for Julia" – the title echoes Herrick and also smacks of a double-entendre – is another examination of the fear of sex: Here the heroine, Julia, in bed with her husband, steels herself against the ordeal of sex by first taking an imaginary journey of suffering through cold and friendless, homeless and wearisome streets until she is finally in a mood to turn toward her mate. It is perhaps not superfluous to assert that in West books this popular Freudianism, the crippling power of sex fear, is a common feature.

Offering still another excursion into sex is "Mother's Day," a brilliant commentary on the pluses and minuses of conventional marriage, which gains its punch from a double-surprise ending. We see the events of the narrative through the eyes of Merlin, a California wife with conventional ideas. Filled with outrage, Merlin's mother complains to her that Aunt El-Dora's husband must have broken the aunt's spirit to make her share him with another woman for five days out of seven. Poor El-Dora. She ought to rebel. Urged by her mother, Merlin then goes with her pampered husband, Alban, to check on the rumor. But it comes as a jolt when this pair peeps into El-Dora's house and sees her and her weekend husband together, cooing and billing as if they were newlyweds, as if the interloping "other woman" did not even exist. What they saw was an El-Dora, desperate to have at least a share of her husband but fearful of driving him away by claiming all her due, who dotingly "hovered [by him] . . . touched, fed, listened, in agony" (*Crimson Ramblers*, 152). El-Dora was grateful to have him to herself even for a weekend. But Merlin can only think of the misery her aunt must be in. Alban, on the other hand, announces that the split ménage arrangement was simply wonderful – imagine, the husband, who loves music, can have the loving attentions of his wife *and* those of the mistress with the beautiful singing voice! In this story West touches on the secret wish fulfillment of what must be many a husband who had surrendered his heart before he understood how polygamous he was and dared to follow that instinct into practice.

"Mother's Day" also gives us good examples of the author's skill at using nature for descriptive and symbolic effect. Merlin's mother, espousing safe, old-fashioned values when it comes to marriage, has at her home an attractive greenhouse made of lathes and wisteria. Here is what the narrator, who shares those values, thinks of it before visiting her Aunt El-Dora: "The lathe house under its canopy of blossoming wisteria was a big purple cave. So beautiful! I felt loving toward the whole human race simply to think that it was capable of developing a vine like the wisteria and of training it over a support like a lathe house so that for a week or two in spring there would exist a room lined with amethyst and scented like honey. The light was lavender colored. Bees seemed to be hanging in the air" (*Crimson Ramblers*, 141). Now let us turn to Merlin's thoughts again, this time after she visited the house of the fawning El-Dora and realized that her own conventional, monogamous life has not led to happiness: "[I heard] the palms clattering again with what I suppose is their true sound – a sound in the desert, of dryness and loneliness and vast infertile wastes of sand. But here amidst our irrigated groves and our stucco bungalows we have long since learned to associate that sound with home" (*Crimson Ramblers*, 153).

In "Live Life Deeply" West fictionalizes the near-tragic conflict she had had with the neurotic college English teacher mentioned in *To See the Dream*. Here again the teacher is identified as a Miss Fisher (evidently the real name). For various reasons the story does not convey the horror and anguish that must have been in the real-life experience.

"Child of the Century" chronicles the sad but somehow grimly comic misadventures of one Oliver Young, whose birth at precisely the turn of 1900 is interpreted by his ambitious mother as auguring conspicuous success for him. The story hinges on the problem of too much parental influence on the young – a common theme in West books. Finally a pharmacist, Oliver has got about as far in life as the farmer in the old joke, who was praised for his success of being outstanding in his field.

"Like Visitant of Air" is a thrilling discovery for many West devotees, partly for the fact that it brings together two bachelor-recluses and nature lovers who in real life were among the author's favorite writers, and both of whom died young from TB: Henry D. Thoreau and Emily Brontë. The lonely literary bachelor Emily Brontë, obscure and brusquely independent like Thoreau and living a frustrated life in far off Yorkshire, chances to be listening to the rain at the same time as he is and yearning, as he is, for the soul mate that was never to be. The time in the story is the winter of 1845, when Thoreau was living alone, and presumably *lonely*, in his cabin at Walden Pond, and Emily was living in almost-equal isolation in a parsonage on the stormy moors at Haworth. Charlotte has just found Emily's secret poems that speak of passionate yearnings for some lover and soul companion as yet unmet. Practically at the very moment when Emily affirms the reality of that companion somewhere but knows in her despairing heart that she will never meet him in this world, Thoreau across the Atlantic stands in the doorway of his cabin, and reaches out into the darkness, and asks urgently, "Where are you? . . . Where are you?" (*Crimson Ramblers*, 202). The story gains effectiveness by using two people whose lives showed mystical tendencies.

"The Heavy Stone" is not the sort of story that came naturally to West – "it was outside me in spirit," she reports – and derives from a factual account told to her by a friend who had lost a son in battle recently on Luzon. The story has the slickness and sentiment that popular women's magazines look for, although it was not written with that market in mind (West's 28 August 1970 letter to me).

The still-shorter "Gallop Poll," originally published also in *American Magazine*, is more sophisticated and thought engaging. In a cocktail lounge a woman in her thirties abruptly asks the other patrons to guess her age, the result to decide whether she will accept the proposed nuptials made by her very young escort. Meanwhile our attention is turned to the upholstered "coffin lid" ceiling of the room that hovers over the participants in this little drama, reminding the reader of the mortality that hems us in and makes present youth and present love all the more precious for being so fleeting.

"Up a Tree" is much more subtle. As this murder mystery begins a husband has murdered his wife and hauled her body up to a platform in the eucalyptus trees where it can be devoured by buzzards. Motive: She had refused to give this philanderer a divorce. It just so happens that she had long voiced the opinion that bodies should be disposed of as the Indians had done in the old days. The whole story is told from the viewpoint of the daughter, Eugenia, who was ashamed of the Indian blood in her mother but loved her father inordinately. Eugenia is the first to discover the bones on the platform; afterward she tries to get her father out of jail by planting evidence that the death was a suicide. Of course, she sees to it that

the police notice the right clues, such as the fabricated farewell note
and the Seconal pills hidden in a tree bole. What makes the story
unusual and challenging is that the protagonist in this situation
would ordinarily be thought of as the *bereaved* daughter, and as
such deserving of our sympathies, whereas we have to be on our
guard at all times in listening to her voice, for nowhere does Eugenia
admit, even to herself, that she is guilty of complicity. It is only as we
notice her slips of tongue, her being the first to find the note and the
pills, and her cold-blooded calm in going to sleep up there beside
her mother's bones – the bones of this mother who was so gentle,
so tolerant of her husband's infidelities, so sensitive to the beauties
of nature – that we feel the full horror and realize that here is
another filial monster. The perfect family coverup.[50] This is one of
West's most chilling stories.

   Among the stories in *Crimson Ramblers* we especially note the
frequent presence of the female narrator, the problem of love and
marriage, the overinfluence from the parent, and the beguiling
adolescent. The tuberculosis theme, so marked in the earliest West
stories, is in decline. Disappointed love and marriage problems
figure in more than a third of the stories, specifically "Up a Tree,"
"There Ought to Be a Judge," "Crimson Ramblers," "Night Piece for
Julia," "Like Visitant of Air," "Mother's Day," and "Child of the
Century," a record illustrating that West was absorbed – and would
be to the end of her career – in domestic affairs of the heart as they
pertain to youth and marriage. And this interest carries over into her
final novel. "The Ouija Board"[51] and "The Blackboard"[52] should
have been retrieved for the collection but were not, nor were these
included in the posthumous *Collected Stories*.[53]

Remembrance of Times Past

West's last novel was *The State of Stony Lonesome* (1984). This
posthumous novel occupies a situation analogous to that of
Melville's *Billy Budd*, being a work that the author evidently did not
complete before she died, and thus being open to several interpreta-
tions. More on this problem later. *The State of Stony Lonesome*
nevertheless contains such a charming nostalgia for the era in which
West grew up in Orange County, California, that her fans will be
grateful anyway, even though the book is hauntingly ambiguous. She

used in the novel a subplot from the short story "For One Golden Moment" published back in 1963.[54] As for the main plot in the novel, the Uncle Zen-Ginerva relationship, this is entirely new.

The State of Stony Lonesome starts off in 1921 with Ginerva Chalmers, a young, affianced woman going alone to visit her beloved Uncle Zen McManus, a former Indianan now sick with TB and living in his house in the country. These are the two major figures in the novel. Upon her arrival they reminisce about their past, beginning with 1915 and then running on through 1917 and 1919 and up to 1921 again. The focus of narration is fragmented, like in *The Friendly Persuasion*: The work begins as Ginerva and Zen's story and ends that way, and the author devotes a few intervening chapters to the consciousness of Ginerva's father and mother, and even one chapter to her boyfriend Dell. Shifting around this way is not in itself bothersome, but the fact is we cannot always read the state of mind of Ginerva and Zen in those chapters devoted to their consciousness; still less can we read the state of mind of these lesser figures, even when we are seeing things through their eyes. As readers we get the feeling that certain important things that should have been said are left unsaid.

On the other hand, the reader is likely to take a strong interest in the engaging, vital characters, as charming a group as one is likely to meet in West's corpus. One soon learns that lusty Uncle Zen has had a woman living with him out of wedlock for the preceding two years, but Ginerva, through whose consciousness we learn this part of the story, is not at all disturbed by such unconventional behavior; nor is she jealous, even though she herself had once dated this man and continues to love him in what appears to be a Platonic fashion. To her way of thinking, she loves him unselfishly as a friend; they share memories of a beautiful past together.

Through flashback we retreat a few years to the heart of the story, to the time when Ginerva was a teenager in high school in the southern California town of Valencia that is pretty much like the one Cress Delahanty knows. But compared with Cress, Ginerva is a much better student, more precocious in her reading, and more active in heading off trouble that might threaten her loved ones. She is also more physically aggressive than Cress, as we can see in the scene where she flattens the nose of the school foulmouth, Pete Finney.

Ginerva, who has had a dream in which her father sang a love song to the attractive Mrs. Ashton, becomes suspicious when her father pays too much attention to the woman. Shrewd and wary though she is about her father's supposed weakness, she is naive and unsuspicious when her Uncle Zen, a prosperous car salesman 18 years her senior, courts her with kisses on the mouth, unchaperoned drives about the countryside, and promises of a brand-new Hup automobile for her birthday. It seems that everyone except Ginerva smells trouble in this April-September match. Her mother tells her – and she certainly ought to know her own brother – that all a girl needs to do to get a bad name is go out with Zen a couple of times. Even her father, Reno, is certain that Zen never makes gifts to women except on a quid pro quo basis; in one instance he gets so fed up with the way the car salesman is carrying on with Ginerva that he knocks him down. In this bit of fisticuffs there is no pushing or shoving or wrestling, no screaming, no cursing, no sound of a blow being struck, no attempt by Reno to get a second blow in, no vows of revenge or even feelings of regret on the part of the victim. Not even a self-righteous protest by Uncle Zen that he bears honorable intentions toward the girl. In any event, violence is always quickly over with in West books, and readers are likely to believe they are missing out on some of that raw, manly feel that lesser writers have no trouble conveying. Probably West underplayed violence here in order to preserve the air of sweet nostalgia that hovers over the novel like fragrance from a garden of old-fashioned roses; maybe she underplayed physical love for the same reason.

In the center of this storm stands Ginerva, living a charmed life, seemingly indifferent to the threat of erotic hanky-panky. In almost any other contemporary novel, even in the early ones by West herself where incest sometimes raises its ugly head, Ginerva would have lost her virginity right away and the reader would never be in the least doubt about the deflowering. One of the weaknesses in *The State of Stony Lonesome* consists in the coy absence of details that would let us learn for sure just how far Uncle Zen, known for his couplings, succeeds in courting the vulnerable Ginerva. At what point does Ginerva reject her uncle's advances – if indeed she does?

As an example of the ambiguity in the story, note what happens at the close of chapter 14. Ginerva is now wearing a fake mustache from a Charlie Chaplin contest she has just been in and she is out driving with Uncle Zen. Out of sentimental regard for the man she asks him to hand her the eyeglasses that Zen's dead girlfriend, Love, had once worn, an item he carries about with him as a keepsake. He has treasured the glasses all these years. Zen snatches the eyeglasses out, puts them on Ginerva's nose, and kisses her while both she and he pretend that she is Love. Thus coyly the chapter ends. Ginerva obviously likes his kisses. Whether Zen kisses her again at this time and whether these demonstrations of affection go any further as they drive, and whether she ever has to restrain his ardor we are simply not told. It would have helped if we could read the minds of these people – or at least learn the author's view – but the method of narration does not permit us such luxuries.

Chapter 17 ends with similar inconclusiveness, with once again the couple in the car and the eyeglasses and the make-believe and the kissing – and this time 16-year-old Ginerva responds eagerly to her uncle's lips. Unanswered questions flock into the reader's mind: How far is Ginerva willing to go? Does the uncle try to take further advantage of her in this game of make-believe? Again West supplies no certain answers.

One of the subplots deals with the mother, Birdeen, who enters an elocution contest at the temperance league; she faints during her recitation of the poem "Kentucky Belle," but Ginerva, eager to help out, takes over for her at the crucial moment and wins the prize. The judges do not even mention Birdeen's contribution.[55] (This taking over and winning for the mother is a kind of allegory for what happened when West used her mother's anecdotes about the old days in Indiana to write *The Friendly Persuasion* stories and win recognition for herself.) More humor follows when Birdeen signs up Ginerva for the Charlie Chaplin impersonation contest.[56]

Perhaps the funniest scene of all takes us far back into Zen's life. As a widower courting his second wife, Lavelle Saunders, he goes to her house for an ice cream supper. While Zen is kneeling in the darkened parlor to take off Lavelle's wet shoes, her rabid atheist of a father, used to shouting his scorn at believers, chances to peek in at the doorway and mistakes Zen for a certain local preacher kneeling at prayer. He reviles the unsuspecting guest and tells him that he will not permit that posture in his house, that Zen can go to church and pray there if he wants to. Zen, unable to resist mischief, begins praying aloud for God to protect him from the "pestilence" that is abroad that night. On hearing this old Saunders hurls a boot at him and hits him in the ribs. Lavelle saves her beau from getting hit next with a stove poker by lying that he was proposing marriage – news that Zen does not have the heart to contradict, for he had been lonesome a long time and is hungry for a woman's touch. The title of the novel comes from the state of lonesomeness in which he has lived for so long.

Back to the recent past. Zen is a widower now. The enterprising postmistress Sarah Loomis finally does something about Zen's foolish pursuit of the niece because she wants him for herself. Accordingly, when Sarah learns that Zen plans to give his niece a new Hup automobile as a birthday present, she arranges for the boy called Dell to enter the competition for the girl by bringing the gift of a new bicycle that she, Sarah, will furnish; the idea is to shame Zen into realizing his age and relinquishing the field for someone younger. And the plot works handsomely. The Hup that Uncle Zen plans to give away happens to be out of tune and barely crawls up Ginerva's driveway. Dell, peddling valiantly from behind on the bicycle, passes the car and wins a symbolic victory.

Although Zen has a reputation for amorous pursuits, even once having impregnated a woman, we never see him engaging in or talking about affairs. His foreplay never goes beyond hugs and kisses: too ardent for an uncle; too reserved for a lover. And yet the sophisticated reader knows in his or her heart that the threat of incest and statutory rape hangs like a dark cloud on the horizon of an otherwise sunny landscape.

The last chapter returns the reader to the present, 1921, with Ginerva, now a grown woman, evidently saved from mischief for the time being by reason of Uncle Zen's health – he has had occasional relapses. She is now alone with him in his house, sitting cozily on his lap reminiscing, but one who reads this passage in the context of the whole story realizes that she is, despite her air of innocence as a loving friend, sitting on a razor's edge between friendship and something more – a dilemma all the more important now that she is engaged to another man. Luckily for her virtue she will be marrying young Dell soon. But considering that Uncle Zen is unquestionably the real man in her life, one is left wondering why Ginerva will marry anyone else, especially a young man that she had never viewed before as a groom and apparently not even kissed (at least, no dating scene is allotted to this pair). If by marrying Dell she is taking the graceful way out of an incestuous match that her heart actually favors, what led her to this decision? Perhaps the answer lies in some chapter that never got written. Does she end up filled with tender sadness that she will never marry Uncle Zen? No. At least we never learn about it. Evidently we are supposed to believe, despite all the kisses, that West meant the Ginerva-Zen relationship to be mostly platonic on both sides. Even so this belief puts a strain on the reader's credulity, at least when it comes to the womanizer we know as Zen.

Birdeen is patterned after Grace West physically and temperamentally. Both are plain-featured, active Hoosiers: Tiny women ridden with sex fears; good at elocution; and suspicious of drinking and card playing – women who feel devoted and yet superior to their husbands from ne'er-do-well families. And, of course, there is plenty of evidence that the author has projected herself emotionally into the role of Ginerva.

The State of Stony Lonesome went ignored by the journals, many of which had praised West's books in years past. Perhaps the very shortness of the book (only 184 pages in the hardcover edition) had something to do with the neglect. But the newspaper reviews, few in number, were uniformly favorable: "What a sweet, poignant, wry and humorous novel it is," went the *San Francisco Chronicle*[57]; "Jessamyn West's last novel is a tribute to her ability to evoke a time and place," went the Raleigh, North Carolina, *News and Observer*[58]; "gem of a small book," went the *Kansas City* (Missouri) *Star*.[59] Possibly none of these reviewers even perused the novel. Linda Rolens of the *Los Angeles Times* was apparently the only commentator who had read West's earlier work and the only one who analyzed the story in any detail.[60] But Rolens somehow missed the tantalizing ambiguities of the relationship between the heroine and her uncle. And none of the reviewers had any notion that the novel as it exists in print was not actually completed by West herself.

By 1983 a succession of little strokes had left West incapacitated for getting *The State of Stony Lonesome* ready for the press. She had been working on this novel for years, as her husband indicates, and had talked to him so often about her Uncle Walter Milhous (her mother's younger brother) that he had no doubt whatever that she was portraying Uncle Walter in the novel. Walter had been the

"rascal," the wild one in the family, the skirtchaser, the tippler with a
gift for words; like Uncle Zen in the novel, he had gone out West
from Indiana to cure himself of TB and ended up living in the Yorba
Linda district. Dr. McPherson reports the family belief (shared by
West herself) that it was probably Walter who communicated his
disease to little Jessamyn by picking her up and holding her in his
arms.

Three to four months before West died she surprised her
husband by asking him in a pitiful voice from the bedroom whether
he would help her with *The State of Stony Lonesome*: "We've got to
get it all together and I don't know where it is."[61] She was almost in
tears. What she wanted was not merely to find the separate chapters
or sections that were filed away in various places, one part in a
drawer, another in a trunk, but to get his help as editor (a function
he had never performed before) in assembling them in the proper
order, and not only that but he was to edit a work that he had never
discussed with her before, unlike the case with her earlier books.
About all he knew was that the story contained an avatar of Uncle
Walter. What a sad pass for a woman who had up to now fiercely
guarded her independence as a writer! In her prime she had
resented an editor changing even as much as a comma.

Dr. McPherson brought her the files of material that he recog-
nized as belonging to the story and sat down on the bed beside her,
but she was forgetful, and confused, and not sure which section
ought to be placed first. Dr. McPherson, however, proved unequal to
the task of editing – almost anyone would have – and suggested
that the project be placed in the hands of her Harcourt Brace
Jovanovich editor, Julian Muller, to whom she had dedicated
Massacre at Fall Creek and in whom she placed considerable trust.
To this she readily agreed. From this point on Muller did not consult
West personally on what needed to be done, nor did he send galleys
to be corrected. Her mental decline precluded any of this. He was all
on his own with a set of lovely fragments to piece together. Dr.
McPherson and his son-in-law, Alan Cash, believe that Muller then
rewrote some materials and introduced others in order to give
greater coherence to the separate sections.[62] But what exactly did he
do? When I queried him on this matter, he flatly declined to answer
my letters.

Almost certainly West had not completed the novel to her satisfaction, even though she seemed convinced that she had it figured out in her mind, and the remedy now was not a mere matter of assembling the separate chapters and tying them together with a little transitional material. Consequently, her editor, Julian Muller, did only a patchwork job at best, presenting the world with a sentimental story that raises questions, a story whose mood is a throwback to the *Cress Delahanty* period, before West began her realistic phase. The world in this narrative is innocent and pre-Freudian, except where Uncle Zen is rumored to have done such-and-such things with his women – acts discreetly placed in the background of the story. My own impression is that, had West's powers remained undiminished, she would have clarified Ginerva's relationship with the uncle, improved the narrative point of view, and unified the separate chapters that now hang together so loosely. But one may never know what West's final intentions were. As it is, *The State of Stony Lonesome* is a delightful failure for which the author herself cannot be blamed.[63]

Chapter Four

Learn to Say Goodbye

Limitations and Strengths

Surely, in view of her late start, Jessamyn West should have spent more time writing fiction and less time writing other things, such as her poems and her 40-plus volumes of journals. One might add that the fiction is insufficiently varied; the author kept too close to the domestic scene where violent action is practically nonexistent, using very few of the character types from popular novels, certainly no spies, professional killers, terrorists, thieves, outlaws, pirates, police officers, detectives, big game hunters, bullfighters, aviators, explorers, tramps, tycoons, politicians, revolutionaries, or soldiers at war; nor cabaret dancers, actresses, singers, waitresses, or international adventuresses; nor any Europeans at all.

Then there are other limitations. All of the novels and short stories, save "Hunting for Hoot Owls," are restricted to the American setting, and all the major characters live in or near some farm or ranch in a place like North Vernon or Yorba Linda. The father is nearly always independently employed as an agriculturist or asylum keeper or small-business man. And the mother is strictly a housewife who is almost always more articulate and witty than her husband. Even so, far more famous writers than West have labored under narrower limitations than these. Aeronautical engineers are said to have stated that the hummingbird, because of the disproportion of wingspan to body weight, ought not be able to fly, but the hummingbird, ignorant of the wise pronouncements, goes ahead and flies beautifully anyway.

Although several of the West novels lack strong plots, they redeem themselves in other ways, such as the impressive characterization of women and children and the admirable sense of place. The typical teenage heroine in the California stories finds the school the center of such activities as picnics, athletics, and musical and

dramatic events, and her problems are typical of adolescents everywhere in small-town America and often mirror the author's experience. The typical older heroine is a resourceful and durable young
woman of Protestant (commonly Quaker) background who was born
in Kentucky or Indiana during the nineteenth century. Partly because
she was too eager to please her mother, who is ridden with fears
about sex, the young married heroine either suffers from an inade-
quate sex education or has a husband who never took that course
either. Such a woman is more memorable than any of the men in the
story, partly because West used real-life models in several instances.
If this heroine has a brother, he is likely to be a favorite sibling and
go into the ministry. Though it is difficult to generalize about sisters
because well-drawn ones are scarce, the sister in *A Matter of Time*
comes straight from life. (None of the brothers or sisters show the
least taint of villainy.)

The heroine's grandparents are likely to own a plant nursery or
operate a poor farm. Relatives in the family die off not from violence,
or accident, or old age but from TB. And if anyone in the family
moves away from the state, the goal is sure to be a small community
in the Los Angeles area. The Napa region rarely figures in these
stories, curiously enough, despite West's more than 40 years of resi-
dence there, for hers is mainly a literature of nostalgia, of remembered or imagined scenes from her childhood or familial accounts.

From *Friendly Persuasion* onward West seemed intent on
proving the critics wrong, proving that she could go beyond the
bounds of Quaker experience, be more than a one-book writer, and
be *un*ladylike whenever she pleased. As her husband wrote to me in
his notes circa 4 April 1991, "J. often [after completing such a book]
said something along this line: '*That* will stop them thinking of me as
just a Quaker writer!' This seemed to bother her more than most
critics' comments." A reader who has read nothing further of West's
than the Jess Birdwell and Cress Delahanty stories might make the
mistake of believing that she never dealt with the dark aspects of life.
But all one has to do is read *Witch Diggers*, *South of the Angels*, *The
Life I Really Lived*, and *Massacre at Fall Creek* to see the other side
of the coin. Comparatively speaking, nevertheless, hers was usually a
quiet voice heard amid the hubbub of the multitude. Probably owing
to her Quaker background, West had a disconcerting habit of avoid-
ing violent confrontations, for the most part ignoring popular trends,

writing to please herself rather than the passing whims of the reading public, while all the time following the precedent of her beloved Thoreau in marching to a different drummer.

A fairly large proportion of the male scoundrels in West's fiction commit adultery, sex abuse, or tyranny over women. Nevertheless, truly wicked men are scarce in her books, partly for the reason that, as she declared, she did not know such people. In the interview with Marshall Berges, West admitted that she would often be angry at first with her scoundrels, but when she stepped inside them and began to understand what made them as they are, she grew sympathetic. Having identified herself with such people, and being a writer who liked herself, she rationalized that she had no alternative but to be sympathetic. Tennessee Williams seems to have reached the same pitfall. The worst of the lot, the rapists and sodomists and castrators, all commit their outrages offstage, and we are never privy to the details. For a long time Dr. Chooney was probably the most diabolical of them all, until, suddenly, a whole pack of them came along in *Massacre at Fall Creek*. The lone degenerate in the gallery, namely Lon (Alonzo Dudley), is hardly believable. Even the lechers never talk dirty or rip bodices or ravish their victims; they tend to be easygoing, gallant figures who make a leisurely sport of venery.

Probably the most realistic instance of sex abuse occurs not in West's fiction but in her autobiographical *Double Discovery* where, during a train ride, an Irish masher in the next seat slides his knee under her skirt and puts a scissors lock on her knee for the rest of the journey (96). In general, she had trouble creating vividly drawn men, whether they were wicked or not, and John Flanagan is at least partly right when he praises the Quaker men "whose firm virtues she can sincerely admire and whose peccadilloes and gentle stubbornness she can review with smiling tolerance" (Flanagan, 309). Jess Birdwell is, of course, the shining example in this group.

West often gives her villains a foolish ignorance of external nature or relates these people to nature's cruel features. Dr. Chooney watches with pleasure a woodpecker devouring his prey; Mary Abel disfigures the earth with diggings and burns pigs; Tom Mount, too occupied with carnal quests in *South of the Angels*, cannot tell a buzzard from a hawk; Mr. Wallenius (*Cress Delahanty*) drowns snakes for the fun of it; Mr. "Senator" Whitehall ("The Battle of the Suits") hates bees even though they once saved his life; and

Mrs. Prosper tells the singing birds outside her window they are fools, regrets not having seen a certain monkey drown, and is the proud owner of a cat whose specialty is biting flies.

The boys are usually more believable than the men because the author had from early to late an uncanny skill at peering into the lives of children, evoking a poetic mood through appropriate detail and gesture, and giving us at once a penetrating and charming view of adolescence: The conflicts with parents, the fears, the confusions, the crushes, the rejections, the heartbreaks, and the tender and ineffable sadness. All this she conveys in a manner worthy of her idol, Katherine Mansfield. One does not have to be an adult, West says, to know what tragedy is. In one of Sir James M. Barrie's early books he observes that genius is the capacity to prolong one's childhood. Whether measured against any other criterion or not, Jessamyn West beyond all dispute qualifies here for her numerous figures of non-idealized children. Nor does she subordinate the intrinsic interest in these to the purpose of moral contrast with adults, unlike the purpose of J. D. Salinger and William Golding. In West's detailed sketches of pert, intelligent, and nearly always engaging youngsters, she attains a success enviable in any literature and in any period. The believable handling of children in stories suitable for an adult audience calls for powers of no mean order. Accordingly, some of the stories in *Cress Delahanty*, *Crimson Ramblers*, and *Love Death* are among the best things she ever wrote.

The reader might wonder why West did not enlarge her scope by using more imagination, as did Robert Louis Stevenson, a man who was similarly afflicted with TB and yet produced a string of novels with a fairly wide range of settings. Several answers apply: For one thing, at the time she discovered she had TB, West was far more ill than Stevenson had been at the outset of his career, and she was not as economically independent, either. It is a wonder that she survived death to write a single line. For another thing, Stevenson had in his formative years a considerable amount of travel and physical adventure, greater by far than hers, experience that he could and did draw on for his writings.

Certainly she followed too long the theory of V. S. Pritchett that literature is created by examining the author's inner self, by finding out who the author is. This introspective theory led her all too easily to rely on family or personal experience and thus become repetitive.

142   JESSAMYN WEST

On the other hand, unlike writers who never sink roots, who scatter their energies in too many directions and thus never gain an intimate knowledge of any region or people, West had the good fortune to discover in the past of her ancestors and in her own childhood a rich lode of story material. She often told would-be authors: *Write what you know most about.* The historical novel *Massacre at Fall Creek* showed her departing from this rule, breaking into fresh new ground away from her usual locales and subject matter. The success of this work boded well for her career. But by then, 1975, she was an elderly woman about to suffer a series of debilitating strokes.

The later West shifted her output from short stories to novels, and in the novels experimented increasingly with such techniques as multiple interlocking plots, flashbacks, stream of consciousness, first-person narration, and symbols, all of which were by that time well-established features of English and American literature. Otherwise she never strained after some revolutionary new style, such as John Dos Passos used in his *U.S.A.*; or one that ran the risk of making her prose practically unreadable, as was the case with the later Henry James and James Joyce. Many critics and professors put a high premium on experimentation, as if that were the very index of belletristic skill, but W. Somerset Maugham reminds us that all the foremost novels in world literature from generations past – the familiar "classics" that are read and admired by generations of discriminating people – employ a straightforward narrative technique without the literary "tricks" that make so many modern novels wearisome. *South of the Angels* (1960) is probably West's most beautifully structured novel, and marks the acme of her novel-writing experience, but it is a work that is still largely ignored by the critics and the public. Still, there are fine things in all her novels, save perhaps *Leafy Rivers*, right up to the very end.

Final Position

It is not useful to compare West with such Hoosier writers as Theodore Dreiser, Edward Eggleston, Ross Lockridge, James Whitcomb Riley, Booth Tarkington, and Lew Wallace, but she does contrast interestingly with James Baldwin (1841-1925). Among the Hoosiers the greatest similarity of all is with Gene Stratton-Porter, author of such once extremely popular sentimental novels as *Freck-*

les (1904) and *A Girl of the Limberlost* (1909). Both authors use a definite backcountry Indiana locale, sympathetically render teenaged heroes and heroines, show a knowledgeable interest in natural history, and, moreover, employ at least one Thoreau figure in their respective books. Both women prepared some of their work for Hollywood filming.

As for differences, West's style has none of that saccharine fatuity that marks Stratton-Porter's work, is considerably more polished, and appeals not merely to young people but to adults as well – even intelligentsia. Further, unlike Stratton-Porter, she made no claim that fiction should be morally improving, even though some portions of her *Friendly Persuasion*, *Except for Me and Thee*, and *Cress Delahanty* exude a subtle moral atmosphere.

One facet of West's writing often remarked upon by critics is her polished style. Quotable passages abound. At its best the style is well husbanded, natural sounding, melodious, even poetic. Obviously she was much in love with words, especially with their connotations and sensuousness – conscious, too, of the rhythmic effect of words when used singly or when strung like beads in a sentence. Yet hers is not the language of cool, alpine distances; it is warm and of the valley, full of generous feeling and aspiration.

It is hard to place the distinctive manner of Jessamyn West. As valid a comparison as any is that of the early Willa Cather. The two women share much in common, including a poetic, melodious style; both of them read and admired Virgil. In developing the comparison beyond style we may also note that they share an interest in the midwestern pioneer and like to lay their stories in the distant past of their native region. But whereas Cather worked steadily backward in time in her sequence of books, West generally worked forward until she reached the period of her own childhood and then made occasional trips back into the nineteenth century. Just as Cather had tended to idealize her pioneer characters Antonia Shimerda and Alexandra Bergson, West did likewise with Jess and Eliza Birdwell. Of course, there is a lot more sex in the West books.

Some of West's contributions to national and world literature show up in her stories about Quaker life in such works as *Friendly Persuasion* and *Except for Me and Thee*. No one else in recorded literature has ever treated of the Quakers – definitely not the American branch of the sect – so extensively, so humanly, so entertainingly, and yet so faithfully to history even though some of the stories are idealized. Some readers with no special interest in Quakerism would prefer productions like *Crimson Ramblers* and *Love Death* because of their skillful handling of wry understatement, wit, symbolism, and psychological depth, for in some ways the Birdwell books are textually simple. Nevertheless, their main characters are not "flat" ones in the sense of illustrating one or two dominant traits at the expense of depth. They do come alive – very much so. And that is what matters, after all. Luckily, as readers, we do not have to choose between the two types of stories; if we did, though, our taste would turn reluctantly in favor of the *Friendly Persuasion* people – not because we dare not face up to evil, think deeply, or contemplate the ambiguities of human experience but because of a desire left unsatisfied these days by the many specimens of raw and blatant naturalism that clamor for our attention on the market, each of them hawking its own sensational brand of artistic "truth" or "reality."

West's second distinction – although it is not a unique one – is her literature about adolescence. Of course, stories about adolescence have long been plentiful, and there are many good ones; nevertheless, West's books *Friendly Persuasion, Cress Delahanty, Witch Diggers, South of the Angels*, and some of the stories in *Love Death* and *Crimson Ramblers* stand out in this class in a twofold way: (a) They contain high merit with respect to sensitivity of characterizations, restraint, genuineness of feeling, psychology, and delightful humor, and (b) the first two books listed, as well as some stories in the last two, appeal not only to adults but to children.

The scholarly presses, which more often than not wait until an author is safely deceased before beginning an autopsy, have devoted relatively little attention to West's writings. Besides, twentieth-century America has yielded a flood of excellent writers, and it is easy for talent to go among them unnoticed – and be forgotten after death. Another difficulty is that most of the influential male critics (and they are in the majority) still consider women writers as anomalies in the stream of literature and give them only grudging acceptance. In the case of West, she deserves to be better known. She wrote a lot of excellent stories that have nothing to do with Quakers or Indiana or idyllic life in the nineteenth century.

Yet she is no Balzac or Tolstoy or Dickens. Nor would she fit into the rank with Fielding and Flaubert and Melville. For the time being it is safe to rank her as a minor but intriguing artist several rungs down the ladder of greatness, a biregionalist in the literature of America, exploring in sometimes exquisite prose what was left of the frontier experience. She being unique, it is difficult to compare her with any particular writer, and critics run the risk of being sexist if they put her into the same camp with local colorists like Sarah Orne Jewett and Kate Chopin. But she is fit company for many figures who get mentioned more often than she does today in literary histories, people like Willa Cather, Ernest Hemingway, Eudora Welty, and John Updike. Her repute as short story writer is likely to survive that as novelist, and her late work shows a falling off in power. Nonetheless, Jessamyn West has woven some stories of considerable beauty, such as those in *Friendly Persuasion, Cress Delahanty, Love Death,* and *Crimson Ramblers,* and through such books has gained many enthusiastic and discriminating readers throughout the world.

Notes and References

Chapter One

1. See my *Maxwell Anderson* (New York: Twayne Publishers, 1976), 24-25, and *The Life of Maxwell Anderson* (Briarcliff Manor, N.Y.: Stein & Day, 1983), 54-56.

2. Speech by West at the "Book and Author Benefit Luncheon" sponsored by the Wellesley College Club, Sheraton Dallas Hotel, Dallas, Texas, 26 September 1970. I attended this event.

3. Most of the information on West's parents and ancestors is taken from two West letters (9 August 1965 and 2 May 1967) to me; to a lesser extent, from a short, unpublished holograph biography of Joshua Vickers Milhous, prepared by his daughter, Martha J. Ware (original owned by Jessamyn West, as is true of family letters and letters from editors to her); and from the memoirs *To See the Dream* (New York: Harcourt, Brace, 1956) (hereafter cited in text as *Dream*), *Hide and Seek: A Continuing Journey* (New York: Harcourt, Brace, 1973), *The Woman Said Yes: Encounters with Life and Death – Memoirs* (New York: Harcourt, Brace, 1976) (hereafter cited in text as *Woman*), and *Double Discovery: A Journey* (New York: Harcourt Brace Jovanovich, 1980). Today the two largest repositories of manuscript material on West are Whittier College and, to a lesser extent, Stephen F. Austin State University.

4. Almira P. Milhous, *Thoughts in Verse*. With Life Sketches of Franklin and Almira P. Milhous (n.p.; c. Christmas 1950), 5. Privately owned booklet of 44 pages. Copy owned by Allie Clark, a West relative in North Vernon, Indiana.

5. Letter from Jessamyn West (7 April 1960) to a Mr. Mock (given name and address not specified), who had inquired about the possibility of making *The Friendly Persuasion* a kind of campaign biography of Richard M. Nixon. Hereafter cited in text.

6. Taken from two unnumbered pages of a 1944-45 notebook on southern Indiana farm life prepared at Jessamyn West's request by her parents. The mother's contribution, from which the nursery's name and other information on fruit are taken, occupies the first and final thirds of this notebook owned by Jessamyn West. Jess Birdwell's nursery is also called Maple Grove.

7. Letters from Grace Anna West, in Whittier, California (undated – internal evidence suggests late summer or fall 1947), to Jessamyn West, who

by then was living in Napa. Grace's frequent talk about her Indiana past are mentioned in the letter to Mr. Mock, cited earlier.

8. "Yes" (the affirmative side of a debate with Paul Engle entitled "Should This Father Raise His Son?"), *Ladies' Home Journal* 83 (May 1966): 149. Hereafter cited in text as "Yes."

9. Ann Dahlstrom Farmer, *Jessamyn West*, Boise State University Western Writers Series, no. 53 (Boise, Idaho: Boise State University, 1982), 7. Hereafter cited in text as Farmer.

10. Ray Mast, "*Friendly Persuasion* Author Recalled," (Fullerton, California) *News Tribune*, 22 December 1965, A2. Hereafter cited in text as Mast.

11. From a note under a photograph of the West home illustrating Mast's article (see note 10).

12. "Bare Hills Become Orchards as Pioneers Plan Future," *Yorba Linda Star*, 17 October 1947, 1. This special commemorative issue of the *Star* celebrates 30 years of the town's development and contains early photographs and articles of local history. Hereafter cited in text as "Bare Hills." Incidentally, during six months in 1924, West wrote society notes (unsigned) for this paper.

13. " 'Those Good Old Days' by One Who Can Really Tell It," *Yorba Linda Star*, 17 October 1947, 1. (Article signed: Jessamyn West McPherson).

14. Valdo Smith, "It Took Lots of Fight to Build Yorba Linda Water Company," *Yorba Linda Star*, 17 October 1947, 1. Hereafter cited in text as Valdo Smith.

15. West letter (9 August 1965) to me. The prosperity is verified in a letter from Gladys Gauldin, La Habra, California (7 February 1967) to me. My sole but reliable evidence for the realty business is the letterhead "Eldo R. West Representing Strout Realty Co.," which is found on several letters from Grace West, c. 1940s.

16. West readily confessed this in her letter to me (30 January 1967). Gladys Gauldin verified this incident for me (see note 15).

17. "The Three R's," *Wilson Library Journal* 31 (October 1956): 157; hereafter cited in text as "Three R's." Also, *Dream*, 252.

18. West letters to me (9 and 18 August 1965). Except as otherwise noted, these have furnished me with all details about her reading and tastes in this direction.

19. West letter to me 28 March 1966.

20. West letter to me 9 August 1965.

21. Lowry C. Wimberly letter (13 April 1940) to West, in which, as editor of *Prairie Schooner*, he offered her constructive criticism about her story.

22. West letter (7 May 1966) to me. In a letter to her (8 April 1940) Dudley Wynn of the *New Mexico Quarterly* said that she might become the Mary Wilkins Freeman of the 1940s, a compliment she at that time felt to be insulting.

23. "Jessamyn West" by herself in *New York Herald Tribune Book Review*, 18 February 1951, 2, ed. John K. Hutchins.

24. Jane S. Bakerman, "Jessamyn West: A Wish to Put Something into Words," *Writer's Digest* 56 (January 1976): 28.

25. Quoted in interview by Carolyn Doty, "Jessamyn West," *Paris Review* 18 (Fall 1977): 148-49. Hereafter cited in text as Doty.

26. Whittier College transcript of Mrs. Maxwell McPherson (Jessamyn West). For a long time West would not authorize me to obtain a transcript, for fear that I would see her birthdate on it (she felt that disclosing her age would discourage youthful readers of such works as the *Cress Delahanty* stories). But once I learned the birthdate from a letter by Jessamyn's mother to a relative of hers in North Vernon, Indiana, and told Jessamyn about it, she readily furnished me with a transcript.

27. *New Pleiades* (Fullerton Union High School and Fullerton Junior College Weekly), vol. 3 (17 December 1920), n.p.

28. Letter from Dr. William T. Boyce, Claremont, California (24 February 1966), to me. The new library at the college was named in his honor in 1957. At the dedication ceremony, West surprised everyone by donating a fairly large sum of money to establish a "William T. Boyce Fund in Creative Writing." Hereafter cited in text as Boyce.

29. *Pleiades*, Fullerton Union High School (1919), 39.

30. Letter from Esther Lewis Mendenhall, Santa Ana, California (30 March 1966), to me.

31. *Dream*, 254-57. Also, West letter (8 April 1966), to me. Also, "Three R's," 159.

Jack Smith, newspaper columnist, had the following revealing conversation with West in 1982, after she gave a speech at a dinner sponsored by the Friends of the San Marino (California) Library: "Miss West," I asked, "if the reservoir hadn't been boarded and fenced, would you have done away with yourself?" "Don't you think I would have?" "No. You'd have seen the morning sun shining on the water, and you'd have said, 'Live life deeply.' " She smiled mischievously. "Besides," I said, "you wouldn't have wanted to ruin that white skirt." The real Jessamyn laughed. "You see right through me," she said. Jack Smith's column "Nothing Ventured," *Houston Chronicle*, 26 March 1982, as taken from the Los Angeles Times-Washington Post News Service, copyright 1982.

32. Quoted from West in "Where Do Stories Come From?" *Adventures in Appreciation*, ed. Walter Loban et al. (New York: Harcourt, Brace & World, 1958), 9; hereafter cited in text as "Where."

33. Transcript of grades, Whittier College.

34. "Love," *Women Today: Their Conflicts, Their Frustrations, and Their Fulfillments*, ed. Elizabeth Bragdon (Indianapolis: Bobbs-Merrill, 1953), 87.

35. Letter from Paul S. Smith, president of Whittier College (9 February 1966), to me.

36. "Report of a Sociology Trip to Los Angeles," by M. J. West. Copy furnished to me courtesy of Paul S. Smith, owner of the original.

37. West letter (4 February 1966) to me.

38. Letter from Esther M. Dodson, Altadena, California (11 March 1966), to me. Dodson is West's cousin.

39. *Love Death and the Ladies' Drill Team* (New York: Harcourt, Brace, 1955), 234; hereafter cited in text as *Love Death*.

40. Letter from Richard Scowcroft, Stanford University (5 December 1966), to me.

41. West letter (24 October 1965) to me.

42. Marshall Berges, "Jessamyn West & Harry McPherson," *Los Angeles Times* (Home Q&A section), 10 October 1976, 38. Hereafter cited in text as Berges.

43. My interview with Dr. Harry Maxwell McPherson at his home in Napa, 26-27 December 1990. Unless otherwise stated, all subsequent statements that I attribute to West's husband stem from this interview and subsequent letters from him to me. See also Jessamyn West's "The Trouble with Doctors Is Me," *Ladies' Home Journal* 82 (March 1965): 42, 44-45.

44. *Crimson Ramblers of the World, Farewell* (New York: Harcourt Brace Jovanovich, 1970); hereafter cited in text as *Crimson Ramblers*.

45. West letter (9 August 1965) to me.

46. West letter (28 January 1966) to me.

47. Photocopy (owned by Stephen F. Austin State University) of the copy sent to Jessamyn by her mother. Undated but undoubtedly close to June 1947.

48. Carbon copy of a three-page, unpublished autobiography typescript (undated) that West prepared for some as-yet-unidentified person. Hereafter cited in text as "unpublished autobiography typescript." Also, West letter (24 October 1965) to me and *Dream*, 258.

49. West letter (9 August 1965) to me.

50. Berges reports her as saying that the first story was accepted. Much the same information appears in the personal interview with West recorded in Dan Tooker and Roger Hofheins's "Jessamyn West," *Fiction! Interviews with Northern California Novelists* (New York: Harcourt Brace Jovanovich/ William Kaufman, 1976), 181-91; hereafter cited in text as Tooker and Hofheins. See also "Grandma" Sue Lucas, "On the River" column of 5 March 1970, in *Parker Pioneer* (Parker, Arizona). West made a habit of parking her motor home in the trailer park run by "Grandma" Lucas, a part-time newspaper writer.

51. West letter (4 February 1966) to me. Also, evidence in letter from Wimberley to West (13 April 1940).

52. The story "99.6" was later collected into *Crimson Ramblers*, "Homecoming" into *Love Death*, and both of them into *Collected Stories of Jessamyn West* (San Diego: Harcourt Brace Jovanovich, 1986).

53. West letter (26 May 1966) to me.

54. *Dream*, 46, 269-71. West letter (2 May 1967) to me.

55. West letter (22 May 1966) to me.

56. All quotations and other details relating to the Limerick episode are taken from West's letters of 9 February and 22 May 1966 to me; pp. 119-27 of *Double Discovery*; Ann McCarthy Cash's (1 March 1991) letter to me; and my personal interviews with Dr. Maxwell McPherson, Ann McCarthy Cash, and her husband Alan Cash on 26-27 December 1990. At the time the first edition of *Jessamyn West* was being written, West permitted me to give only a few innocuous details about this affair for fear of hurting the girls' feelings. *Crimson Ramblers* is dedicated "To my Irish girls, Ann McCarthy Cash and her daughters Lisa and Molly."

57. Julian Muller, ed., "By Way of Introduction," *Collected Stories of Jessamyn West* (San Diego: Harcourt Brace Jovanovich, 1986), vii. (For many years Muller was West's editor at this publishing house.) Farmer, who had interviewed West, reports that the writer received honorary degrees from Whittier, Mills, Swarthmore, Indiana University, Indiana State College, Western College for Women, Juniata, Wheaton, and Wilmington College in Ohio. West also won the Indiana Author's Day Award and the Thormod Monsen Award.

58. Not all obituaries give the same date of death, but the following report the death as occurring on 23 February: *New York Times*, 24 February 1984, B16; *Newsweek*, 5 March 1984, 91; and *Current Biography 1984* (New York: H. W. Wilson, 1987), 481. A letter to me (24 April 1991) from Marianne Pecoulla, of the Medical Records office, Queen of the Valley Hospital, clinches the matter by giving the date as the 23rd also. And Dr. McPherson agrees. The details of West's last hours are derived from my telephone conversations with Dr. McPherson on 10 September 1990 and 9 April 1991, as well as his notes mailed to me c. 4 April 1991.

59. Details are in *Dream* and in Elizabeth Poe, "Credits and Oscars," *Nation* 84 (30 March 1957): 267-69.

60. West letter (7 September 1965) to me.

61. I derive some of my description of the estate and West's writing habits from Carolyn Doty; Jane S. Bakerman, "Jessamyn West: A Wish to Put Something into Words," *Writer's Digest*, 56 (Jan., 1976), 28; and West's own letters to me. Some also comes from my visit to Napa 26-27 December 1990, at which time I interviewed Dr. McPherson and his adopted daughter, Ann, along with her husband, Alan, as well as the novelist Karen Ray, who from childhood had been a friend of West's.

62. West letter (10 October 1966) to me.

63. Her husband told me also during the interview I had with him in Napa (26 December 1990): "She didn't ever want to know about [how he had invested her earnings]. Once a year I made her sit down and I'd have a board of directors meeting with her of what we owned and what was accumulating. . . . And her eyes would kind of glaze over, 'Well, that's nice.' But . . . I never got a feeling that she ever was aware, really, of what we were

doing. Ann [his adopted daughter] tells me that during the last three years
. . . she would call Ann occasionally and say, 'Max just told me we had
passed another mark' or something, you know, but did [Jessamyn] ever let
me know? *Never once* did she ever indicate to me that she wanted to keep
informed of what we were doing."

64. More of my sources for material on how West did her work are
Tooker and Hofheins; Farmer; Ellen Whittle, "50 Plus Beauty," *50 Plus* 20
(March 1980): 54; *Dream*; Doty; and miscellaneous letters to me from West.

65. Confirmed in Doty, 152.

66. Jessamyn West letter to Mr. Mock (see earlier).

67. "The Story of a Story," *Pacific Spectator* 3, no. 3 (1949): 266. In this
essay West appears to take for granted that the fictionist (certainly herself)
employs the "organic development of the narrative." Dr. McPherson told
me a few more details about this house, which is said to be still standing.

Chapter Two

1. Much of the following material is taken from John T. Flanagan's
excellent article "The Fiction of Jessamyn West," *Indiana Magazine of
History* 67 (1971): 299-316; hereafter cited in text as Flanagan.

2. *The Friendly Persuasion* (New York: Harcourt, Brace & World,
1945), 152, 171. Hereafter cited in text as *Persuasion*.

3. Quoted in David Dempsey, "Talk with Jessamyn West," *New York
Times Book Review*, 3 January 1954, 12. Hereafter cited in text.

4. Letter from Ken McCormick (8 August 1941) to West. Photocopy
furnished to me by West.

5. West angrily described this attempt at censorship in two letters to me
(25 and 27 January 1966). Doty, 149, supplies some details.

6. West covers this problem in a philosophical way in her essay "The
Slave Cast Out," in *The Living Novel*, ed. Granville Hicks (New York:
Macmillan, 1957), 206.

7. Nathan L. Rothman, review of *The Friendly Persuasion*, *Saturday
Review* 28 (17 November 1945): 14.

8. Katherine Simons, review of *The Friendly Persuasion*, *New Mexico
Quarterly* 17 (Spring 1947): 117.

9. Richmond P. Miller, review of *The Friendly Persuasion*, *Friends
Intelligencer* 15 (November 1945): 724.

10. *The Friend: The Quaker Weekly Journal*, 29 November 1946, 971.
Unsigned review of *The Friendly Persuasion*.

11. Letter from Clarence J. Robinson, of Winchester, Pennsylvania, in
Friends Journal, 8 December 1956, 791.

12. "Music on the Muscatatuck" was first published in *Prairie Schooner*
14 (1940): 79-92. The other stories first appeared as follows: "Shivaree
before Breakfast," *Collier's* 113 (22 January 1944): 22 passim; "The Pacing
Goose," *Collier's* 116 (11 August 1945): 36, 48-50; "Lead Her like a
Pigeon," *Atlantic Monthly* 174 (December 1944): 60-63; "The Battle of

Finney's Ford," *Harper's Magazine* 191 (September 1945): 273-84; "The
Buried Leaf," *Atlantic Monthly* 176 (September 1945): 72-76; "A Likely
Exchange," *Atlantic Monthly* 174 (July 1944): 56-61; "First Day Finish,"
Atlantic Monthly 174 (August 1944): 88-92; " 'Yes, We'll Gather at the
River' " under the title "Carnal Room," *Collier's* 116 (21 July 1945): 33, 44,
47; "The Meeting House," *Atlantic Monthly* 176 (July 1945): 78-83; "The
Vase" under the title "A Pretty Thing," *Ladies' Home Journal* 62 (July
1945): 35, 91, 93; "The Illumination," *Harper's Bazaar* 77 (October 1943):
101 passim; "Pictures from a Clapboard House," *New Mexico Quarterly* 15
(Summer 1945): 176 passim; "Homer and the Lilies," *Ladies' Home Journal*
62 (August 1945): 18-19.

13. Robert B. Heilman, "Comment" on "Shivaree before Breakfast," in
Modern Short Stories: A Critical Anthology (New York: Harcourt, Brace,
1950), 108.

14. When West was recovering from TB, she had living in her bedroom
a kitten named Samantha, to whose playful company she credits much of
her recovery. Jessamyn West, Introduction to *Categorically Speaking*,
photographs by Lynn Lennon (New York: Viking, 1981).

15. "And I believe that I have to some extent been handicapped in my
writing by this lingering belief in the hero as [a] man who withdraws."
West's letter (18 August 1965) to me.

16. "Yes." Part of a debate with Paul Engle on the Question: "Should
This Father Raise His Son?" *Ladies' Home Journal* 83 (May 1966), 149.

17. All quoted matter, as well as some other information about the
sources of *Friendly Persuasion*, are taken from West's letters (25 and 26
January 1966) to me. Hereafter cited in text. Material on Homer comes not
only from the 26 January letter but an undated letter written by Grace West
to Jessamyn. Much information on Joshua is taken from the unpublished
holograph biography of Joshua Vickers Milhous.

18. James Baldwin, *In My Youth: From the Posthumous Papers of Robert
Dudley* (Indianapolis: Bobbs-Merrill, 1914). Later reissued (1923) carrying
the title *In the Days of My Youth: An Intimate Personal Record of Life and
Manners in the Middle Ages of the Middle West.*

19. Jessamyn West helped write the script for the film *Friendly Persuasion*, which was directed by William Wyler of Allied Artists Productions. The
film's success, however, did not improve the sales of the book. More than
50,000 copies of the hardbound edition were sold prior to the motion
picture, and about that number afterward. Letter from Julian P. Muller (13
October 1965) to me. *Index Translationum* reveals that *Friendly Persuasion* has gone through numerous translations.

20. *Except for Me and Thee: A Companion to "The Friendly Persuasion"*
(New York: Harcourt, Brace & World, 1969.) Hereafter cited in text as
Except.

21. "Little Jess and the Outrider," *Ladies' Home Journal* 72 (October
1955): 68, 126, 129-32.

22. S. L. Steen, review of *Except for Me and Thee*, *Library Journal* 94 (March 1969): 1022.

23. Zena Sutherland, review of *Except for Me and Thee*, *Saturday Review* 52 (May 10, 1969): 62.

24. Carlos Baker, review of *Except for Me and Thee*, *New York Times Book Review*, 11 May 1969, 35.

25. Referred to in a letter from Dudley Wynn (8 April 1940) to Jessamyn West. Stephen F. Austin State University owns an almost complete copy of the story.

26. Although West made no secret of having used the Jennings County Poor Farm as the setting, I "discovered" the place on my own on 22 April 1966 and took some photographs that I then forwarded to West. The ingenuous letter of reply from her (7 May 1966) more than confirmed my impression. Subsequent letters from her (esp. 30 May 1967) left no doubt in my mind that here was indeed the model.

27. *The Witch Diggers* (New York: Harcourt, Brace, 1951), 202. Hereafter cited in text as *Diggers*.

28. West letter (29 January 1966) to me. Also, in another letter (31 May 1967) she writes: "I disliked Lib for instance – but the more I wrote about her the more I understood her and sympathized with her. The seeds of the story I'm sure lie deep in my unconscious."

29. Jane S. Bakerman, "Surrogate Mothers: The Manipulation of Daughters in Works by Jessamyn West," *Midwestern Miscellany* 10 (1982), 54.

30. She did not know there was an actual cemetery connected with the Jennings County poor farm until I described it to her in a letter. Yet in the novel there is one on the property, a short distance from the main building and near a creek – almost precisely where the real one is. Nor did she know that an earlier version of the real barn, like the one in the novel, had burned down around the turn of the century, killing a colt (no lover). All that we need to know are a few key pieces, West says in one of her letters to me, and then the other pieces naturally fall into place.

31. West letters (11 and 17 May 1967) to me. Hellen [*sic*] Ochs, in a letter (2 May 1967), has kindly furnished me with copies of old North Vernon newspaper clippings that describe life at the farm shortly after the turn of this century. As the daughter-in-law of a former superintendent there, she is much impressed with the verisimilitude of *Witch Diggers*.

32. John K. Hutchins, "On an Author," *New York Herald Tribune Book Review*, 18 February 1951, 2. "I think *Witch Diggers* is a better book than *Friendly Persuasion* and I resent being thought of as a one-book author." West letter to me (7 September 1965).

33. Eudora Welty, review of Jessamyn West's *The Witch Diggers* in *New York Times Book Review*, 14 January 1951, 5.

34. E. W. Wilson, review of *The Witch Diggers*, *Saturday Review* 34 (3 February 1951): 17.

35. Quoted by Lee Graham, "An Interview with Jessamyn West," *Writer's Digest* 47 (May 1967): 24-27. Hereafter cited in text as Graham.

36. Page 56 of one of West's unpublished, 175-page writing notebooks, this one being associated with her first three books. The entries are largely undated. West loaned this item to me. Hereafter cited in text as writing notebook.

37. Quoted by Dan Wyant, "Author Here for 'First Performance,' " *Eugene* (Oregon) *Register-Guard*, 22 May 1958. Information about the production appears in a series of publicity articles published in this newspaper in May 1958, on the following dates: 5, 16, 18, and 19-24. Also, I have used copies of pages from the *Annual Report of 1957/58* of the University Theater of Oregon, kindly furnished to me by its business manager, Wilhelmina Bevers. Horace W. Robinson, director of the University Theater, has supplied to me in two letters (4 November 1965, and 17 February 1966) much additional information of an evaluative nature.

38. Dan Wyant, "Premiere of Musical is Set for Weekend," *Eugene* (Oregon) *Register-Guard*, 20 May 1958.

39. *A Mirror for the Sky: An Opera Based on an Original Conception of Raoul Péne duBois for Portraying the Life of Audubon in a Musical Drama*. Costume sketches by Raoul Péne duBois (New York: Harcourt, Brace, 1948).

40. Letter by Mrs. William J. Pease, Jr., of Eugene, printed in *Eugene* (Oregon) *Register-Guard*, 28 May 1958.

41. Quoted in letter from Alyce R. Sheetz, of Eugene, Oregon (24 January 1966), to me. Informant's name withheld on request. Sheetz is a high school journalism teacher.

42. Letter from Robinson (17 February 1966) to me.

43. *Leafy Rivers* (New York: Harcourt, Brace & World, 1967); hereafter cited in text as *Leafy*. The novel had the dubious distinction of being abridged for *Reader's Digest*.

44. In West's letter (28 March 1966) to me she states that she had put down *Leafy Rivers* "3/4 finished" in order to complete *A Matter of Time*, a book to which, in an earlier letter, she assigned a priority for publication. In still another letter to me (8 March 1967) she confesses to having rewritten the last third of *Leafy Rivers* after it was first submitted to the publishers so that was now "much improved." She said, without explaining, that I would not like the book.

45. "[*Leafy*] is filled with symbols." West letter (6 September 1967) to me.

46. Also, see Chancellor's adverse judgment of Reno (p. 10): The schoolmaster struck him as a "careful man," one who "wouldn't take a chance."

47. West letter (6 September 1967) to me.

48. Joan Joffe Hall, review of *Leafy Rivers, Saturday Review* 50 (7 October 1967): 45.

49. *Massacre at Fall Creek* (New York: Harcourt Brace Jovanovich, 1975). Hereafter cited in text as *Massacre*.

50. Oliver Hampton Smith, *Early Indiana Trials and Sketches* (Cincinnati: Moore, Wilstach, Keys, 1858).

51. *Encyclopaedia Britannica* (1962), s.v. "Indian, North American."

52. Kay Kinsella Rout, "The Social Morality of *The Massacre at Fall Creek*," *Society for the Study of Midwestern Literature* (Fall 1983), 2 (East Lansing, Mich.; newsletter). Hereafter cited in text as Rout.

53. Mary Ganz, "Jessamyn West's Persuasions," *Houston Post*, 23 January 1977, 28. Hereafter cited in text as Ganz.

54. Elisabeth Fisher, review of *Massacre at Fall Creek*, *New York Times Book Review*, 27 April 1975, 32; P. S. Prescott, review of *Massacre at Fall Creek*, *Newsweek* 85 (14 April 1975): 86; Sister Joseph Marie Anderson, review of *Massacre at Fall Creek*, *Best Sellers* 35 (May 1975): 22.

55. Anonymous review of *The Massacre at Fall Creek*, *New Yorker* 51 (5 May 1975): 143.

Chapter Three

1. In Doty's essay, pp. 145-46, we learn that Grace West was shocked by reading in Jessamyn's journal that her daughter had labeled her a slattern. Eldo West, on learning of the discovery, sat the daughter down and cried. Jessamyn wrote much the same account to me in one of her letters.

2. Farmer, 41. Said to be based partly on a personal conversation with West on 5 May 1980.

3. *The Life I Really Lived* (New York: Harcourt Brace Jovanovich, 1979), 3, 5; hereafter cited in text as *Life*.

4. Nancy Hale, review of *The Life I Really Lived*, *New York Times Book Review*, 16 December 1979, 16.

5. Lucille de View, review of *The Life I Really Lived*, *Christian Science Monitor*, 2 January 1980, 17.

6. Jean Strouse, review of *The Life I Really Lived*, *Newsweek* 12 (November 1979): 119.

7. *The Pismire Plan*, in *Cross Section 1948: A Collection of New American Writing*, ed. Edwin Seaver (New York: Simon and Schuster, 1948), 1-96.

8. Original title: *Little Men*, in *Star Short Novels*, ed. Frederik Pohl (New York: Ballantine Books, 1954); reprinted in book-length form as *The Chilekings* (New York: Ballantine Books, 1967). Both are paperbound editions.

9. The separate stories in *Love Death* were first published as follows: "A Time of Learning," *Ladies' Home Journal* 63 (March 1946): 26-27, 194, 196-97, 199; "The Mysteries of Life in an Orderly Manner," *New Yorker* 24 (27 March 1948): 29-30; "Love, Death and the Ladies' Drill Team," *New Yorker* 27 (22 September 1951): 33-37; "Homecoming," *American Prefaces* 4 (Summer 1939): 164-67; "The Battle of the Suits," *New Yorker* 30 (5 February 1955): 32-36; "Tom Wolfe's My Name," *New Mexico Quarterly* 14

(Summer 1944): 153-65; "Learn to Say Good-bye" under the title "The Lesson," *New Yorker* 27 (11 August 1951): 25-30; "A Little Collar for the Monkey" under the title "A Gift for the Bride's Mother," *Woman's Home Companion* 75 (February 1948): 30 passim; "Public Address System," *Harper's Magazine* 197 (October 1948): 93-102; "Foot-Shaped Shoes" under the title "You've Got to Grow Up Sometime," *Saturday Evening Post* 227 (12 March 1955): 31, 80-81, 84-85, 87; "Horace Chooney, M.D.," *Mademoiselle* 24 (February 1947): 225, 302-7; "The Linden Trees," *The Tanager, A Quarterly Review* 18 (February 1943): 3-8; "Breach of Promise," *Harper's Magazine* 206 (April 1953): 46-57; "The Singing Lesson," *Harper's Magazine* 190 (January 1945): 145-50.

10. Carlos Baker, review of *Love Death and the Ladies' Drill Team*, *New York Times Book Review*, 16 October 1955, 4.

11. Christopher G. Katope, "West's *LOVE, DEATH AND THE LADIES' DRILL TEAM*," *Explicator* 23 (December 1964), item 27.

12. Edward C. Aswell, "A Note on Thomas Wolfe," in Thomas Wolfe, *The Hills Beyond* (New York: Harper & Row, 1964), 146.

13. Harrison Smith, review of *Love Death and the Ladies' Drill Team*, *Saturday Review* 38 (3 December 1955), 27.

14. West letter (7 September 1965) to me: "I can't think *what* Harrison Smith was thinking about when he wrote of Dr. Chooney. His version of the story came out of *his* head, not out of my narrative. Your interpretation is the right one."

15. *Cress Delahanty* (New York: Harcourt, Brace & World, 1953), 25-26; hereafter cited in text as *Cress*. The 16 separate *Cress* stories were first published in altered form under the following titles: "The Child's Day," *New Mexico Quarterly* 10 (Winter 1940): 233 et seq.; "The Mush Pot," *Foothills* 1 (Winter 1939), six unnumbered pages; "Mr. Powers," *New Yorker* 24 (24 July 1948): 24-26; "The Hat," *Ladies' Home Journal* 65 (May 1948): 46-47, 141-44, 146; "Recapitulation," *Ladies' Home Journal* 68 (October 1951): 53, 239-40, 243-45; "Road to the Isles," *New Yorker* 23 (21 February 1948): 27-30; "A Few Lines for Mrs. Charlesbois," *Woman's Day*, 16th year, 3d issue (December 1952): 52-53, 106-19; "Arma Virumque Cano," *Harper's Magazine* 198 (January 1949): 72-77; "The Sump Hole," *New Yorker* 22 (14 December 1946): 39-44; "King Midas in Reverse," *Colorado Quarterly* 1 (Summer 1952): 58-66; "Summer of Signs and Portents," *New Yorker* 24 (28 August 1948): 21-25; I have not been able to locate the two stories corresponding to "Fourteen: Summer II" and "Fourteen: Spring"; "You Can't Talk about It," *Ladies' Home Journal* 70 (July 1953): 28, 74-76; "Mr. Cornelius, I Love You," *Collier's* 130 (22 November 1952): 2021 passim; "Grandpa Was Her Mirror," *Harper's Magazine* 192 (May 1946): 439-42.

16. Boyce letter (24 February 1966) to me.

17. "Grandpa Was Her Mirror," *Harper's Magazine* 192 (May 1946): 442.

18. Boyce letter (24 February 1966) to me.

19. Edward Weeks, review of *Cress Delahanty, Atlantic Monthly* 193 (January 1954), 80.

20. Riley Hughes, review of *Cress Delahanty, Catholic World* 178 (March 1954), 472.

21. Dan Wickenden, review of *Cress Delahanty, New York Herald Tribune Book Review*, 3 January 1954, 3.

22. Frances Gaither, review of *Cress Delahanty, New York Times Book Review*, 3 January 1954, 3.

23. Eleanor M. Scott, review of *Cress Delahanty, Saturday Review* 36 (9 January 1954), 19.

24. The composition of *South of the Angels* must have begun not much earlier than February 1956, for at that time West still considered the work a "new" one. But she was far enough along to regard the Copes as the main people. See *Dream*, 4.

25. Gladys Gauldin letter (7 February 1967) to me.

26. Valdo Smith. Incidentally, a West short story that was reworked and made part of the novel is "The Leppert," *Senior Scholastic* 46 (23 April 1945): 21-22, 28-30.

27. Tuberculosis (herself, her husband, an uncle, and a cousin); cancer (Grace West, Carmen, and three grandparents – the last four of these having died of it – plus Eldo West); crippling arthritis (Myron); migraine (herself).

28. *Dream*, 88. But this was far from being the first time. She said in her *New York Herald Tribune Book Review* article, "Jessamyn West," that she had read Thoreau and his notebooks "more often than any other writer." The very first entry in her writing notebook consists of a short quote from him describing fireflies ("bronze light").

39. For the story, see *Crimson Ramblers*, 192-202; also, *Collected Stories*, 414-22.

30. *Love Is Not What You Think* (New York: Harcourt, Brace & World, 1959), 23. Hereafter cited in text as *Love*.

31. *South of the Angels* (New York: Harcourt, Brace, 1960), 102. Hereafter cited in text as *Angels*.

32. William Hogan, review of *South of the Angels, Saturday Review* 43 (23 April 1960), 23.

33. Orville Prescott, review of *South of the Angels, San Francisco Chronicle*, 28 April 1960, 29.

34. Edward Weeks, review of *South of the Angels, Atlantic Monthly* 206 (July 1960), 94.

35. R. T. Bresler, review of *South of the Angels, Library Journal* 85 (15 May 1960), 1939.

36. West's letters (22 May and 10 October 1966) to me.

37. Webster Schott, review of *A Matter of Time*, "A Gentle Storyteller Challenges Death," *Life* 61 (21 October 1966): 8.

38. *A Matter of Time* (New York: Harcourt, Brace & World, 1966), 163. Hereafter cited in text as *Matter of Time*.

39. Felicia Lamport, review of *A Matter of Time*, *Book Week*, 6 November 1966, 8.

40. West letter (22 May 1966) to me. Earlier Julian Muller in a letter (17 February 1966) to me wrote that West was at that time performing "extensive revisions" in the work.

41. Elaine Gottlieb, review of *A Matter of Time*, *New York Times Book Review*, 16 October 1966, 64.

42. Charles Poore, review of *A Matter of Time*, *New York Times*, 27 October 1966, 45.

43. Rita Estok, review of *A Matter of Time*, *Library Journal* 91 (1 October 1966), 4704.

44. The Reverdy in Jessamyn West's "Love," *Ladies' Home Journal* 66 (September 1949): 68-69 passim, has an unfortunate childhood. The husband of this Reverdy is also named Everett. Like Tassie and Blix, she has a severe illness. And she has already gone through several marriages, presumably because of false, prudish attitudes toward sexual love. But unlike Tassie, she finally arrives at the conviction that love is of the flesh as well as of the spirit.

45. "Another Word Entirely," *New Mexico Quarterly* 17 (Spring 1947): 63-71.

46. West letter (10 October 1966) to me. But on 28 March 1966 she had written to me, "Carmen is the central figure in *A Matter of Time*. You are *not* to say and I will call you a liar if you do. . . . I put down *Leafy Rivers* to write about her. The book is about 85 percent factual."

47. My autographed copy of Charles Cooper's *Whittier: Independent College in California* (Los Angeles: Ward Ritchie Press, 1967), containing a preface by West, is inscribed in her handwriting: "For Alfred Shivers, who knows Pilgrim College and therefore will not find this strange." Incidentally, the beneficiary of the West manuscripts, personal library, and, apparently, donations of money is this same Whittier College that she finds so much fault with in the novel.

48. And what were West's avowed feelings toward her family? Dr. Boyce wrote to me on 24 February 1966: "I want to say that Jessamyn's love and devotion for her immediate family – father, mother, brother has been impressive. I think she must have had a most happy home life." Judging, however, from her letters to me as well as her stories, where her three siblings appear in various guises, and particularly from my conversation with her husband, I conclude that her relations with her brother, Myron, were cool at best.

49. The stories in *Crimson Ramblers* were originally published as follows, with the exception of those labeled "new," which made their first appearance in the book: "Up a Tree" (new); "There Ought to Be a Judge," *Mademoiselle* 23 (June 1946): 134-35, 212-17; "Gallup Poll," formerly titled

"The Love Ballot," *American Magazine* 140 (August 1945): 42-43; "Alive and Well," *Harper's Bazaar*, 81st yr., no. 2829 (September 1947): 223, 266, 268, 270; "I'll Ask Him to Come Sooner," *The Tanager, A Bi-Monthly Review* 12 (December 1941): 9-16; "Hunting for Hoot Owls," *Harper's Magazine* 228 (January 1964): 86-94; "Crimson Ramblers of the World, Farewell" (new); "Night Piece for Julia," *Rocky Mountain Review* 8 (Fall 1943): 10-12; "Live Life Deeply" (new, and not to be confused with an unpublished essay by that title that West wrote at Whittier College); "Mother's Day," *New Yorker* 46 (30 May 1970): 32-37; "The Heavy Stone," *American Magazine* 145 (March 1948): 22-23, 126, 128-30; "99.6," *Broun's Nutmeg* 3 (10 June 1939): 7; "The Day of the Hawk," *Foothills* 1 (Fall 1939), nine unnumbered pages; "Like Visitant of Air," details of magazine publication uncertain, but story anthologized in *Modern Reading* 14, ed. Reginald A. More (London, 1941-46), and later in *Collected Stories*; "The Condemned Librarian," *Harper's Magazine* 211 (July 1955): 45-53; "Child of the Century," *Woman's Day*, 16th yr., 2d issue (November 1952): 54 et seq.

50. This interpretation is confirmed in West's letter to me (28 August 1970).

51. "The Ouija Board," *Yale Review*, New Series, 39 (December 1949): 255-62.

52. "The Blackboard," *Town and Country*, 100 (November 1945): 124, 152, 154, 156, 159. Reprinted in *O. Henry Memorial Award Prize Stories of 1946*, ed. Herschell Brickell and Muriel Fuller (Garden City, N.Y.: Doubleday, 1946).

53. These collected stories, according to her editor, represented "all of the independent short fiction that she [West] wished preserved." Julian Muller, "By Way of Introduction," *Collected Stories*, vii. Of the items in this edition, most had already appeared in *Love Death* and *Crimson Ramblers* after first having magazine publication. Those few for which I have been unable to find any previous publication are "Probably Shakespeare," "The Calla Lilly Cleaners & Dyers," "Aloha, Farewell to Thee," and "The Second (or Perhaps Third) Time Around."

54. "For One Golden Moment," *Good Housekeeping*, 157 (November 1963): 79, 139-40, 144, 146, 148, 150, 156.

55. In *Woman*, p. 12, we read about "Kentucky Belle," West's favorite narrative poem that her mother used to recite to her and the other children. The horse Kentucky Belle was a beautiful equine heroine that was stolen by Yankee soldiers who went marauding through Kentucky. The owner never saw his horse again.

56. An event that actually happened, except that, unlike Ginerva, West refused to go through with it. *Woman*, 16.

57. Anonymous review of *The State of Stony Lonesome*, *San Francisco Chronicle*, 30 November 1984.

58. Gail Smith Wallace, review of *The State of Stony Lonesome* (Raleigh, N.C.) *News and Observer*, 19 May 1985.

59. L. G. Harvey, review of *The State of Stony Lonesome*, *Kansas City* (Missouri) *Star*, 13 January 1985.

60. Linda Rolens, review of *The State of Stony Lonesome*, *Los Angeles Times*, 23 December 1984.

61. My interview with Dr. Harry Maxwell McPherson at his home in Napa, California, 26 December 1990.

62. My interviews with Dr. Harry Maxwell McPherson, Ann McCarthy Cash, and Alan Cash in the West home at Napa, California, 26-27 December 1990; also Dr. McPherson's notes mailed to me c. 4 April 1991.

63. When I questioned Dr. McPherson and his daughter and son-in-law, I found that they had no idea what West's plans were for the Ginerva-Uncle Zen relationship in *State of Stony Lonesome*. The only unpublished version of the novel owned by the Wardman Library at Whittier College is the final typescript. And this typescript contains no indications of corrections or editing. Letter to me from Philip M. O'Brien, Library Director, Wardman Library, Whittier College, Whittier, California, 31 January 1991.

Selected Bibliography

PRIMARY WORKS
Only those short stories are listed which were not collected by West or reworked by her into some book. For those stories which have gone into her books, see the appropriate entries in the Notes and References section.

Books

The Friendly Persuasion. New York: Harcourt, Brace, 1945.

A Mirror for the Sky: An Opera Based on an Original Conception of Raoul Pene duBois for Portraying the Life of Audubon in a Musical Drama. Costume sketches by Raoul Pene duBois. New York: Harcourt, Brace, 1948.

The Witch Diggers. New York: Harcourt, Brace, 1951.

The Reading Public. New York: Harcourt, Brace, 1952. Privately printed for friends and publishers.

Cress Delahanty. New York: Harcourt, Brace, 1953.

Little Men in *Star Short Novels*. Edited by Frederik Pohl. New York: Ballantine Books, 1954. Later published as *The Chilekings*. New York: Ballantine Books, 1967.

Love Death and the Ladies' Drill Team. New York: Harcourt, Brace, 1955.

To See the Dream. New York: Harcourt, Brace, 1957.

Love is Not What You Think. New York: Harcourt, Brace, 1959.

South of the Angels. New York: Harcourt, Brace, 1960

The Quaker Reader. Selected and introduced by Jessamyn West. New York: Viking Press, 1962.

A Matter of Time. New York: Harcourt, Brace & World, 1966

Leafy Rivers. New York: Harcourt Brace & World, 1967.

Except for Me and Thee: A Companion to The Friendly Persuasion. New York: Harcourt, Brace & World, 1969.

Crimson Ramblers of the World, Farewell. New York: Harcourt Brace Jovanovich, 1970.

Hide and Seek: A Continuing Journey. New York: Harcourt Brace Jovanovich, 1973.

The Secret Look: Poems by Jessamyn West. New York: Harcourt Brace Jovanovich, 1974.

The Massacre at Fall Creek. New York: Harcourt Brace Jovanovich, 1975.

The Woman Said Yes: Encounters with Life and Death – Memoirs. New York: Harcourt Brace Jovanovich, 1976.

The Life I Really Lived. New York: Harcourt Brace Jovanovich, 1979.
Double Discovery: A Journey. New York: Harcourt Brace Jovanovich, 1980.
The State of Stony Lonesome. New York: Harcourt Brace Jovanovich, 1984.
Collected Stories of Jessamyn West. New York: Harcourt Brace Jovanovich,
   1986. Posthumous. Introduction by Julian Muller.

Uncollected Stories

"Footprints beneath the Snow." Written about 1940, this is one of her
   unpublished stories. Original owned by West estate.
"The Snow Is Dancing." *Yankee* 7 (January 1941): 11-12.
"The Stove That Had the Devil in It." *Decade of Short Stories* 3 (November-
   December 1941): 32-39.
"The Leppert." *Senior Scholastic* 46 (23 April 1945): 21-22, 28-30.
"A Little Walk with Brother." *Woman's Home Companion* 81 (September
   1945): 21, 100, 102-3.
"The Blackboard." *Town and Country* 100 (November 1945): 124, 152,
   154, 156, 159. Reprinted in *O. Henry Memorial Award Prize Stories of
   1946.*
"Presumed Missing." *Mademoiselle* 22 (January 1946): 130, 232-36.
"Spring of Life." *American Magazine* 14 (April 1946): 50-51, 136-39.
"There'll Come a Day." *Collier's* 117 (11 May 1946): 11, 61-64.
"Another Word Entirely." *New Mexico Quarterly* 17 (Spring 1947): 63-71.
"Perigord." *Ladies' Home Journal* 65 (January 1948): 50-51, 140-41.
"The Pismire Plan." In *Cross Section 1948: A Collection of American Writ-
   ing,* edited by Edwin Seaver, 1-96. New York: Simon and Schuster,
   1948.
"Love." *Ladies' Home Journal* 66 (September 1949): 68-69, 221-27.
"For One Golden Moment." *Good Housekeeping* 157 (November 1963): 79,
   passim.

Articles, Speeches, and Introductories

"Meet an Overseas War Bride." *Ladies' Home Journal* 62 (August 1946):
   127-32, 194.
" 'Those Good Old Days' by One Who Can Really Tell It." *Yorba Linda Star,*
   17 October 1947, 1.
"Story of a Story." *Pacific Spectator* 3 (Summer 1949): 264-73.
"Home for Christmas." *Mademoiselle* 29 (December 1949): 52, 120-24. Not
   to be confused with the story by that name in *Except for Me and Thee.*
"Jessamyn West." *New York Herald Tribune Book Review,* 18 February
   1951, 2. Edited by John K. Hutchens.
"Jessamyn West." *New York Herald Tribune Book Review,* 7 October 1951,
   18.
"Is Love Enough?" *Mademoiselle* 36 (February 1953): 100, 166-70.
"Life Where You Are." *Mademoiselle* 38 (January 1954): 68, 128-29.

"Four Years – for What?" *Addresses by Richard Nixon and Jessamyn West.* *Whittier College Bulletin* 47 (December 1954): 15-24.

"The Choice of Greatness." *Journal of the American Association of University Women* 49 (January 1956): 82-84.

"West, A Place to Hang Your Dreams." *Women's Home Companion* 83 (May 1956): 46-47.

"The Three R's." *Wilson Library Bulletin* 31 (October 1956): 155-59.

"Hollywood Diary." *Ladies' Home Journal* 73 (November 1956): 70-71, passim. Condensation of *To See the Dream.*

"Secret of the Masters." *Saturday Review* 40 (21 September 1957): 13-14, 44.

"The Slave Cast Out." In *Living Novel*, edited by Granville Hicks, 194-211. New York: Macmillan, 1957.

"Where Do Stories Come From?" In *Adventures in Appreciation*, edited by Walter Loban et al., 1-13. New York: Harcourt, Brace, 1958.

"On Words and Men." *Jessamyn West on Words and Men; Richard Nixon. The Independent College.* Whittier College *Bulletin,* 53 (May 1960): 1-2. Speech.

Foreword. In *Letters of a Woman Homesteader*, by Elinore Pruitt Stewart, v-vii. Lincoln: University of Nebraska Press, 1961.

"Violence." *Redbook* 120 (January 1963): 35, 104-5.

"On Friendship between Women." *Holiday* 35 (March 1964): 13-17.

"Prelude to Tragedy." *Redbook* 123 (July 1964): 53, 84-92.

"The Trouble with Doctors Is Me." *Ladies' Home Journal* 82 (March 1965): 42, 44, 46. Contains autobiography.

"Yes." Part of debate with Paul Engle on the question "Should This Father Raise His Son?" *Ladies' Home Journal* 83 (May 1966): 88, passim. Contains autobiography.

"Her Unmistakeable Style." West's contribution to a symposium entitled "The California Woman." *Ladies' Home Journal* 84 (July 1967): 76, 115-16.

Preface. In *Whittier: Independent College in California*, by Charles W. Cooper, ix-xvii. Los Angeles: Ward Ritchie Press, 1967. Contains autobiography.

"Getting Personal." *PTA Magazine* 63 (September 1968): 5-7.

"Jessamyn West Talks about Her Cousin President Nixon." *McCall's* 96 (February 1969): 69-70. Contains description of Yorba Linda and some material on family background.

"The Good Life on Earth." A symposium by Jessamyn West, Jean Stafford, M. F. K. Fisher, et al. *McCall's* 97 (January 1970): 29-38, 95.

"On the River" (article included in this column), edited by "Grandma" Sue Lucas, *Parker Pioneer* (Parker, Arizona), 5 March 1970, 4.

"Marina Oswald Porter: Seven Years after Dallas." *Redbook* 135 (August 1970): 57-59, 129-32, 134-35.

"Toward Peace." *Redbook* 135 (September 1970): 75, passim.

"Be Gentle, Be Happy – And Give Your Child the Stars for Christmas." *Redbook* 138 (December 1971): 66-67, passim.

"From Billy Sunday to the Beatles." *McCall's* 103 (April 1976): 204-5, passim.

"Jimmy Carter's Sister: How Faith Can Heal." *McCall's* 104 (April 1977): 32, passim.

Introduction. In *Categorically Speaking*. Photographs by Lynn Lennon. New York: Viking Press, 1981. Four unnumbered pages.

"Examining the Childhood Roots of Women's 'Fears.' " Review of *The Cinderella Complex*, by Colette Dowling. *Los Angeles Times Book Review*, 24 May 1981, 2.

"Criticism." In *The Complete Guide to Writing Fiction*, edited by Barnaby Conrad and the staff of the Santa Barbara Writers' Conference, 258-61. Cincinnati: Writers' Digest Books, 1990. See p. 263 for a short summary of West's remarks to the conference during a 1978 speech.

Letters and Miscellaneous Writings

The great majority of the following West letters to me deal in some way with autobiography, explication of stories and novels, or bibliographical problems. Save for excerpts herein, none of the West correspondence has yet been published. Nor have any of her numerous journals.

Letters written in 1965: 15 July; 9, 18, August; 7 September; 24 October. In 1966: 20, 25, 26 (last two in same envelope), 27, 28, 29 January; 1, 4, 5 (last two in same envelope) 9 February; 28 March; 3, 8 April (last two in same envelope); 7, 17, 22, 24, 26, 27 May; 20 June; 10 October; 17 (note on Christmas card), 20 December. In 1967: 30 January; 18 February; 8, 16, 20 March; 12 April; 2, 11, 17, 22, 25, 27, 30, 31 May; 6, 29 September; 23 October. In 1969: 17 December. In 1970: 4, 28 August. Originals of the letters are owned by the Ralph Steen Library, Stephen F. Austin State University. Copies of the other materials are owned by the same library.

Unpublished writing notebook. 175 pp. Covers *Friendly Persuasion* and *Witch Diggers* writing period. Entries largely undated. Original owned by West estate, along with several other writing notebooks.

Unpublished three-page autobiography typescript (undated). Original owned by West estate.

"Report of a Sociology Trip to Los Angeles." Written for Professor Paul S. Smith's class, Whittier College school year 1922-23. Original owned by Smith.

Notebook, 1944-45, on Southern Indiana farm life prepared at West's request by her parents. Unnumbered pages. Owned by West estate. Although not showing any direct sources for story plots, it gives a first-hand account of everyday domestic life and furnishes the kind of concrete detail that might have stimulated West's imagination.

Film

My Hand – My Pen. Video cassette manufactured by Davidson Films. "Writers on Writing Series." 231 "E" Street, San Francisco, CA 95616. Produced and directed by Arthur M. Kaye. 1970.

Screenplays

The Big Country. With Robert Wyler from a novel by Donald Hamilton. United Artists, 1958.

The Friendly Persuasion. With Robert Wyler. Allied Artists, 1956.

Stolen Hours. Remake of *Dark Victory.* United Artists, 1963.

Films Made from West's Works

Friendly Persuasion. Directed by William Wyler. Allied Artists Productions. Released 1956. Starring Gary Cooper as Jess Birdwell.

Learn to Say Goodbye. Produced for television by Ronald Reagan, Universal Studios, in 1960. Transferred to video in 1988 at the request of Dr. Maxwell McPherson. 24 minutes, 42 seconds. Starring Ronald Reagan, Colleen Gray, and Michael Burns (as the boy). In color.

Horace Chooney, M.D. Produced by William Rose Productions, 360 Oxford Ave., Palo Alto, California, in 1988. In video format. 18 minutes. Executive producer, Charles Orgish. Adapted by William Rose, a Stamford University graduate student. Starring Frank Morsman, Debra Emerson (as Miss Chester), and Priscilla Oliver (as Mrs. Chooney). In color.

SECONDARY WORKS

Bakerman, Jane S. "Jessamyn West: A Wish to Put Something into Words." *Writer's Digest* 56 (January 1976): 28-29. Based on a personal interview with West, this enthusiastic essay contains biographical material about how West began to write, her writing habits, her admission that she did not know who her reading audience would be, her journal keeping, and her source for *The Massacre at Fall Creek.*

_____. "Surrogate Mothers: The Manipulation of Daughters in Works by Jessamyn West." *Midwestern Miscellany* 10 (1982): 49-58. Bakerman pursues the thesis: "Always the love between parent and child is potentially strong, and always the mothers intend to be supportive and nurturing, but they make crucial errors." Limited to an examination of *Witch Diggers, Leafy Rivers, South of the Angels, A Matter of Time, The Massacre at Fall Creek,* and *The Life I Really Lived.*

Berges, Marshall. "Jessamyn West and Harry McPherson." *Los Angeles Times* Home Q & A section, 10 October 1976, 38-39, 41, 43. A personal interview with West and her husband. Tells how Dr. McPherson's nagging was crucial in getting West to market her first stories. Illuminating insights into her writing techniques.

Doty, Carolyn. "Jessamyn West." *Paris Review* 18 (Fall 1977): 140-59. Consists of revealing notes from an interview Doty had with West in her home in Napa, c. 1976. About West's beginning to write, her ordeal with TB, her husband's influence (minor but supportive), her writing strengths and weaknesses, her then-present involvement in constructing *The Life I Really Lived.*

Farmer, Ann Dahlstrom. *Jessamyn West.* Boise, Idaho: Boise State University, 1982. Boisie State University Western Writers Series, no. 53. Documented critical-analytical pamphlet of 51 pages based on a careful reading of the literature, an interview, some correspondence, and numerous published articles and reviews. Sympathetic and comprehensive. Good bibliography.

Flanagan, John T. "The Fiction of Jessamyn West." *Indiana Magazine of History* 67 (1971): 299-316. Valuable, sympathetic article on West's fiction as a whole. Covers well her strengths and weaknesses as a fiction writer by discussing narrative structure, "control of the physical locale," "use of authentic and specific colors and objects," characterizations, and command of language (with emphasis on colloquial and folk diction). Flanagan locates her main strengths in the last two areas.

_____. "Folklore in Five Midwestern Novelists." *Great Lakes Review* 1 (1975): 43-57. Treats in the last four pages West's use of folk speech in the Jess Birdwell stories and in two novels. Flanagan says that in the Indiana stories she "reveals a sure ear for the cadences and a fine understanding of the folk mind."

Graham, Lee. "An Interview with Jessamyn West." *Writer's Digest* 47 (May 1967): 24-27. Contains useful information about the author's intentions in *A Matter of Time* and about her writing in general.

Heilman, Robert B. Comment on "Shivaree before Breakfast." In *Modern Short Stories: A Critical Anthology*, 107-8. New York: Harcourt, Brace, 1950. Analysis brief but perceptive.

Katope, Christopher G. "West's 'LOVE DEATH AND THE LADIES' DRILL TEAM.' " *Explicator* 23 (December 1964), item 27. Except for its note of optimism concerning the heroine's final state of mind, this explication alluding to Shelley's "Ode to the West Wind" is novel and convincing.

Kempton, Kenneth Payson. Comment on "Love, Death and the Ladies' Drill Team." In *Short Stories for Study*. Cambridge, Mass.: Harvard University Press, 1953. Mentions the wind symbolism elaborated on by Katope; contains a few questionable assumptions that detract from the value of the explication. For instance, Imola's "childhood environment" does not seem to have been far away; it is only her lover who is referred to as being a "Mexican." Also, there is nothing indicating that Emily and John love each other – in fact, the earlier story in the *Love Death* collection suggests that they do not get along well together.

Rout, Kay Kinsella. "The Social Morality of *The Massacre at Fall Creek*." *Society for the Study of Midwestern Literature* (Fall 1983): 1-11 (East Lansing, Mich.; newsletter). Measures West's achievement in the novel against what John Gardner (*On Moral Fiction*) says is the only valid aim for art: transmitting truth. Rout finds the achievement satisfying.

Shivers, Alfred S. *Jessamyn West*. Boston: Twayne Publishers, 1972. The first extended scholarly study of West's life and work. Like this revised edition, it made use of family papers, letters, interviews, photographs, galleys, a writing notebook, and so forth. Covers West's work through 1970.

Tooker, Dan, and Roger Hofheins. "Jessamyn West." *Fiction! Interviews with California Novelists*, 181-91. New York: Harcourt Brace Jovanovich/William Kaufman, 1976. About West's writing habits, her preference for the Indiana locale, and her difficulty in writing about evil.

Index

The Author

Alfred S. Shivers is a professor of English at the Stephen F. Austin State University in Nacogdoches, Texas, where he specializes in American literature. He is the author of three books on playwright Maxwell Anderson, including the first book-length biography, which helped him win the Regents Professor Award at his university. He also wrote the first edition of *Jessamyn West*. Among his dozens of shorter publications, the 1969 article "Jack London: Not a Suicide," first published in *Dalhousie Review* and reprinted in *Critical Essays on Jack London* in 1983, used medical-literary methods to establish what is now the current view among scholars, that Jack London did not kill himself, contrary to what almost all earlier biographers had claimed.

The Editor

Frank Day is a professor of English at Clemson University. He is the author of *Sir William Empson: An Annotated Bibliography* and *Arthur Koestler: A Guide to Research.* He was a Fulbright Lecturer in American Literature in Romania (1980-1981) and in Bangladesh (1986-1987).